12-50

EXPERIENCING COMPREHENSIVE EDUCATION

EXPERIENCING
COMPREHENSIVE
EDUCATION

A STUDY OF
BISHOP McGREGOR SCHOOL

ROBERT G. BURGESS

METHUEN   LONDON AND NEW YORK

First published in 1983 by
Methuen & Co. Ltd
11 New Fetter Lane, London EC4P 4EE

Published in the USA by
Methuen & Co.
in association with Methuen, Inc.
733 Third Avenue, New York,
NY 10017

© 1983 Robert G. Burgess

Typeset by Keyset Composition,
Colchester

Printed in Great Britain by Richard Clay,
The Chaucer Press, Bungay, Suffolk

British Library Cataloguing in
Publication Data
Burgess, Robert G.
Experiencing comprehensive
education.
1. Comprehensive high schools –
England – Case Studies
2. Educational sociology – England –
Case studies
I.   Title
373.2'5'0722   LA635

ISBN 0-416-35150-6
ISBN 0-416-35160-3 Pbk

Library of Congress Cataloging in
Publication Data
Burgess, Robert G.
Experiencing comprehensive
education.
(Education paperbacks)
Bibliography: p.
Includes index.
1. Catholic schools –
England – Case studies.
2. Comprehensive high schools –
England – Case studies.
I. Title.   II. Series.
LC506.E5B87 1983   373.2'5
83-12119

ISBN 0-416-35150-6
ISBN 0-416-35160-3 (pbk.)

FOR MY PARENTS OLIVE AND GEORGE BURGESS

CONTENTS

LIST OF TABLES

LIST OF ILLUSTRATIONS

PREFACE AND
ACKNOWLEDGEMENTS

This study is based upon my PhD thesis and has been written with several audiences in mind: teachers, sociologists and general readers who are interested in the social world of schools and classrooms. As a sociologist who has been a school teacher I have provided an account that will I trust contribute to our understanding of comprehensive schools and help to promote debates and discussions about education among the readers of this book.

In common with all social researchers I have received much assistance in preparing this study. I owe a special debt to the headmaster, teachers and pupils at Bishop McGregor School for their help and co-operation. However, in maintaining confidentiality it is not possible to thank individuals by name. I trust that the pseudonyms I have used and the changes I have made will cause no offence and will prevent individuals who were so generous with their time from being harmed in any way. The access I was given to their lives and their work will, I hope, advance our understanding of the experiences of teachers and pupils in a comprehensive school. In addition, I would like to thank the parish priests and officers of the local education authority (past and present) for their assistance with this study and the SSRC who provided financial support.

I am also indebted to a number of other people without whom this study could not have been completed. I owe much to Valdo Pons (now Professor of Sociology at the University of Hull) who originally encouraged me to engage in ethnographic work. He stimulated my initial interest in fieldwork and subsequently read and commented upon drafts of my material. I was also very fortunate to have Wyn Lewis as my PhD supervisor. He spent many hours talking to me about my field experiences, data analysis and the various drafts of each chapter. I have learned much from him about doing research, and about schools and schooling. I have also received very helpful comments on the complete draft of this study from Peter Sidey and the headmaster of Bishop McGregor School. My thanks are also due to David Hargreaves, David Morgan and the late Professor Lawrence Stenhouse for their interest, encouragement and advice in preparing my thesis for publication. More widely, I have been helped by friends and colleagues who have commented upon my field experiences at the school. I have also been fortunate to have once again the expert secretarial services of Valerie Campling, who not only typed a very accurate copy of my PhD thesis but also patiently retyped the manuscript for this book. Finally, I would like to thank my wife Hilary, who has been involved with every part of this study. She has given help, advice, encouragement and moral support for which I am very grateful. However, none of these people is responsible for any inadequacies in the study, which of course are my own.

Robert Burgess

University of Warwick

INTRODUCTION

Morning assembly, registration, tuck shops, school dinners, uniforms and school rules all have a familiar ring about them. For most people feel they are acquainted with the world of schools and classrooms through their own experiences as pupils. Yet these experiences only provide a pupil's view of school and are seldom used to examine the ways in which a school operates. The purpose of this study is to take the everyday experiences of a headmaster, teachers and pupils in order to reveal the way in which a comprehensive school works. The school is a purpose-built, co-educational Roman Catholic comprehensive called Bishop McGregor School, located in the city of Merston.[1]

Although comprehensive schools have been in existence for some years, sociologists have given relatively little attention to their house systems for pastoral care and their departments for subject teaching, to the ways headteachers have defined their roles, to the ways in which they have co-ordinated teachers working in houses and departments and how a comprehensive school works in practice. It is issues such as these that are examined in part one of this study, which focuses upon the day-to-day experiences of teachers in Bishop McGregor School. Meanwhile, part two is concerned with relations between teachers and pupils in the school's Newsom department.[2] Here, the focus is upon pupils who were regarded as the 'less willing' and the 'less able'; those pupils who would have few opportunities to gain success in public examinations. It is now twenty years since the Newsom committee (Newsom 1963) reported on such pupils. How do they and their teachers fare in a comprehensive school? What courses do they follow? How do teachers and pupils relate to each other? How do teachers who work with Newsom pupils differ from 'ordinary' teachers? How do they and their pupils adapt to the school? It is the aim of this study to address these questions in the course of providing an ethnographic description of the social processes and social relationships among teachers and pupils in Bishop McGregor School.

The background of the study

Ethnographic studies of schools have steadily developed in Britain over the last twenty years.[3] However, they are part of a broader tradition of ethnographic work in social anthropology and sociology that has been developed during this century (Burgess 1982a, 1–11). Originally, ethnographers worked in societies other than their own, focusing upon the experiences of the participants in order to understand a way of life from the participants' point of view.[4] While many social anthropologists worked in other societies, sociologists in the USA and in Britain concentrated on their own cultures. In America, this approach was used by Chicago sociologists to study urban settings and institutions,[5] while in Britain sociologists engaged in field studies of urban and rural localities.[6] Both these developments were influenced by the work of social anthropologists because it was argued that ethnographic studies could be conducted in urban locations. Max Gluckman encouraged members of the Manchester Department of Social Anthropology and Sociology to utilize this approach in the study of towns and villages, factories, schools and other social institutions in Britain (Gluckman 1964).[7] As Lacey (1981, xi) remarks, sociologists and social anthropologists in this department were drawn into close collaboration with each other with the result that 'Manchester sociologists pushed much deeper than their contemporaries into understanding social process and the perspectives of actors'. Hargreaves (1967), Lacey (1970) and Lambart (1970) used this approach to conduct a series of interrelated intensive studies of schools.

Until these studies appeared, sociological accounts of educational institutions consisted of speculative essays in which sociologists examined the organizational characteristics of schools and developed abstract models which summarized how it was *thought* they worked. However, there was little empirical evidence about how they were actually organized and worked. Indeed Ottaway (1960, 195) was forced to remark:

> One has the feeling that nobody knows what goes on in schools, not even those who work in them, and least of all those who work and live in them. It needs the outside observer; it needs the anthropologist visiting the savage tribe.

This suggestion that sociologists should observe and analyse social relations in schools was taken up in several British studies: of grammar schools by King (1969), Lacey (1970) and Lambart (1970; 1976), of a secondary modern school by Hargreaves (1967), of an independent school by Wakeford (1969), of comprehensive schools by Mays, Quine and Pickett (1968) and Ford (1969). These studies had much in common, concentrating on patterns of informal social relationships among pupils in particular schools.

The studies by Lacey and Hargreaves were of special interest as they were broadly concerned with the school as an institution and focused on internal processes within schools. Both researchers utilized their former teacher status by taking teacher roles to collect data. However, several gaps could be identified within these studies. Firstly, the researchers were not directly concerned with the formal organization of the school and the activities of teachers. Secondly, there were no detailed accounts of departments or of teachers' classrooms. Finally, there was little material on the content of education. It was therefore my intention to take up some of these issues by studying the social organization of a comprehensive school. Subsequent developments in the sociology of education have resulted in further school studies[8] and analyses of social processes that occur within classrooms.[9] This study therefore examines the social processes and experiences of comprehensive education, focusing on the ways in which members of one school define and construct their social world.

The theoretical framework of this study is based broadly upon symbolic interactionism[10] but does take into account decisions and definitions of situations that were external to the school. Evidence from other parts of the educational system therefore complements the analysis of interaction in the school and classroom. In focusing upon the meanings that participants attribute to social situations I used the 'definition of the situation', a concept that was developed by Thomas (1928)[11] and has been used by Stebbins (1974; 1975) in studying social interaction in schools and classrooms. This allowed me to examine how situations are defined and how the definitions are interpreted by different groups and individuals. In turn, I looked at the strategies, negotiations and bargains that are used in defining and redefining situations. The focus is therefore upon the way in which the meaning of 'school' is constructed by the participants and the way in which 'school organization' is defined. In this sense, the different ways in which the school is defined depend upon the different groups and individuals and their pattern of social relations and social interaction. The school is therefore seen as a social creation which arises out of the processes of definition, redefinition and interpretation that continuously occur among teachers, between teachers and pupils and among pupils. However, for the purpose of this study, attention has been concentrated predominantly on teachers on a school-wide basis and teachers and pupils in one department.

The fieldwork

The kinds of questions that were initially used to orientate the study have already been located within the substantive literature in the sociology of education and linked predominantly to the theoretical perspective that is encompassed by the term *symbolic interactionism*. At this point we can now make further links between the problems posed, the theoretical approach that informed this study and the fieldwork methods that have been used. As Bechhofer (1974) has argued, there is no best method or single method of social investigation. He follows Denzin (1970) and argues for a variety of methods being used to study a social situation. Nevertheless, the methods that are used have to be appropriate for the problems posed.

In this study, the questions concerned the way in which a comprehensive school worked and in particular the ways in which individuals and groups defined and redefined the situation in which they were located. Such questions, as Stebbins (1967) has indicated, require the observation of events, situations, groups and individuals within a school. Detailed observation was needed to acquire the definitions and meanings that were attributed to social situations. The study is therefore based on fieldwork which was conducted between April 1973 and July 1974. During this sixteen-month period I took a part-time teacher role in the school. I taught a Newsom group on a regular basis for four periods each week and also took many substitution lessons in other departments in the school. As a part-time teacher I was a member of a house and a department. I could therefore do participant observation, conduct unstructured interviews with teachers and pupils, and collect documentary evidence.[12]

The organization of the book

All the chapters in this book deal with teachers' and pupils' experiences of comprehensive education in Bishop McGregor School. The study is presented in two parts. Part one locates the school in a social context and examines the extent to which the house system influenced the headmaster's conception of the school (chapter two) and the definitions and redefinitions of the situation by house and departmental staff (chapter three). In chapter four there is a detailed analysis of the operation of the school.

While the first part of the book is principally concerned with the teaching staff in the whole school and the way in which the school structure operated, the second part focuses on teachers and pupils in the Newsom department. This study of the department is used to examine relationships between teachers, pupils and teachers, and pupils. While this brings the pupils into view, it also extends and elaborates on some of the themes that were explored on a school-wide basis in earlier chapters.

After introducing the department (chapter five) there are chapters on Newsom pupils (chapter six), becoming a Newsom teacher (chapter seven) and a discussion of the definitions, redefinitions, strategies and bargains that were used in classrooms (chapter eight). The conclusion considers the major themes of the study together with some implications for further research and for the practising teacher.

Notes

1 All names of institutions, places and people that are used in this study are pseudonyms in order to maintain anonymity.
2 The Newsom department provided courses for pupils for whom the maximum expectation of success in public examinations seemed likely to be three CSE (Certificate of Secondary Education) grade fives or less.
3 For a review of school studies including ethnographic work see Burgess (1981c, 11–24) and Tyler (1982) which contains an excellent bibliography.
4 For discussions of the ethnographic approach see, for example, Spradley (1979; 1980) and Wolcott (1975), and for its use in the study of schooling see Popkewitz and Tabachnick (1981), and Spindler (1982).
5 For the Chicago School approach see Park (1952) (originally published in 1916), Anderson (1923), Cressey (1932), Shaw (1930), Thrasher (1927), Wirth (1928) and Zorbaugh (1929).
6 See, for example, Frankenberg (1957) and Stacey (1960).
7 For further details see Gluckman (1945), the commentary by Hannerz (1980, 128–31) and Frankenberg (1982).
8 See, for example, Ball (1981), Hargreaves, Hester and Mellor (1975), King (1978), Sharp and Green (1975) and Woods (1979).
9 For an extended review of classroom ethnography see Hammersley (1980). For a British text on classroom research see Delamont (1976). For collections of papers on classroom research see Chanan and Delamont (1975), Stubbs and Delamont (1976), Hammersley and Woods (1976), Woods and Hammersley (1977), Eggleston (1979), Hargreaves (1980) and Woods (1980a; 1980b).
10 For a discussion of symbolic interactionism see Blumer (1969) and Rock (1979), and for its use in the study of education see Delamont (1976) and Hargreaves (1972).
11 See Thomas (1928, 584) when he stated: 'If men define situations as real, they are real in their consequences'.
12 For a discussion of the methodology used in this study see Burgess (1982b; 1984a; 1984c).

PART 1
SOCIAL RELATIONS
IN THE SCHOOL

1

THE PHYSICAL AND SOCIAL

STRUCTURE OF THE SCHOOL

Schools in common with other organizations do not exist in a social and cultural vacuum. They are products of the past and of the social context in which they are located. In this respect, Bishop McGregor School was no exception as it embodied several traditions which it derived from the pattern of comprehensive schooling that had been established by the Merston local education authority in the 1950s. This chapter will therefore briefly examine the way in which the authority developed comprehensive schools and the extent to which the physical structure of Bishop McGregor School influenced the social structure of teachers and pupils.

The social context of the school

Under the 1944 Education Act both local education authorities and the churches which had established denominational schools were required to provide separate secondary schools.[1] In Merston, debates about new secondary schools focused upon equality of educational opportunity: according to Charles Bridges (deputy director of education, 1937–47, and director of education, 1947–69) local education officers were unhappy about official pronouncements that children could be subdivided into three distinct groups on the basis of a selection examination at the age of eleven.[2] Furthermore, the Labour group who controlled the city council wanted to develop multilateral schools, which it considered would over-come local problems of school accommodation and provide schooling appropriate for young people who would work locally. Thus, although Ministry of Education circulars[3] inclined towards tripartitism, Merston advocated multilateral schools. In the city's 1946 Development Plan, the authority proposed to establish ten eight-form entry multilateral schools, a scheme that was criticized by the Ministry of Education who advised Merston to construct ten-form entry schools in order to produce viable sixth forms.

In 1953 the authority submitted a revised development plan to a Conservative Minister of Education in which they proposed to establish a group of purpose-built ten-form entry comprehensive schools. Merston obtained support for this scheme on the understanding that each of the schools 'is to be regarded as experimental and the authority will ensure that it is possible to use the buildings for separate schools later should this be found desirable'.[4] As a result the city's comprehensive schools had to be built in such a way that they could, if the need arose, be restructured as separate grammar, technical and modern schools. The new schools there-fore carried a comprehensive label but contained elements of tripartitism as they provided different types of education on one site.

The ministry indicated that these schools would demand some re-thinking, especially about school organization. Among the problems they thought demanded solution were those associated with size: physical space and traffic control in buildings, loyalty to the school and to teachers, and the provision of buildings in which the whole school could meet for morning assembly. The authority was therefore asked to consider the ways in which size could be handled. The director said in numerous reports and letters to other authorities[5] that he considered school size would influence the tenor of relationships between teachers and pupils. He maintained that even if the schools were large, 'It is important that children should feel themselves part of an organization which is in itself a microcosm of society'.[6] The director was aware that several devices could be used to break down large numbers in comprehensive schools.[7] One approach was the division of the school into lower, middle and upper sections as a means of decentralization. However, he considered the 'house' system as used in English boarding schools ideal.[8] He believed this approach to school organization would help to integrate the large school, provide a base where pupils could develop a sense of loyalty and where staff could supervise the moral welfare of their pupils. Further-more, as each house would have social and teaching facilities it would, he thought, help to develop links between the house and the school.

This pattern of school organization was also approved by the city architects who considered that a physical house system would help to solve problems of space, traffic control and school design. Accordingly, each comprehensive school that was established in the city was sub-divided into physical units which were known as houses. The officers of the authority therefore considered that they had found a solution to the problems of comprehensive school size and that they had helped to promote the social and academic integration of pupils.

By the time Bishop McGregor School was planned and built in the late 1960s, it was evident that comprehensive schools were no longer an experiment in Merston and in England.[9] As it was the policy of the Catholic church to fit in wherever possible with the local education authority's secondary school scheme, it was decided to 'go compre-hensive' in the Catholic sector of the city and to operate McGregor as a co-educational comprehensive school.

The school site

The school was built in four phases. In phase one, house facilities were constructed that included accommodation for teaching, dining and social activities.[10] Each block had accommodation for two houses on the ground floor and for one or two departments on the first floor. Identical accom-modation was provided on each side of the block. Inside the houses the decorations were in house colours. On the ground floor there were no classrooms because the accommodation consisted of a hall (used for morning assembly, dining, teaching and social activities) which could be subdivided for each house, a study for each house head and one working staff room for the teachers in the two houses.

On each side of the house block narrow staircases opened out on to landings around which were suites of classrooms that were used by departments. Each large department (for example, English and mathe-matics) had four or five classrooms, while smaller departments (for example, history and geography) had only two or three classrooms. The decoration in the classrooms was a murky yellow engrained with the marks and (in some cases) the messages left by pupils. However, pictures, posters, and children's work provided some colour that brought the rooms 'alive' when teachers and pupils were not present.

While the house blocks, established in the first phase of building, provided the basic accommodation, subsequent building provided specialist accommodation. The science and art block consisted of seven science laboratories and three art rooms. There was a specialist block for needlework and home economics and further accommodation for wood-work and metalwork. A project unit housed the library and the music department on the first floor, while the ground floor was dominated by one large room which had the appearance of a derelict science museum: empty cupboards, dilapidated workbenches and broken machines. The headmaster considered this room 'suitable for use as project bases in technical activities and for audio-visual purposes'.[11] Some science was taught here and it was where the Newsom department was housed. Dominating all the other buildings was the sports complex: sports hall, gymnasium, swimming-pool and tennis courts. The most significant allocation of accommodation was to houses after which many of the blocks were named. Only departments that required specialist equipment merited a whole block or part of a block. As a result, there were divisions between houses and departments and between departments themselves and further divisions between specialist and non-specialist accommodation.

The administrative block, located near the main entrance, contained separate offices for the headmaster, deputy head and school secretaries. Above these offices was the staff common room which was 'out of bounds' for pupils. The only exception to this rule that could be recalled by teachers was when an art master had obtained special permission from the Common Room Association to allow a group of pupils to paint a mural. This painting, staff notices and the odd exercise book were the only direct reminders that this room was part of the school.

The buildings provided a physical structure within which the social structure could operate. As Smith and Keith (1971, 171–208) state in their study of Kensington School, the physical structure of a school embodies the wishes of the architect, the planners and educational innovators, but it is the teachers and pupils who transform these wishes in their day-to-day activities. As Stebbins (1974; 1976) has shown, it is the physical context of a school that can influence teacher–pupil relationships. School buildings may embody certain messages which the makers communicate to the teachers and pupils. However, the way in which these ideas and messages are accepted, transformed, defined and redefined is revealed in the daily activities of the school. Indeed, the physical structure may well be an important factor in determining some sets of social relations (see chapters three and four).

At Bishop McGregor School the house system had been specifically designed to overcome some of the problems associated with large schools. Each block was specifically related to houses and specialized departments. While it was argued that this helped to promote cohesion among small groups, it also helped to subdivide the school into a number of small, distinct physical and social groups. The separate buildings therefore helped to create a number of different groups that advanced different definitions about the school structure and the way in which it should operate (see chapters three and four).

Subdivisions into houses and departments allowed staff and pupils to work in smaller groups and helped to promote a sense of 'community' while overcoming the problems of anonymity and traffic flow. A teacher could therefore belong to the school, to Westminster House and to the

English department. Teachers could also work with small groups of colleagues and small groups of pupils. Pupils were members both of the school and of houses, but it was to departments that they went for their classes.

While the physical structure helped promote the work of the school by overcoming problems associated with size, it also created other problems. The physical distinctions that were made between different houses and different departments resulted in the identification of specific physical territory for each group. I saw several situations that illustrated how teachers used the physical characteristics of the buildings to make distinctions between groups. Westminster House used the mathematics department's rooms on the first floor of the house block for social activities in the lunch hour. During one term the head of the mathematics department complained to the head of house about the mess that remained in the rooms each time his pupils used them. These rooms became the subject of house notices in assembly when the house head told his pupils it was important to leave the rooms in the way they found them as, he remarked: 'these rooms belong to the maths department. We are only guests in their rooms. We should, therefore, leave the rooms tidy just as guests do.' Here, a distinction was made between houses and departments based upon territorial distinctions embodied in the design of the school. Areas within the block were said to 'belong' to one group, with the result that the other group became 'guests' in that area. In this particular case, a concept of 'ownership' of physical territory was employed.

Ideas which incorporated territory and subdivision of the physical context were used at various times in the year when members of the school had to come to terms with the problem of litter. Although litter bins were provided around the site, it was still possible to see apple cores lodged on window ledges, crisp-packets trapped in mud and chocolate-wrappers blowing along pathways. When the headmaster considered that the school was untidy he would promote anti-litter campaigns by dividing the site into six areas each of which were allocated to the six houses. Each house had to keep a particular area free from litter and in return was awarded a number of house points. In this situation, physical territory was used to create a competition among teachers and pupils and reinforced the physical divisions. House assemblies were used by house heads to encourage pupils to maintain the appearance of 'our area' in order that house points could be obtained and the competition won. But the majority of teachers considered that the competition was really between house heads whom they suspected of picking up litter themselves to help their house win the competition. So physical territory helped to promote competition and subdivide members of the school. Distinctions between pupils in different house groups were also maintained on a territorial basis. One head of house announced in an assembly that pupils who belonged to other houses were not to be brought inside 'our' house block during lunch hours and break times. Similar statements were also made by other house heads. The house blocks were therefore used to promote ideas of territory and membership. While this helped to promote the notion of a 'community' pupils belonged to, it also emphasized lines of demarcation, division and subdivision within the school.

The departments were also associated with particular blocks. However, the science department claimed the right to use further rooms outside its own territory including the project area. At the beginning of the autumn term I found I was timetabled to use this room with a Newsom group. At the same time a science master was also timetabled to use the same room. The science master claimed that it was 'his' room. He argued that as the room was fitted out with plugs, cupboards and workbenches which would be required for science lessons, it should be his room, a point which was supported by the deputy head who provided me with a house hall in which to teach my Newsom class. Later that day the science master apologized to me for the fact that I would have to move classrooms in the middle of a double lesson each week, but he added that he still thought the room belonged to the science department because of the way in which it was equipped.[12]

Although the city architect and educational planners had envisaged the different buildings as a way in which problems of school size could be overcome, some redefinition of their ideas had taken place. The physical context of the school, the site and its buildings were used by teachers to create territories, boundaries, divisions and subdivisions within the school. In addition, it influenced the pattern of teacher recruitment and methods of teaching and learning. In short, the structure of the school supported various groups and different sets of social relationships which in total comprised Bishop McGregor School.

The teachers

A new school with new buildings requires new equipment, new staff and a new head. The first task for the governors was to appoint a new head. They told me that they had looked for someone who was regular in his faith and morals, a man[13] of principles, an individual who was capable of forming personal relationships with parents, pupils and teachers and who was committed to Catholic schools and to comprehensive schools. In appointing a headmaster, the governors were in part dependent on the views of the director of education's representative (an inspector of schools in Merston who was a Catholic) and the parish priests. However, they were virtually unanimous in their selection of Mr Geoffrey Goddard as the first headmaster of Bishop McGregor School.[14] On the basis of his experience and his ideas for the new school, the governors considered that

Mr Goddard was the ideal man to develop a new purpose-built, co-educational Roman Catholic comprehensive school. One governor summed this up by saying: 'Mr Goddard really stood out to me. His enthusiasm for the job and for every aspect of comprehensive teaching made him the man for the job. His personality just oozed.'[15] Other governors who had been present at the interview agreed. They considered that in Goddard they had found a good Catholic with boundless enthusiasm for his work and who they thought would make McGregor a great school.

Mr Goddard was in his early forties and had experience of teaching in several Catholic schools. In a short biography that he wrote for me, he summed up his teaching experience:

> I taught at All Hallows Grammar School in Leyton for a year. I was employed as a teacher at St Augustine's Secondary Boys' School (in Merston) becoming Head of Science in 1957 and Head of House in 1958, . . . before going . . . to St Mark's Comprehensive, outside Leyton. I became Head of Science in 1960 and stayed until 1964 when I became the Head of St Edmund's Boys' School in Oldtown.[16]

As a Catholic Mr Goddard had always worked in Catholic schools and was committed to comprehensive schooling. He told me, 'I had been in grammar schools and done several years in secondary moderns, but realized that it made no sense until you put the two together'. Goddard considered that a comprehensive school consisted of several school traditions brought together on one site. Here, the comprehensive school was seen in terms of some elements of a tripartite framework: a notion that was embedded in the ministry's thinking about comprehensive schools in the early 1950s. In these circumstances, Goddard could capitalize on his teaching experience. He had held different posts (head of department, head of house and headmaster) in comprehensive and secondary modern schools respectively. He also had some teaching experience in Merston and knew the schools and the Catholic sector of the city. However, he had never before had to organize a comprehensive school or a new school.

In common with other headteachers, Mr Goddard saw that there were several advantages to being appointed head of a school that was new.[17] Everything could be planned from the beginning. Unlike his experience at St Edmund's, Goddard found there were no staff, buildings or equipment to inherit. He could therefore develop this school within the overall plan for the Catholic sector and for comprehensive schools in Merston.

When he was appointed, Goddard had been told that McGregor would be a purpose-built comprehensive established on the Merston house system. Furthermore, the school would be built and developed over a number of years so that it would be some time before a complete staff could be recruited. It was against this background that Goddard had to think about staff appointments. Staffing required some care, especially

Table 1.1 Staffing at Bishop McGregor School, 1969–74

Academic year	Major appointments	Total staff
1969–70	Headmaster Deputy headmaster Four heads of houses One head of department (English) Teachers in charge of subjects	18
1970–1	Two heads of houses Four heads of departments One teacher in charge of a subject	30
1971–2	One head of department One teacher in charge of a subject (Major internal promotion begins)	45 (plus 4 part-time)
1972–3	Senior mistress	57 (plus 3 part-time)
1973–4	Director of studies	69 (plus 6 part-time)

Source: Documents prepared by the headmaster for the governors and for the Diocesan Schools Commission.

because it would be five years before the school would be at full strength. The pattern of staff appointments is summarized in table 1.1.

The first appointment that Goddard made was that of deputy head. He summed up the qualities that he looked for in a deputy as:

> Someone who would be a head in five years' time, who was going to the top, who wasn't afraid of hard work and who had knowledge and experience of comprehensive schools. Basically, I wanted someone who would complement me and who wouldn't have my faults.[18]

The man he found for this post had several of his qualities but was in many respects his opposite. Frank Lloyd, a Catholic in his mid-forties, was quietly spoken, cautious where Goddard was bold and conservative where Goddard was liberal, but like Goddard had a capacity for hard work. Together they made a team who were to lead the school for eight years.[19]

The first set of further particulars for posts at McGregor requested detailed applications from experienced teachers for the positions of heads of houses, heads of departments, and general subject staff. The type of people required were 'teachers of varying experience, but possessed of drive and imagination' who might find the school 'offers scope both for the exercise of their talents and for some meeting of their ambition'. Nevertheless, the headmaster did add that 'This must not, however, be read as a promise that all promotion will be internal'.[20] These requirements were considered too demanding by the local education authority's chief inspector of schools, who thought that the head had set his sights too high; in the past he had found difficulty recruiting highly qualified Catholic staff to Catholic schools. However, Goddard told me that he deliberately made the standard requirements very high because 'I didn't want anyone coming to McGregor for an easy ride. I did it quite deliberately to put people off. Getting the application form in was the first hurdle so that some people eliminated themselves.'[21] He considered this strategy was successful as he knew that several local teachers had not applied to McGregor because they thought the demands would be too heavy.[22]

The physical structure of the school determined the order in which assistant teachers were appointed and the staffing pattern established (see table 1.1). The house heads were consequently the first group of assistant teachers to be appointed. As the archbishop of the diocese considered that all pastoral posts in Catholic schools should be held by Catholics, it was necessary to appoint Catholic teachers as heads of houses. The type of teachers that the headmaster wanted for these posts were 'people with a capacity for growth, people with compassion and with five to seven years' experience'[23] because he thought it vital to appoint teachers who were more concerned with pupils than with teaching subjects.[24] Four house heads were appointed when the school opened and two further appointments were made when other house blocks were completed. At this stage, these were the only specific appointments to the house system. However, all heads of departments, teachers in charge of subjects and general subjects teachers were house tutors in addition to their posts in a particular area, a situation which was never indicated in any set of further particulars issued to applicants for posts. The result was that most departmental staff did little apart from marking a register and looking after a tutor group, because they did not consider it part of their job to do what they considered to be house duties.

At McGregor, the recruitment of heads of departments followed the appointment of house heads. In a new school with few pupils it was not possible to provide posts of responsibility in all departments. But the head did attempt to attract well-qualified Catholic teachers to be heads of departments. The type of teachers he wanted for his departments were:

The best brains and people with adventure and enthusiasm. It wasn't a number one priority to believe in comprehensives. I saw that we had to convince people that comprehensives were the answer as I was not prepared to settle for a comprehensive protagonist for a second-rate head of department.[25]

At McGregor only one head of department was appointed as there were so few suitable applicants. Several teachers were in charge of subjects but official oversight of departments was given to heads of houses: a situation that held implications for future relationships between heads of houses and heads of departments (see chapter three). In 1970–2 departmental responsibilities were strengthened. More heads of departments were appointed and several staff were given responsibilities in subject and non-subject areas. Among the latter group were positions for careers, Newsom work, and remedial education. Finally, two senior appointments were made: a senior mistress in 1972 and a director of studies in 1974. In addition, general subjects teachers were appointed to departments, many of whom were probationary teachers.

Table 1.2   Catholic and non-Catholic teachers at Bishop McGregor School, 1973–4

Year	Catholic teachers	Non-Catholic teachers	Total
January 1973	33	24	57
January 1974	36	29	65

Source: School census for the Catholic Education Council.

The staffing pattern therefore appeared to reflect the major division on the site between houses and departments. House heads controlled more teachers and pupils than the heads of departments and therefore commanded higher salaries. But this makes far too basic a distinction, as there were further divisions. The headmaster had attempted to attract large numbers of highly qualified Catholic teachers to the school. By the time I joined the staff, the proportion of Catholic to non-Catholic teachers was as shown in table 1.2. While there was no open conflict between Catholic and non-Catholic teachers, there was a noticeable division between them as the former held all the posts of responsibility for pastoral work and some of the posts of responsibility for departments. The result was that higher salaries and greater power were concentrated in the hands of Catholic teachers.

However, the position was still more complex. Many non-Catholic teachers, like Catholic teachers in the departments, also did pastoral work because they acted as group tutors in the houses. Similarly, heads of departments worked in houses while heads of houses worked in departments. At McGregor these groups of teachers put forward different ideas about the school and about the type of education that should be provided (see chapters three and four).

The pupils

McGregor's pupils lived in the Catholic parishes surrounding the school in the south-west corner of Merston. These children attended their local Roman Catholic primary schools until they reached the age of eleven, when they were automatically transferred to Bishop McGregor School. The school, therefore, had a completely Catholic intake.[26]

Just as the pattern of buildings and staffing had been by instalments,

Table 1.3   The pupil population in Bishop McGregor School, 1969–73

Year groups	Academic years				
	1969	*1970*	*1971*	*1972*	*1973*
1st	240	220	256	288	255
2nd	160	240	227	255	281
3rd		160	238	227	254
4th			157	233	227
5th				113	228
6th					24
7th					
Totals	400	620	878	1116	1269

Note: The number of pupils are those who were in attendance during September each year.
Source: (1) Appendix to the governors' report, October 1971.
(2) Letters to the Diocesan Schools Commission, September 1972 and September 1973.

so the size of the pupil population developed in a similar way. The first group of children to join the school in September 1969 consisted of second-year pupils who transferred to McGregor from other Catholic secondary schools in the city, together with a first-year intake from Catholic primary schools in the catchment area. The developments in the size of the pupil population are shown in table 1.3.

In five years McGregor trebled in size. By 1973 it qualified for the description of 'large comprehensive school'.[27] For the head, the critical point was reached in September 1972 when he had over one thousand pupils: he started his entry in the school log book with the words, 'The beast has changed'. The question of size was very real but the house system was seen as the 'solution' to this 'problem'. When first-year pupils arrived in the school they were automatically allocated to a house to help them come to terms with school size. Pupils were distributed at random among the houses, except for those who had older brothers and sisters in the school and were therefore allocated to their siblings' house; it was considered easier for parents to communicate with the same house head. In the houses, all pupils belonged to mixed-ability groups called tutorials in which they remained until they were to leave school or transfer to the sixth form. In tutorial groups, registers were taken, letters distributed to parents, social and charity work organized and competitions held. These groups were the focus of formal social organization among pupils.

Alongside the social organization was the academic organization of teaching groups. For first-year pupils the mixed-ability tutorial was the basic teaching unit. Here, pupils were predominantly taught by their house staff as this gave teachers an opportunity to get to know the members of their house and to establish house rules and routines. The academic organization of the school therefore helped to reinforce the social organization of the school among first-year pupils. In the second and third years, pupils were allocated to sets according to their ability in mathematics, languages and science subjects. Although in theory pupils were not supposed to know the rank order of sets, it was usual for them to refer to themselves as the top set or second set or, 'in the bottom set because we're dim'.[28] However, even those in the bottom sets took comfort that they were not in the remedial group for work in reading and arithmetic, as in their terms that indicated you were 'really dumb'. In the fourth and fifth years, pupils were divided into various teaching groups when they followed a common core of subjects, subject options for examination courses and the non-examination (Newsom) course. Finally, in the sixth form, pupils were relatively free to select their own subject groups.

The pupils therefore belonged to a number of formal subgroups: houses, tutorials, mixed-ability groups, sets and option groups. Each pupil's membership of the school involved simultaneous membership of several groups. These groups constituted basic divisions within the school's formal structure and gave strength to the idea that the school was not a single group or 'community'. Instead, the formal organization resulted in a series of subgroups and 'communities', all of which advanced different norms and values on the basis of different sets of social relations, patterns of social interaction and beliefs about the school and about education.

The curriculum

The curriculum was linked to the pattern of academic organization in the school (cf. Hargreaves 1982). In years one to three, the pupils were introduced to the major subjects in the secondary school curriculum. Meanwhile, in the fourth, fifth and sixth years, the pupils followed specialized

Table 1.4 Option groups for fourth- and fifth-year pupils, 1972–4

Group A	Group B	Group C	Group D	Group E
French (O)	History (O)	Spanish (O)	Commerce	Typing
Physics	Biology (O)	French	Motor vehicle maintenance	Home economics
Art	Needlework	Geography (O)	Technical drawing	Metalwork
Economics	Human biology	Music	History	Art and craft
Typing	Art	Shorthand	Physics (O)	Biology (O)
Geography	Typing	Chemistry (O)	Physics	Additional maths (O)
Technical drawing (O)	Metalwork (O)	Biology (CSE)	Physics	General science
Woodwork (O)	Motor vehicle maintenance	Building construction	Spanish	German
Motor vehicle maintenance			Latin	Religion (O) and (CSE)
				Understanding industrial society

Notes: 1 Arrows ←——→ indicate linked subject choices.
2 (1) Subjects marked (O) indicates GCE Ordinary-level courses.
   (2) Subjects marked (CSE) indicates CSE courses.
   (3) Subjects unmarked indicates course level to be decided.
3 All choices by pupils had to include one science subject.
4 Only one subject could be chosen from each group.

courses that were taken to different levels for public examinations and for non-examination purposes.

At the end of the third year, parents, pupils, house and departmental staff were involved in the selection of subjects for the fourth- and fifth-year courses.[29] All pupils were required to take a core course consisting of religious education, English, mathematics, games and physical education. In addition, pupils who wished to follow an examination course had to select a further five subjects from the option groups (see table 1.4) which would allow them to take either Ordinary-level courses for the General Certificate of Education (GCE), or a series of courses leading to the Certificate of Secondary Education (CSE) or a mixture of both. Pupils who wished to take non-examination courses had to follow the common core and take a series of options selected from art and craft, motor vehicle maintenance, typing, woodwork, home economics, metalwork and needlework together with the Newsom course that included project options and courses provided by the technical college. Such a division between academic (examination)-based courses and practical (non-examination) courses suggests that within this comprehensive school there were elements of tripartite school organization in the fourth and fifth years, based on the distinction between the academic education that had previously been provided by grammar schools and the practical education that had been defined as the core curriculum of the secondary modern school.[30]

At McGregor, the curriculum generated sets, options, examination and non-examination groups. Together with the pattern of school organization it helped to produce specific groups in which education was defined in numerous ways.

Summary and conclusion

This chapter has examined the physical and social contexts in which teachers and pupils found themselves when they became members of Bishop McGregor School. Although I acquired this knowledge throughout the fieldwork, I have used it at this point in the study for three reasons. Firstly, it provides a picture of the physical and social setting of the school. Secondly, it outlines the context of the situations and events that I discuss in my analysis. Thirdly, some of the physical and social features of the school raised questions which were used in my fieldwork and are discussed in subsequent chapters.

Bishop McGregor School was subdivided into a number of separate buildings. Based on this subdivision was the house system, and staff and pupil organization followed directly from it. Teachers and pupils were organized in a number of distinct groups that constituted important social divisions within the school. The main formal division was between houses and departments: while most staff were recruited to departments some overlap did occur when departmental staff worked in the houses and house staff worked in the departments. Alongside these formal groups were informal groups whose composition reflected the formal structure of the school. Among pupils the basic house and departmental structure influenced the formal groups to which they belonged for social and academic purposes. All pupils simultaneously belonged to a house group (tutorial) and to mixed-ability groups, sets and option groups in the departmental structure. Alongside the formal groups were informal groups that cut across this structure.

The salient features of the physical and social structure of the school presented a series of initial questions that were used to guide my field-work. These questions concerned the ways in which the 'school' and 'education' were defined by different groups at Bishop McGregor School. I began by examining the distinction between teachers appointed to houses and those appointed to departments. How did the headmaster operate the school with these basic groups? What norms were held by the members of these groups? How did the social organization of the school influence the curriculum? How was teaching and learning conducted and defined? How were the pupils educated and how was their education defined? In short, I posed questions about the social and academic organization of the school, definitions of the school and the way in which education was defined within it. To address these questions, I focused my attention on sets of social relationships and patterns of social interaction among different groups. The remaining chapters in part one examine the ways in which the school and education were defined by teachers, while part two examines similar themes in relation to teachers and pupils in the Newsom department.

Notes

1 See Education Act (1944), and for commentaries on church, state and education see, for example, Murphy (1971), Archer (1979, 498–505).
2 Interview with Charles Bridges.
3 See Ministry of Education (1945; 1947).
4 Letter to the Merston local education authority from the Minister of Education, 1 July 1953.
5 Letters responding to enquiries about the internal organization of Merston schools.
6 Memorandum on comprehensive schools prepared for the authority, 20 March 1953.
7 For a review of decentralizing schools in England see, for example, Halsall (1973) and for data on the USA, Plath (1965).
8 The director had experience of this system as he was a governor of an inde-pendent school.

9 Nationally there was a Labour government that had issued Circular 10/65 (Department of Education 1965) requesting local education authorities to submit schemes for the reorganization of secondary education along comprehensive lines. For further discussions of the development of comprehensive education in England see, for example, Bellaby (1977) and Fenwick (1976).

11 General information on the school written by the headmaster in 1969.

10 For a discussion of the house system in comprehensive schools see, for example, Benn and Simon (1972, 328–34, 336–7, 413). For a critical comment on the house system in comprehensive schools see, for example, Pedley (1978, 118–20).

12 The science master had good reason to think in this way, as in further particulars for appointments in the science department, the headmaster and the head of the science department had referred to this room as follows: 'the technical activities room – a science laboratory/workshop equipped with lathes and various other machine tools . . . is designed for project work with some of the older children'.

13 All the governors told me that they specifically wanted a headmaster for the school.

14 The governors told me that only one of their number had to be persuaded that Mr Goddard should get the position.

15 Interview with a school governor.

16 Extract from short autobiography written by the headmaster.

17 For accounts of starting new schools by headteachers see, for example, Chetwynd (1960), Boyson (1974), Colgate (1976) and Holt (1978).

18 Interview with the headmaster, which like all interviews with teachers and pupils was tape-recorded. For a further discussion of the appointment of a deputy head to a new comprehensive school see Chetwynd (1960, 26).

19 In 1977 Frank Lloyd obtained a headship in a comprehensive school.

20 Further particulars for posts at Bishop McGregor School issued by the headmaster in 1969.

21 Interview with the headmaster.

22 Cf. Chetwynd (1960, 26) where she discussed her policies for staffing a new comprehensive school. She wanted teachers who were not too attached to the 'old' traditions and who would adjust themselves to new ways of thought and a different approach to education.

23 Interview with the headmaster.

24 Cf. Chetwynd (1960, 27) where she discusses her requirements for house heads. She wanted teachers for these posts who were more concerned with teaching in the broadest sense than with teaching subjects.

25 Interview with the headmaster. Cf. Chetwynd (1960, 27–8).

26 At the time of the study, the demand from Catholic parents meant that no places could be allocated to non-Catholic children.

27 According to the Department of Education and Science statistics for January 1973 (Department of Education and Science 1974) there were 5159 maintained secondary schools in England and Wales. Of these schools, 3.2 per cent had less than 300 pupils, 30 per cent had 301–600 pupils, 39.8 per cent had 601–1000 pupils and 26.8 per cent had over 1000 pupils. (See Department of Education and Science 1974, table 4, 12.)

28 For similar findings in a junior school see Nash (1974).

29 For a discussion of subject choice see Woods (1979, 25–62), and for the pattern of the fourth-year curriculum in secondary schools see Department of Education and Science (1979, 21–37).
30 For further discussion of the education provided by grammar schools see, for example, Rée (1956), Stevens (1960), and studies by King (1969) and Lacey (1970). For further discussion of education in the secondary modern school see, for example, Loukes (1956), Newsom (1963), Taylor (1963), the study by Hargreaves (1967) and the account by Partridge (1968). For trends in secondary education see Department of Education and Science (1979), and for critical comment Hargreaves (1982).

2

THE HEADMASTER'S

CONCEPTION OF THE SCHOOL

It has become traditional in the English school system for considerable power and authority to be vested in the office of headteacher. Headteachers have been given responsibility for internal organization, the recruitment of teachers, the distribution of resources and the control and discipline within schools. In short, as Baron (1955) has remarked, heads have become the pivot and focus of their schools.

Despite the relative importance of headteachers, there are few accounts of what they do. This is not to suggest that accounts have not been available as there are numerous discussions of how headteachers should organize their schools, what issues need consideration and how they should be handled.[1] Individual accounts by headteachers such as Chetwynd (1960), Boyson (1974), Holt (1978) and Dawson (1981) have provided some insights into the ways in which particular headteachers claim to perform their tasks. Meanwhile, public attention has been drawn to the way in which individual headteachers have interpreted their role.[2]

In turn, there have been relatively few sociological studies of headteachers, and those that are available tend to be somewhat speculative. Firstly, there are accounts of the role of the headteacher (cf. Bernbaum 1976; Hughes 1976; Baron 1970). Secondly, there are accounts of the changes that confront headteachers (Taylor 1973) and thirdly, there are some discussions of headteachers as leaders, managers and sources of authority within the schools (Taylor 1976; King 1973b). However, there is very little empirical material specifically on headteachers.[3] A notable exception is a report by Bernbaum (1974) on the social origins, educational and work experiences of a sample of headmasters in the East Midlands. Meanwhile, ethnographic studies of secondary schools by Hargreaves (1967), Lacey (1970), Woods (1979) and Ball (1981) have devoted little attention to the headmasters of the schools other than incidental remarks that relate to various facets of school organization.[4]

This chapter is therefore intended to fill a gap in the current literature by focusing on the headmaster at Bishop McGregor School. In particular, attention will be devoted to the way in which he defined the internal organization of the school and the content of the curriculum.

Defining headship

Baron has shown how the concept of headship has been linked to particular schools. He discusses how the structure of public schools and grammar schools gave rise to heads who ran the schools and shaped them according to their own ideals (Baron 1955, 3). This has been partly taken over by headteachers in state schools as Banks remarks:

> Traditionally the headmaster or headmistress of an English school is expected to function as a leader rather than as a part of an administrative bureaucracy. All the teaching methods and procedures, all matters relating to curricula, the relationships with parents and the control of teachers and their duties are recognized as matters for the head to decide and education committees will rarely try to interfere. (1976, 134–5)

While the headteacher may be relatively free from interference, he or she does operate within constraints that are, in part, determined by the local authority. In Merston, the director of education considered that large new comprehensive schools demanded 'good' headteachers who would adapt to working in the authority's new schools. In an address to housemasters and housemistresses on 5 February 1958 he explained that these schools demanded a new concept of headship as he remarked, 'I thought of our large schools rather as universities where the head, like the vice-chancellor, is more a chairman of the senate than dictator'. Here, there was an expectation of some movement away from the traditional autocratic concept of headship. However, the director still maintained that the headteacher was all important in the school as he stated: 'It is abundantly clear that nothing can take the place of the man or woman at the top in any educational institution – the tone and the quality of the person who in the ultimate resort is responsible for it'. This position is similar to that of Bernbaum (1974) and Taylor (1973) who see the head occupying an important but nevertheless modified position within the school as a result of changes in the size and complexity of the institution. In particular, Taylor (1973, 11–12) summarizes changes in the style of headship when he states:

> It is no longer so easy for the head to be in close personal contact with the staff and pupils, to be able to claim that he knows everyone in the school. He must necessarily delegate a good deal to senior colleagues. The skills involved in co-ordinating the work of several departments and house units, in interpreting the school to the community which it serves, in initiating innovation and encouraging others to innovate, all become of greater importance; the head must add managerial skills to his existing commitment to educational objectives and the needs of children.

In Merston's comprehensive schools headteachers required a diverse set of skills as they had to manage large schools, co-ordinate, and innovate and present the school to the community. So the selection of the head-teacher was crucial to the development of each school.

The governors of Bishop McGregor School appointed Mr Geoffrey Goddard, a Catholic in his early forties, to be the first headmaster. When Mr Goddard was appointed to lead McGregor he had been a teacher for thirteen years, five of which had been spent as headmaster of a secondary modern school. In comparison with Bernbaum's sample of heads he had been appointed relatively early to a headship in a secondary school and to the headship of a comprehensive school.[5]

His ideas about how to run a school were, as in the case of most headteachers, based on his early teaching experience and from positions of responsibility that he had held in other schools. But in Mr Goddard's case he had an experience of teaching and of headship from his own family as both his parents had been teachers and his father had been headmaster of the Roman Catholic school in his home town.

Originally, Mr Goddard had reacted against teaching. On leaving school he decided to train for the priesthood, but by the mid-1950s he had resigned from the Order to follow a teaching career. His first teaching post was at St Augustine's Secondary Boys' School in Merston. He was highly successful here: at the end of his first year the headmaster singled him out for special mention in a governors' report by stating, 'Mr Goddard has been outstanding in his devotion to work and in his extreme thoroughness and conscientiousness'.[6] At St Augustine's he gained experience in several areas of secondary modern school work. He was soon promoted to be head of the science department which allowed him to gain experience in preparing classes for external examinations. Mean-while, he also gained some pastoral and organizational experience as a head of house. Outside the school he quickly earned a reputation for his vigorous participation in the Catholic Teachers Association and the local branch of his teacher union.

Four years later he was to leave Merston for St Mark's Roman Catholic School in Leyton, a new Catholic comprehensive school which had quickly established a reputation for itself and where promotion was rapid. Mr Goddard became head of chemistry and head of science having responsibility for twelve teachers and a block of science laboratories. While he was at St Mark's, a parish priest encouraged Goddard to apply for headships. The priest thought that Goddard had sufficient experience for such a post. His first application was unsuccessful, but a further application resulted in his appointment to the headship of a secondary modern school for boys in Oldtown. At St Edmund's School in Oldtown Mr Goddard's ideas about schools, about teaching and more particularly about headship were put to the test.

An early but formative experience of headship was drawn from his father. Mr Goddard recalled his father bringing much of his day-to-day administrative work home with him, principally because he had spent the whole day working with classes. In this way, Goddard learned that being a headmaster meant working with pupils: a belief that was to serve as his basic model, because he had gained his success through teaching and believed that he could demonstrate his own abilities to staff and pupils through his classroom work. As a consequence, difficult classes and substitution lessons became part of his daily routine at St Edmund's. He believed that teaching the difficult pupils indicated their importance for him and allowed him to demonstrate to the staff various methods of working. Demonstrating his beliefs was central to his style as he considered that if a head 'wants an attitude developed in a school, he must demonstrate it to the people he is with. He must demonstrate it to the staff and pupils.'[7] In addition, he considered that a headteacher should be seen around a school. In this sense, as headmaster at St Edmund's, Mr Goddard delivered letters to teachers, met his staff and pupils, took classes and a share of substitution lessons.[8] For Goddard, being the head meant taking the lead: 'I became convinced that the more a head was about, the more he led. I was a field officer, not a staff officer. I led from the front and it worked for me.'[9] Mr Goddard therefore defined the role of the head as manager, co-ordinator, decision-maker, organizer and teacher. To him, the head was the main participant in the school.

It was these qualities that persuaded the governors that he should be appointed as head of Bishop McGregor School. Here was a challenge given to relatively few teachers: namely, to open a new school.[10] When Mr Goddard was appointed to the post, McGregor was little more than an idea, a building site with several blocks that had to be made into a school. It was Goddard's task to bring this site alive, to recruit staff, allocate pupils and construct a curriculum.

While Boyson (1974) argues that a head in this position has a relatively free hand, the situation at McGregor highlights the constraints within which a head operates. McGregor was a purpose-built comprehensive school with house accommodation; factors which were to influence staff recruitment and the definition of the curriculum. In common with other secondary school heads the terms of Goddard's appointment were defined in the Articles of Government:

> The headteacher shall control the internal organization, management and discipline of the school, shall exercise supervision over the arrangements for school meals so far as is necessary for the purpose of school discipline and organization and over the teaching and non-teaching staff.

While this presents few immediate problems for headteachers in established schools with traditions and routines, at McGregor a pattern of organization, management and discipline had to be created. The way in which Mr Goddard decided to establish his school was to start by, 'selling the idea of this school to teachers, parents, pupils, to industry and the city. I told them my ideas about running the school and what might happen.'[11] In this respect, Mr Goddard considered communication to be of paramount importance in defining the structure and identity of the school.

The first discussion paper[12] which Goddard produced concerned communications. In particular, the paper suggested that communications were vital in a new school so that, 'the right image is projected to the public in general and to individuals who have a special interest (e.g. parents)'.[13] Public relations were to be the head's responsibility, but as all teachers would to some extent become involved in the system it was argued that 'it is important that all members of the staff are fully conversant with the philosophy and policy of the school'.[14] It was envisaged that this could be done through meetings that the head would hold with the staff or through written communications. Finally, it was suggested that the pupils should also be involved in the process of communications through tutorial groups and the record system.

While this paper indicated that meetings and further notes and papers were the ways in which the head would communicate with groups, in practice it was more flexible and wide-ranging as Mr Goddard communicated with parents, staff and pupils by attending meetings, social events and school assembly, teaching different classes, talking to individuals and walking around the school. Goddard defined his role in terms of communication with others and through his actions and activities within the school.

Goddard considered the office of headmaster at Bishop McGregor School meant being the main participant: manager, co-ordinator, consultant, decision-maker, planner and teacher. Indeed, he saw himself occupying all these roles and summarized it by saying, 'I'm a sort of educational supercook who mixes the different jobs together: the Katy Stewart of teaching'.[15] As a consequence of his participation, Mr Goddard found that McGregor 'whether I like it or not or whether I want it or not, is at least in fair measure shaped by me. I'll be blunt. That worries me. I have an influence and it is an important influence, I'll accept.'[16] However, he found that, 'if I'm away for a month it changes. When I went to the engineering works for three weeks little things changed.'[17] But he considered 'This is right and proper as the school shouldn't be a monument to me'.[18] As a headmaster who considered his duty was to participate with parents, teachers and pupils it provided an opportunity for Mr Goddard to define the way in which the school should operate.[19] He was none the less aware that his ideas, hopes and plans for McGregor were manipulated, changed and redefined by various groups in the school. However, we begin by looking at the way in which Bishop McGregor School was initially defined by the headmaster.

Presenting the school to the parents

There was a range of formal and informal meetings between the teachers and the parents: house meetings, year group meetings, social evenings, dances, fêtes, individual meetings with the headmaster and his staff and regular contact with school events through letters and notices which were sent home with the pupils. These contacts provided opportunities for the headmaster to communicate his ideas about the school, its image and the way in which it should be organized. Among the meetings he attended were those held each summer term with the parents of pupils who were to start at McGregor in the following September. Here, he could outline his aims and objectives for the school.

Goddard used the summer term before the school opened to prepare for the new intake in the autumn and to meet parents of new entrants. While the Catholic community were not strangers to Catholic schools or to the new comprehensive schools that had been built in Merston, they had no experience of their own comprehensive school. In this sense, Bishop McGregor School was a pioneer in the city.

This situation demanded attention. Mr Goddard decided that he would have to talk to parents about the way in which he wanted a new Catholic comprehensive school to operate. At the end of the summer term in 1969 he visited all the junior schools in McGregor's catchment area to talk about 'comprehensive education and Bishop McGregor School'. In this talk he discussed the image and identity that he wanted to establish for McGregor as a Catholic comprehensive school as he stated:

It is my hope that for the future, Bishop McGregor will join the list of comprehensive schools known and admired in the first ten years of its life. That within twenty the Catholic community will consider it an outstanding example of what a Catholic school should be, and that when the history of education, given in the schools of England and Wales in the second half of the twentieth century, comes to be written, the part played by this school of such promise and high hopes will be seen to have justified the foresight of the people and clergy of Merston who planned and paid for it, and the trust that you, the parents of our first pupils, placed in us its first staff.[20]

McGregor would be based on traditions that could be derived from Catholic and local authority schools. He explained that from the grammar school he would take streaming, setting and high standards; from the secondary modern school technical courses and Newsom options and from the comprehensive school the idea of houses and pastoral organiz-ation. He therefore suggested that the organization of the school was to be based on elements of the tripartite model of secondary education.

The social or pastoral organization was to consist of the physical house system which had been pioneered by Merston. Each house was to be subdivided into a number of mixed-ability tutorial groups which would, according to Goddard, give the children an opportunity to experience success and excellence. Meanwhile, academic organization would be based on different forms of knowledge in the first three years, an option system in the fourth and fifth years which would provide 'special courses towards specific goals' and an academic and non-academic sixth form. The result would be a series of divisions based on the pastoral system developed by the authority and a curriculum that was derived from secondary schools before comprehensives were developed.

However, the headmaster stressed that McGregor was a Catholic school which would provide a Catholic education. He explained that the church provided schools to encourage children to grow up as Christian men and women and that the school would therefore involve a com-munality of purpose between the church, parents, teachers and pupils. It would emphasize the idea of shared beliefs and values for a fuller life. In short, the headmaster established the identity of the school in terms of its Catholicism, its internal organization based on the house system and its specialized curriculum for the individual pupil; all of which were regularly reinforced in letters and in meetings.

When the parents visited the school, they were visibly reminded of its internal structure by the individual house blocks. The contact they had with the school was through the house system and the house staff, since on open evenings, social occasions and even for individual meetings the house staff were approached first. Parents' evenings were an opportunity for members of the school and part of the community which it served to come together; a time when teachers and parents could meet. It was also an occasion when the headmaster could present further ideas about the school structure and its curriculum.

A third-year parents' evening that I attended was held in the Westminster and Arundel house halls. Over one hundred parents attended this meeting where the headmaster discussed the option system in the fourth year. Here, Mr Goddard not only discussed the option system but also presented the academic organization of the school. He explained that all pupils had to take English, mathematics, religious education, physical education and tutorial as part of the core curriculum which made up nineteen periods on the timetable. This meant that sixteen periods could be divided between the option pools. He explained that the option system allowed children to choose a combination of subjects which would represent an academically orientated curriculum: geography, history, biology, economics or French, or chemistry, or technical drawing and physics. It was also possible to select a less academic orientation by choosing to take a group of subjects which included woodwork, motor vehicle maintenance, history, physics or art, or home economics, or human biology and geography.

A further scheme available was the Newsom course. Mr Goddard explained that this was designed for pupils who did not wish to do examinations exclusively or for whom an examination course was considered undesirable or harmful. He claimed that the Newsom course was 'an adult course to be looked at in an adult way' and included options in film making, wine making and wood carving. However, he also indicated that some Newsom pupils could take examinations in first aid and mothercraft which were specially arranged by the staff.

This parents' evening demonstrates the way in which the headmaster presented the school to the parents. While he talked about academic organization and the option system, he was also defining the way in which the school operated. In this presentation Mr Goddard highlighted three basic features of the upper school curriculum. Firstly, an academic curriculum represented by a range of academic subjects. Secondly, a technical/commercial curriculum represented by academic and practical subjects. Thirdly, a modern school curriculum which was represented by the Newsom course with an emphasis on practical work. The academic organization in the fourth and fifth years appeared to be rooted in the tripartite tradition of secondary school organization. Furthermore, these different types of curricula could be used by the school to subdivide the pupils into three broad strata: those who followed a curriculum with an academic orientation, those who followed a curriculum with a less academic orientation and, finally, those who took Newsom courses.

Presenting the school to the teachers

While the headmaster presented his ideas about the life and work of the school to the parents through a variety of meetings and letters, other strategies were used to communicate with his staff. Meetings and letters were used but Mr Goddard also presented his ideas about McGregor when he took assembly, taught classes and took substitution lessons. Teachers were constantly aware that the head was around the school. There were few days and few lessons when he could not be seen crossing the site. He was his own messenger. If a message had to be given to a teacher it would usually be the head who would walk to their classroom rather than a pupil, a secretary, or another teacher. Whatever the head asked his staff to do, they knew that he would be prepared and able to do himself. When they were asked to keep pupils off the grass, the head took part as he would regularly open his windows and shout at pupils to keep off the grass. When staff were asked to travel on school buses, Mr Goddard joined those who boarded buses and when staff were asked to check buildings during bomb scares, it was the head who took the lead. Thus Mr Goddard's numerous directives, suggestions, plans and routines sent to staff were supported by his actions: he was a head who participated fully in the life of his school. This marked the quality of his headship and earned him respect and co-operation from some teachers as it provided a framework within which they could operate. However, others criticized his approach as they claimed there was too much teaching to be done without having to read his notes.

When the school opened in September 1969 there were only five teachers out of a staff of eighteen who had any experience of comprehensive schools. Of these, the individual with most comprehensive school experience was the headmaster. Many staff had no experience of comprehensive schools and little experience of schools in general, because they were in their early years of teaching.[21] As a result, several teachers required assistance, direction and guidance from the head and his senior teachers.

Goddard set about creating a framework within which his staff could operate by establishing a series of meetings in which teachers could discuss school policy. There were full staff meetings, meetings for house heads and department heads, and meetings of house and departmental staff. While these meetings provided a forum in which the staff could contribute their views on school routine, the headmaster held the most powerful position. Since he chaired many of the meetings, he defined the business. Even in his absence Goddard defined the business as the teachers were often presented with discussion papers that he had written. Meetings within the school were therefore a direct line of communication between the headmaster and the teachers. In addition, Goddard also used school assembly to communicate information to his staff. Often the system of verbal communication would be preceded or followed by written notices that were issued to teachers. Every teacher was the recipient of a number of circulars from the headmaster each week. Among the information I regularly received was a news bulletin, notes, minutes of meetings, details about individual pupils, copies of letters that had been sent to pupils' homes, discussion papers, ideas on school procedures and information on the general routines in the school. In some weeks there was so much information that teachers complained they had little time to read it.

However, most teachers found this material helped them in their work. Firstly, it provided basic information about what was happening in different areas of the school. Secondly, it gave guidance on non-teaching duties. Finally, it helped teachers to understand the way in which Mr Goddard wanted the school to work.

Defining the Catholic school

We have already seen that the church considered that the Catholic character of a school could be established and maintained by the appointment of Catholic teachers. Accordingly, Mr Goddard attempted to recruit the maximum number of Catholic teachers. However, a dearth of applications from Catholics resulted in almost half the appointments going to non-Catholics. In an interview with me Mr Goddard admitted that this concerned him as he wanted to give the school a distinct Catholic character.

Mr Goddard took a key role in developing religious education within the school. At the start of each school year he conducted prayers with all his staff, and prayed for the life and work of all members of the school. On three mornings each week, he took school assembly in the houses. Most Wednesday mornings he attended the school Mass and each week he took a share of religious education classes as he was a self-appointed member of the religious education department. Goddard therefore demonstrated to all that religion was for him a crucial element of school life. But the same could not be said for his staff. Many did not attend the weekly mass or share in the teaching of religious education, while less than half the staff in my house regularly attended the morning assembly. Even those who attended did so for a variety of reasons: to be seen (as they thought this would assist with promotion), to demonstrate their loyalty to the school and the house, as well as to participate in daily worship.

Nevertheless, Mr Goddard attempted to make religion a focal point of school life and school routine. Each year he issued a paper to his staff entitled 'Religious cycles in the school year', in which he argued that the liturgical cycle should be integrated with the school curriculum and should be used to promote a number of school activities. In particular he maintained: 'various events of the church's year do come annually and should be reflected in our joint worship, in formal religious education lessons and informally in other subjects where this can be done'.[22] However, as we shall see in the following chapter, his suggestions were taken up mainly by teachers involved in religious education and by heads of houses who conducted daily worship and taught some religious education classes. The majority of staff only participated because religious education was a central part of the programme in their houses.

Goddard suggested that the great church festivals of Harvest and Christmas were times when the school could engage in music and drama. During the time that I was in the school this suggestion was not followed up by any teachers. In the spring term he suggested that Lent could provide a focus for social service in the school when teachers and pupils could celebrate the Passion and death of Christ through the Lenten charities' collections. This suggestion was followed up by the heads of houses who took responsibility for the Lenten charities. House heads' assemblies were turned into sessions when pupils were encouraged, berated and harangued to collect more money than other houses. Teachers did not escape either. House heads encouraged their staff to push the pupils into organizing comic book auctions, 'discos' and sponsored silences. The result was a period in the liturgical cycle which generated competition among pupils and house heads and cynicism, humour and anger among other staff. The Lenten charities therefore reinforced the structural divisions in the school and promoted competition between groups. Certainly, this was not the headmaster's intention as he considered that events in the liturgical year could be used to develop a positive link between activities in the school and in pupils' homes and parishes. The head thought that these activities would help to foster the development of Christian values among teachers and pupils.

On a daily basis, he saw the morning assembly as central to the life of the school. As these daily acts of worship were Catholic in content they were obligatory for all Catholic teachers, but the non-Catholic teachers were encouraged to attend: the head thought this would help to promote a Christian ethos within the school. This in itself suggested some division between Catholic and non-Catholic teachers, at least in Goddard's terms. In addition to starting the day with worship the head also hoped that the end of the school day would close with worship as he told staff 'the custom to end the school day with short prayers . . . is strongly commended to all. For staff who are not Catholics it is always possible to have one or more of the pupils lead short evening prayers.'[23] While this was an activity which the headmaster wanted to see developed within the school, I was never aware of any staff who followed this particular routine, including himself when he taught on the last lesson of the afternoon. However, Goddard did attempt to promote Christian values and principles at Bishop McGregor School. Even if he could not carry the whole of his staff on this issue he did put before them a series of suggestions to link religion, life and work in the school. While his example was recognized by many there were relatively few teachers, beyond the heads of houses and those who were involved in the teaching of religious education, who actively promoted religion within their school programme.

Defining school organization

Headteachers operate within a series of constraints that emanate from within the educational system and the society in which they are located. At McGregor, it was evident that Mr Goddard's ideas about school organization were, in part, determined by the pattern of comprehensive school organization that had been devised by the Merston authority. In particular, the house system determined the character of the school; he informed teachers who applied for posts at McGregor that 'The school is organized into houses and each house has a number of mixed-ability groups, one or two per year, called tutorials'.[24] The houses and departments represented a basic division of responsibilities in the school, as Goddard considered houses were responsible for social and pastoral activities, departments being entrusted with academic affairs.

This basic division was made clear when the head addressed the staff on the subject of discipline. As far as he was concerned the standard of discipline was the responsibility of 'us all collectively: no one teacher, no one group of teachers, senior or junior, departmental or house acting in an isolated manner can put it right'.[25] But he indicated that if this plan was to operate the staff had to be subdivided into groups with special responsibilities. Here again, the basic division between houses and departments was utilized. Houses were to be responsible for assemblies, uniform, attendance, mannerliness and for liaison work between the school and the pupils' homes, while departments were to take the lead on acceptable standards of work, levels of noise, work, layout of work, levels of talk and co-operation between the pupils. However, Mr Goddard foresaw situations in which houses and departments would work together. If pupils misbehaved or would not work in a department, it was suggested that the teacher should enlist the support of the pupil's head of house who 'may have information which may help in understanding why a child is behaving badly'[26] and who 'can often bring not only information to you but pressure to bear upon a child, or they may as a result of your request institute enquiries which lead to fresh knowledge'.[27] This suggests that the headmaster saw a division of labour between his staff. However, departmental staff rarely consulted house staff about pupils as they thought this would undermine their authority. Although theoretically the staff were striving for the same standards the house staff were responsible for behaviour while departmental staff were responsible for subjects. In this context, the basic division in the social structure resulted, as we shall see in the following chapters, in a series of conflicts between house and departmental staff. In turn these subdivisions were also reflected in the organization of the curriculum.

Defining the school curriculum

The idea that the curriculum is no more than a collection of syllabi has been criticized by Jenkins and Shipman (1976, 4-6). They argue that the curriculum consists of an educational proposal that is taught and learned in the school. This view is shared by Musgrave (1973, 41) who defined curriculum as a term which 'refers to those learning experiences or succession of such experiences that are purposefully arranged by formal educational organizations'. In this respect, the curriculum in a school such as McGregor embraces not merely academic and practical subjects but also common sense or behavioural knowledge as expressed in school rules and routines. At McGregor, the house staff had general responsibility for behavioural knowledge while the departmental staff had major responsibility for academic knowledge.[28]

The headmaster's idea about standards of discipline that were to be encouraged in the school indicated the norms and values that he wanted to be promoted and the way in which he wanted the school to operate. His ideas about discipline indicated that the ideal was to prevent actions from occurring rather than to stop misdemeanours. Mr Goddard expected his staff to arrive punctually at lessons if they were to expect the same standard from pupils. He also indicated the standards which teachers should set when he stated: 'No teacher should tolerate insolence or obscenity from a child. If such occurs then an instant apology should be expected and if this is not forthcoming then the class should not proceed until the offender has been removed.'[29] In this sense, it was the headmaster who indicated the basic standards of discipline in the school and by implication the tenor of relationships between staff and pupils. But his ideas were not always followed and even when they were implemented they were interpreted by teachers in various ways.

Goddard wanted his staff not only to note 'bad' behaviour but also 'good' behaviour which could be praised and encouraged. The teachers were, therefore, instructed to:

Be as quick, if not quicker, to commend and praise as to condemn.

Send children to others with good work, use commendations for effort. Encourage, display, praise, give publicity to all who try so that at the very worst the exhibitionist sees this as a more likely road to fame than mischief and more soberly so that hard-working young-sters do not become so dejected that they give up.[30]

School life was therefore defined by the head in terms of qualities which were to be encouraged: punctuality, a readiness to work, effort and hard work. Even those activities which he wished to eliminate indicated the ideals he wanted to create – discouraging insolence indicated a desire to promote good manners, discouraging the obscene indicated a desire to promote the decent and rejecting the exhibitionist involved promoting the modest.

Within these norms, there was an attempt to institute uniform practice within the school. Mr Goddard insisted that if teachers sent pupils to another part of the school, they were to be given a note which would indicate where the children had come from, where they were going and who had sent them. This procedure should have made it difficult for pupils to play truant from lessons. As few teachers followed this pro-cedure, pupils could often be found wandering around the school without any note or form of permission from a teacher.

The headmaster also devised a uniform set of negative sanctions on a school-wide basis which included: 'lines', essays, detention, corporal punishment and suspension. He suggested that while these punishments should be available, they should not be applied uniformly, but with respect to offence, the circumstances surrounding the offence and the previous record of the individual concerned. While this was an ideal which the head expressed, reality was very different. There were distinct differences in the way in which these punishments were applied between different houses in the school (see chapters three and four), with the result that teachers and pupils were critical of the heads of houses.

In many schools it is the head who defines the basic framework of the academic curriculum, decides the areas of knowledge to be covered and the qualities which are to be encouraged in particular subjects. At McGregor, the way in which the head developed subjects indicated his priorities. When the school opened the emphasis was given to the creation of basic subject departments. The first departments to be established were English and mathematics, followed later by 'traditional' subject depart-ments: geography, history, modern languages, science and technical activities. At a later date, these subjects experienced further expansion with the subdivision of the modern languages department into French, German and Spanish and the subdivision of the science department into physics, chemistry and biology.

It was the headmaster's aims and objectives for the development of the school curriculum that revealed the way in which he wanted the content of education defined in Bishop McGregor School. However, there were a number of phases in the development of the school curriculum. In the first phase, basic subject areas were marked out and their standards set. An academic emphasis was revealed in the headmaster's comment on standards within the subjects when he told staff: 'With the two more able pairs of second-year sets, by Christmas every child should be producing work at least up to good second-year "grammar" standards as far as quality is concerned'.[31] On this basis the academic subject work was linked to the grammar school system as developed in the tripartite system (cf. Hargreaves 1982).[32]

A second phase of development took place in the fourth and fifth years when non-subject areas became fully developed and their staff made post-holders. This phase involved non-academic or non-examination areas of the curriculum: remedial work, Newsom work and careers. But it was not until 1972–3 that the headmaster's aims and objectives for the school called for 'the establishment of improved remedial care' and 'further development and expansion of Newsom courses'. Finally, in 1973 the headmaster considered that the major objective for the school curriculum was:

> Consolidation of first five forms with particular reference to remedial care, to non-academic courses in the fours and fives and the guidance to be given to all pupils in their choice of courses, careers and the conduct of their lives.[33]

At the same time as non-subject areas were developed, Mr Goddard also showed an interest in curriculum innovation. Requests were made to the heads of departments to consider adopting a mixed-ability methodology and to develop inter-disciplinary courses in the humanities in the upper school. In addition, the head also planned an open sixth form which was to include academic and non-academic elements.[34]

Goddard's ideas about the school curriculum contributed towards defining the content of education and establishing divisions within the departmental system. Basically, there was a division between the academic/grammar school curriculum and the practical/secondary modern school curriculum. Furthermore, there was a definite hierarchy of subjects ranging from the academic and practical to the non-academic, non-subject areas.[35] This hierarchy of subjects and non-subjects also helped to reinforce divisions between the departments. However, Mr Goddard considered that these divisions would not lead to major problems. He thought that McGregor was united by a common purpose which allowed the school to act as a group, where unity could arise out of the different interests, tensions and conflicts that would occur in different subgroups among the staff.

Defining the school for the pupils

While for the purposes of analysis I have presented the headmaster's system of communication to different groups in separate sections, it is important to remember that any head has to communicate his ideas to different groups simultaneously. Goddard was no exception. The daily duties of a headmaster meant that he was having to communicate regularly his expectations to the pupils. There are a number of ways in which this can be done: directly through morning assembly, during lessons, through the head's presence around the school, indirectly by means of notices and messages from teachers, or by written notices displayed on notice boards throughout the school. Goddard used all these different methods of communication. However, at some stage he would always present his ideas directly to the pupils.

Presenting the school in morning assembly

Section twenty-five of the 1944 Education Act lays down that 'the school day in every county school and in every voluntary school shall begin with collective worship on the part of all pupils in attendance'. These acts of 'collective worship' are ceremonies that can be used by headteachers to focus on school life.[36] At McGregor, the size of the school prevented everyone from meeting together for assembly every morning. Each house, therefore, combined with another house to hold what was known as a school assembly that was addressed by the head or the deputy head or the senior mistress on one morning each week.[37] During these school assemblies the headmaster took the opportunity to talk to the pupils about Bishop McGregor School, the ideas that he wanted it to stand for, the way in which it was organized and the way in which he thought it should work.

Assembly started when teachers marched their tutorial groups to the house halls, where they were expected to stand in straight lines. Here, senior house staff were much in evidence as they were concerned that pupils should stand up straight and stand quietly until the headmaster arrived. Meanwhile, other teachers stood around the edge of the hall, talking to each other, making jokes, and exchanging stories until the headmaster entered to lead prayers.[38]

The structure of the assembly formalized certain distinctions in the school. Firstly, the pupils who stood in groups were representative of different age groups with junior pupils at the front of the hall and senior pupils at the back. Secondly, there was a broad distinction between the pupils who had to attend assembly and stand quietly and the staff for whom assembly was voluntary and who could exercise freedom about where they stood and what they did before the headmaster arrived.

Thirdly, there was a distinction between senior house staff (heads and deputy heads of houses who were paid allowances for their duties) and departmental staff. While the former took an active part in keeping the pupils quiet the latter took little or no part in these proceedings as they often arrived late in the hall or spent the time talking to their colleagues. Finally, the role of headmaster as distinct from teacher was emphasized when Mr Goddard made a separate entrance to a reserved space in the centre of the house halls from which he could address all the pupils and teachers who were present. As each assembly consisted of staff and pupils from two houses (that were said to be a cross-section of the school), it might be concluded that the structure of the assembly was a visual representation of the school in microcosm.

School assembly was used by the headmaster to present ideas about Catholicism, about the structure of the school and about the knowledge both behavioural and academic that he wanted members of the school to communicate. On most occasions, Mr Goddard supported what he had said in an assembly by a written communication as we shall see in our examination of the content of the assemblies.

Presenting Catholicism to the pupils

While every school is required by law to start the day with an act of worship, a voluntary-aided Roman Catholic school such as McGregor had to begin the day with an assembly that was distinctly Catholic.[39] At McGregor, the school assembly always followed a set pattern of prayers as most pupils and teachers recited in unison the Morning Offering, the Lord's Prayer, the Hail Mary and the Grace. The prayers were Catholic in style and content and were intended to remind the worshippers that they were members of a Catholic school and a Catholic community. After prayers, the headmaster (or one of his senior colleagues) gave a short talk about some aspect of Catholicism. The assemblies which were taken by the senior mistress followed major themes used by the head as she emphasized the qualities of Catholics. She reminded the pupils that they needed courage to be Catholics and to follow a Catholic way of life. She considered that if they were to be good Catholics, they should have a knowledge of specific prayers, of Catholic festivals and their meaning for the individual and a knowledge of the holy places and their significance in life.

The headmaster used Catholicism to communicate the expectations of members of the school and also those expectations that were held by the Catholic community. This was illustrated in one assembly when the head told the pupils of a complaint about behaviour that he had received from a lady who had travelled into Merston on a service bus the previous evening. Mr Goddard said that the complainant was a regular attender at

St Catherine's Church who was acquainted with McGregor School and realized that the pupils on the bus attended the school. It was for this reason, he explained, that she had told him, 'I was ashamed to be a Catholic when I knew they [the children] came from McGregor School'. Goddard repeated this statement several times and remarked that the shame was not something that should be isolated but should be shared by the whole school. The school was part of the Catholic community and the pupils who had misbehaved on the buses had not only disgraced themselves, but the school and the Catholic community of which they were a part. Membership of the Catholic community was therefore used to reinforce school norms.

In another assembly the deputy head reinforced the importance of religion when he talked about knowledge and wisdom which he linked to biblical references about the Wisdom of Solomon. He then proceeded to discuss the way in which the school was a place where knowledge could be obtained in order that 'you can prepare for your adult life, use it wisely and give account of yourself to God'. In this context, the assembly and its religious content was used to reinforce an academic norm of gathering knowledge, which in turn would allow the pupils to live their adult lives so that they would be accountable to God. In these assemblies the headmaster and his senior colleagues used religion in general and Catholicism in particular to reinforce the norms and values of the Catholic community and the qualities that they wished pupils to acquire.

Presenting school organization to the pupils

Several school assemblies were devoted to school organization. This was particularly prevalent in assemblies that were taken by the headmaster in the early part of the autumn term 1973. In these assemblies he talked to the new pupils who had come from small junior schools in the city. As these schools were only three hundred strong and subdivided into ten classes, large schools of over one thousand pupils subdivided into houses, tutorials, mixed-ability groups and sets were unknown to them. So it was essential to describe the school structure and explain how it worked. In one assembly I made the following record of Mr Goddard's talk:

> The headmaster began his talk by telling the pupils that they might all come from different schools but they did come from the same area of the city and therefore the idea behind McGregor School was to bring them all together. He remarked that the school was divided into houses. However, he added, Westminster and Arundel were not enemies as they could look at each other and see how they were alike. He said that their similarities were based on the uniform. He added, 'It's no good to go home and say, "Nobody wears the uniform"

because most people do wear it'. He explained that there were people who did not wear some of the uniform but they would probably have a good reason for it and their tutor or their head of house would probably know about it. He told them that in the past the school had had several problems with bullies but when people had told him about it he had sorted it out and cut those bullies down to size. He said that he had done this in the past and that he would do it again. . . . Finally he said that the school was like a family. 'We are all part of a family – the family of the school, the family of God and the family of man.'

This assembly is illustrative of the way in which the headmaster presented the school to new pupils. He introduced the idea of a large comprehensive school by explaining the way in which McGregor drew together pupils from different Catholic schools in the area. However, he also explained the way in which large numbers of pupils were grouped together into smaller identifiable groups called houses. Here, the way in which the house system subdivided the school and its pupils was not mentioned. Indeed, Goddard emphasized consensus between houses. Finally, he drew an analogy between the houses and a family where all individuals were known. While talking about the houses Mr Goddard also introduced the house staff with whom he thought the pupils should be in close contact. He also illustrated the values and norms held by members of the school by discussing bullying as an activity which would not be tolerated at McGregor.

Shortly after this assembly, Mr Goddard issued a written notice which was displayed in all houses and classrooms and stated:

SOME POINTS OF PRACTICE FOR ALL PUPILS

1 All are expected to be at the correct place at the correct time.
2 All are to conduct themselves sensibly and to show consideration for others at all times.
3 All items of clothing and articles brought to school must be marked with the owner's name and either the house initial or the house colour.
4 All are to treat both buildings and school equipment, furniture and books with care and respect.
5 Movement about the site should be purposeful, conducted at a reasonable walking pace and always display courtesy and care for others. In general a keep left policy is used whenever there is congestion.
6 Pupils are expected to conform to the school code governing appearance and for each this is interpreted by the head of house.
7 All are expected to treat everyone with respect and courtesy.
8 All are expected to keep the school tidy.

9 All instructions from teachers and other adults are to be obeyed.
10 All are to refrain from prohibited practices.[40]

At the same time these notes were issued to the pupils, some explanatory notes were also provided for the house staff who were to be responsible for following up the head's talk in assembly and the notice which was displayed throughout the school. The fact that house staff were to present these norms to the pupils emphasized the role of houses in presenting the school's behavioural norms.

The practices themselves emphasized the physical and social structure of the school together with the importance of houses and house heads. House blocks other than their own were only to be entered on invitation from a pupil or a teacher in another house, and within these blocks the house head's office was only to be entered with permission from a teacher. The relative importance which the headmaster attached to the houses and to the heads of houses was therefore implicitly communicated to the pupils. The points of practice also emphasized the position of head of house and the power which these teachers had over the day-to-day lives and activities of the pupils. The pupils' appearance (in terms of cleanliness, tidiness, hair length and girls' make-up) was to be determined by individual house heads. The head of house was also responsible for seeing that pupils came to McGregor in school uniform. Only house heads could give pupils permission to leave the school site during the day, to bring sandwiches to school or to go home to lunch, and to bring a bicycle to school. However, as we shall see (in the following chapter), each house head redefined his or her duties in very different terms.

The way in which the headmaster acquainted the pupils with the physical and social structure of the house system was two-fold. Firstly, by his talk in the school assembly he was able to outline the way he considered the school should operate. Secondly, he could follow up these talks with notices addressed to the pupils in which he re-emphasized some of the points which he had discussed about the house system.

The headmaster also used school assembly to talk about the academic organization of the school and the content of education. Pupils were told about standards of work and about teachers in departments whom they should consult about their work. In one assembly, the headmaster told the fourth-year pupils that this was 'the start of work in the upper school with special options and academic opportunities'. He proceeded to explain to them how it was important to work hard in their selected subjects so that they would pass the public examinations in CSE and GCE. He said that if pupils found their subject teachers made adverse comments about their work then they should discuss those matters with these teachers and with the heads of departments. Similarly, when addressing the fifth-year pupils he explained that this was the year when they would be taking examinations. He said that work in the fourth and fifth years was comparable to training for running the ten thousand metres. However, he added it was important not to give up the examination courses at Easter in the fifth year; otherwise it was like dropping out of the ten thousand metres after having completed nine and a half thousand metres. In these circumstances the head emphasized academic rather than the commercial, technical, or practical courses offered in the school.

Presenting school norms

We have already examined the points of practice which the headmaster issued to the pupils. These incorporated the basic norms of the school, and included ideas about 'uniform standards of practice throughout the school'.[41] These norms which the headmaster expected the pupils to follow were really a less detailed version of the norms that he presented to the staff. The pupils were asked to care for their physical surroundings by treating buildings and school equipment with respect. This requirement was emphasized not merely in regard to school buildings but also in terms of members of the school – 'All are to conduct themselves sensibly and to show consideration for others at all times'.[42] These points of practice also highlighted behavioural as well as academic norms. The pupils were told that 'All are expected to treat everyone with respect and courtesy'.[43] The headmaster also defined those standards which he considered were acceptable and unacceptable to staff, but these were often modified by individual teachers. While the headmaster saw the position of the teacher as all-powerful, in reality the power of the individual teacher was subject to negotiation between teachers and between teacher and pupil (see chapter eight). In general, rudeness was not to be accepted either from pupils to staff, or vice versa; staff were to be addressed by their full names and pupils by their christian names. The pupils were to be encouraged to say 'please', 'thank you' and make polite requests; personal apologies were to be given to individuals who had been offended. The pupils were also expected to be punctual at school and at all their classes. In this respect, the behavioural norms prescribed were assumed to influence academic norms of hard work, and good progress in various areas of the curriculum.[44] Pupil behaviour was considered to influence academic success.

The headmaster considered that these norms and values were designed for the well-being of the members of the school. When he thought that members of the school (both teachers and pupils) had forgotten major behavioural and academic norms, he devoted part of a school assembly to talk about standards which were to be adhered to, within the school. These assemblies reinforced school norms which were defined by the headmaster. During the autumn term Mr Goddard used an assembly to talk about standards; the details of which I recorded in my fieldnotes:

The headmaster began by saying that he was going to talk about four things: manners, standards of work, litter and mud. He said that when speaking of manners he particularly wanted to talk about spitting and swearing. He considered that if something unexpected happened on the football field it was quite acceptable for a boy to swear. However, he thought that it was not so culturally acceptable for a girl to swear.[45] 'But' the headmaster said, 'I will not tolerate swearing between pupils and I will not tolerate the use of swear words, obscenities and vulgar expressions in normal conversation with the staff. We don't swear at you and we don't expect you to swear at us.' He continued by saying that he would use the highest sanction possible against people who behaved in this way which would mean suspension from school as, he added, 'I do not want to be head of a school where it is accepted that people swear at each other'. He said that spitting was a habit which people had got into despite having handkerchiefs and toilets. During the previous week he said that he had found one boy spitting down a flight of stairs on to another boy. This type of behaviour, he indicated, would not be tolerated and would be severely punished. Secondly, he talked about standards of work which he said should be improved so that the coming weeks before the end of term should be used not to slacken off work but to work harder than ever before.

Thirdly, he admitted that while the school site was difficult to manage with large pools of water around it, the addition of litter made it worse. In this way, all tuck shops were to be closed until the general tidiness of the site improved.

Finally, he talked about grass and mud. He said that there was so much mud brought into the school that the place was difficult to clean. He told pupils that they must keep off the grassed areas so as to help keep the place clean and tidy. The headmaster then recapped on his major points and with that the assembly was over.

This assembly highlights the behavioural and academic norms which he saw associated with the school. He indicated areas that he wanted to encourage and aspects of school life which he wished to discourage. In terms of behavioural norms, reasons were given for refraining from particular practices. Swearing was considered undesirable, mud in the school made it difficult to clean. In each case reasons were given for following the norms and an indication was given of the way in which he intended to control these practices. Goddard said there would be 'severe punishment' and 'the highest possible sanction used' to control the pupils' behaviour. The pupils were therefore reminded of the range of sanctions which could be deployed by the teachers. Finally, it was possible to see that Mr Goddard wanted a school which was clean and tidy and where well-mannered pupils worked hard.

Although this assembly was a forum where the headmaster directed his remarks towards the pupils, the staff were also present. It was an occasion when he could talk to staff as well as pupils. Here, he reminded teachers of the framework within which they worked. He gave them an indication of the kind of work and behaviour which he would like them to encourage and discourage and the means by which this could be achieved. Goddard reinforced the ideas which he communicated to teachers in meetings and in circulars. But many teachers had a different interpretation of the school. Goddard's remarks were therefore the subject of discussion in the common room as teachers commented that 'the boss' had a different conception of McGregor and its pupils from their own. One teacher remarked that, 'Whether he likes it or not, he is head of a school where pupils swear at teachers'. Several teachers agreed and told stories to support this comment which indicated that they had different conceptions of the school.

Summary and conclusion

This chapter has been concerned with the task of the headmaster at Bishop McGregor School, and the way in which the headmaster, Mr Goddard, defined activities in the school. In particular, attention has been given to the way in which Goddard had to come to terms with establishing a new school.

Sociological analyses of heads would lead us to believe that a head is nothing more than a manager, a co-ordinator and a decision-maker, yet Mr Goddard's style of headship shows the way in which a head is also a teacher who participates in the school and beyond it. The result is that a head takes on what Mr Goddard referred to as the role of the educational supercook who blends together ideas that have been derived from teaching experience, discussions, conferences and reading. In short, Goddard used his experience to define the school.

At Bishop McGregor School, Mr Goddard had a unique opportunity to define the kind of school that he wished to lead. When he was appointed, the school had only one group of buildings, no equipment, no staff and no pupils. In like manner, the school had no identity, no tradition, and no pattern of organization. Mr Goddard had to create an identity for Bishop McGregor School.

Even at this stage he had a framework within which to work. McGregor was related to the church and its system of values and the ideas and ideals of the comprehensive school movement as interpreted by the Merston authority. These two traditions were utilized by the head in the course of establishing Bishop McGregor School. However, as we shall see in later chapters, his conceptions of the school were modified by teachers and pupils.

Faced with a new school, Mr Goddard had several tasks. Firstly, he had to recruit teachers and gather together the pupils and parents. Secondly, he had to explain to these groups the characteristics which he wanted as hallmarks for Bishop McGregor School. The head used various strategies to present his ideas: meetings with parents, staff and pupils, discussions with staff, and written communications. All these systems of communication were important at McGregor where parents, pupils and teachers had little experience of comprehensive education or of comprehensive schools. In these circumstances, the headmaster had the opportunity to define the school situation as he explained, 'When I said "This is how a Catholic comprehensive works", there were few people who could say "He's wrong" '.[46] When Mr Goddard talked about the school to parents, teachers and pupils he used three major criteria to define it. Firstly, a system of values which were derived from Catholicism, because McGregor was to be a Catholic school for Catholic children. Secondly, a form of internal organization that was based on the local authority's interpretation of the English comprehensive school. Finally, a curriculum which was expressed through a series of norms that referred to standards of behaviour and school work.

Bishop McGregor School, therefore, embodied a number of distinct traditions which were derived from the Catholic church, the comprehensive school movement and the local authority. These different traditions blended together to create Bishop McGregor School. However, despite Mr Goddard's attempts to merge together the various traditions within one school, there was evidence of divisions and of different schools being created on one site.

Nevertheless, the school was influenced by the way in which the headmaster blended together various ideas. When he spoke to parents, staff and pupils he emphasized different qualities in the school. To the parents he stressed the Catholic tradition of the school. To the staff he emphasized the pattern of internal school organization, and to the pupils he emphasized the behavioural and academic norms which governed their daily lives. The head was therefore establishing different versions of the same school.

While Mr Goddard had one version of the way in which the school could operate, teachers had others. Some staff attempted to manipulate the school structure and the education it provided to their own advantage. The result was that Bishop McGregor School took on various guises and operated in a number of different ways on the basis of the relationships, actions and interactions developed by different groups of teachers and pupils. This suggests that rather than the school being a complete social system as has been suggested by some sociologists,[47] it would point to a number of subsystems in operation where different definitions about the way in which the school should operate are advanced.

Notes

1 For an example see Barry and Tye (1973).
2 Cf. Berg (1968) on Michael Duane at Risinghill Comprehensive School and Auld (1976), Ellis *et al.* (1976) and Gretton and Jackson (1976) on Terry Ellis at William Tyndale Junior School.
3 For a discussion of possible reasons for this absence of material see King (1973b, 422) and Shaw (1969).
4 A similar picture emerges in the United States where there are few studies of the school principal, apart from Wolcott (1973) who also reviews those studies that have been done (pp. xi–xv).
5 Goddard had been a teacher for eight years before obtaining his first headship. In Bernbaum's survey only 36 out of 312 headmasters obtained a headship after five to eight years of teaching. Furthermore, of Bernbaum's comprehensive school heads, only 30 per cent obtained headships after twelve years' teaching experience while 35 per cent of the comprehensive school heads did not get a headship until they had completed seventeen or more years' teaching experience. For further details see Bernbaum (1974, 241).
6 Extract from St Augustine's Secondary Boys' School governors' report on the educational year 1956–7.
7 Interview with the headmaster.
8 Mr Goddard followed a similar routine at Bishop McGregor School.
9 Interview with the headmaster.
10 For discussions on opening new schools see, for example, Boyson (1974) and Coulson (1976).
11 Interview with the headmaster.
12 A discussion paper was an internal document for consideration by the teaching staff.
13 Discussion paper on 'Communications'.
14 ibid.
15 Interview with the headmaster.
16 ibid.
17 ibid. The three-week absence relates to a work experience scheme for teachers in which he participated.
18 ibid.
19 For a discussion of the way in which the head is the most powerful reality definer in the school see Sharp and Green (1975, 47–67).
20 Extract from the headmaster's talk which was filed in the school office.
21 In the academic year 1973–4 approximately one-fifth of the staff were probationary teachers.
22 Discussion paper entitled 'Religious cycles in the school year', written by the headmaster.
23 ibid.

24 General information for intending applicants for teaching posts in the school.
25 Discussion paper on 'Sanctions', written by the headmaster.
26 ibid.
27 ibid.
28 For a discussion of the terms 'behavioural knowledge' and 'academic knowledge' see Musgrave (1973, 7–15).
29 Discussion paper on 'Sanctions', written by the headmaster.
30 ibid.
31 Extract from a general note from the headmaster to all staff, autumn 1969.
32 However, as the headmaster has noted this school did develop mixed-ability grouping.
33 Document on the aims and objectives for Bishop McGregor School in 1973–4 as defined by the headmaster.
34 In this context, non-academic had a different meaning. In the sixth form a non-academic course included Ordinary-level GCE and CSE courses taken by sixth-form pupils. For a discussion of the sixth form in the comprehensive school that also makes reference to patterns of recruitment see Benn and Simon (1972, 278–309).
35 The way in which this hierarchy was reinforced was through the scale posts awarded to staff and through the physical resources given to the departments which are discussed in chapter three.
36 For a discussion of the way in which school assemblies are used to focus attention on the school see Waller (1967, 123) and King (1973a, 45–64).
37 School assembly was held in each house block so that two houses combined together for a school assembly on the same morning, for example Westminster and Arundel houses on Tuesdays, Clifton and Lancaster houses on Wednesdays and Hexham and Southwark houses on Thursdays.
38 For a comparison of the structure of school assembly see King (1973a, 52–6).
39 For a discussion of school assembly in a Catholic school see, for example, Cassidy (1967).
40 Copy of document 'Some points of practice for all pupils' (pupil copy), written and issued by the headmaster, September 1973.
41 Extract from the document entitled 'Some points of practice for all pupils' (staff copy) which was written by the headmaster and contained a detailed exposition of each point.
42 'Some points of practice for all pupils' (pupil copy), written and issued by the headmaster.
43 ibid.
44 For a discussion of the links between work and behaviour in schools see Lacey (1970, 82–5).
45 This statement reinforces the point that Delamont (1980) has made, namely that sexism is implicit in schools.
46 Interview with the headmaster.
47 See, for example, Lacey (1970) and Hargreaves (1967).

3

HOUSE STAFF AND

DEPARTMENT STAFF

With the introduction of comprehensive education, questions were raised about methods of organizing a comprehensive school and their influence upon teacher relationships and teacher–pupil relationships. Architects, administrators and teachers considered ways in which large schools could be subdivided into smaller, more manageable units.[1] A survey conducted by Monks (1968) for the National Foundation for Educational Research (NFER) found that the most popular form of internal school organization was the house system. Similarly, Benn and Simon (1972) found that of all the different types of internal organization, it was the house system that was among the most widely discussed forms of vertical unit in the comprehensive school.[2] However, the 'pure' house system was used in only 122 (17 per cent) of the schools they surveyed. This trend was also repeated in the HMI survey of secondary schools as only 59 (15.4 per cent) of the schools studied were organized on a house system (Department of Education and Science 1979, 219) although one-third of the 384 schools in the survey did use houses alongside other forms of internal organization.

A major problem surrounds the term house system as it can involve everything from the purpose-built house to a form of competition used for work or games (Monks 1968, 40). Some schools have adopted the house system to cope with issues that are broadly concerned with 'pastoral care', while academic concerns remain with departments.[3] Boyson (1974, 40) drew attention to the difficulties associated with this system when he stated: 'The danger to be averted is that of a permanent alliance forged by the housemasters against the heads of department, each sector believing that its responsibilities are the real ones and that they are undermined by the other group of staff'.

However, on the basis of studying Nailsea School, Richardson (1975) has argued that a house/departmental system can help a school to handle problems associated with size and expansion, but she maintained that it could create structural divisions between pastoral care and the curriculum. In addition, she considered that these divisions might destroy the integrity of the teacher's task and fragment the leadership role of the headteacher and his or her senior colleagues. This chapter will focus on some of these issues at Bishop McGregor School. However, as McGregor was based on the Merston system it is to that which we now turn.

The internal organization of Merston comprehensive schools

When the Merston authority originally considered the internal organization of comprehensive schools the director of education prepared a background paper in which he summarized the major problems. A key concern was:

> to devise a system whereby the individual pupil is made to feel that he 'belongs' even in a large school of 1500 and in which the careful supervision of progress of the individual is the responsibility of someone who has under his care a manageable number of pupils.[4]

Bridges wanted to: 'take a leaf out of the independent schools' book and to have a house system which was a physical entity'.[5] Indeed, he considered that the authority should not only follow the structural principles of the house system but that it should adopt the principles of staffing used in boarding schools. He proposed that academic and pastoral roles should be linked.[6]

These proposals were considered by an advisory group[7] who appreciated that the advent of comprehensive schooling in Merston would create difficulties for senior staff in secondary modern schools who would find it difficult to obtain posts of similar status in the new schools. Furthermore, they realized that Bridges's proposals would exacerbate the situation as few former secondary modern school teachers would be appointed to a joint position of head of house and head of department. They considered that these difficulties could be overcome if house posts and departmental posts could be separated, since they thought this would give ex-secondary modern school teachers an opportunity to obtain senior posts in the house system. It was this proposal that was accepted by the local authority.

The authority provided detailed guidance on the house system.

Charles Bridges summarized the duties of housemasters and house-mistresses when he stated:

> We have often used the phrase that the housemaster is guide, philosopher and friend to the members of his house. Another way of describing his relationship is to say he is the personal tutor of his pupils even though he may not himself be appearing as their teacher in their formal time-table at any point.[8]

House staff were therefore to be concerned with the educational progress and moral welfare of the pupils, discipline and overall tone of the school, while departmental staff were to be responsible for the curriculum. Although Bridges appreciated that this subdivision between teachers was a very delicate aspect of the Merston comprehensive school system, he maintained that it had some potential as 'provided there is no "empire building" on either side any difficulties should be easily resolved'.[9] However, even if these relationships between heads of houses and heads of departments did operate smoothly, the new schools would still present teachers with some problems, as this pattern of school organization had not previously been used in state schools.[10] Teachers taking positions in houses would have to come to terms with different patterns of work.

The organization of the staff in Bishop McGregor School

When Goddard was appointed to the headship of Bishop McGregor School, the local authority and the governors indicated that the internal organization of the school was to be based upon a house system for pastoral care and a departmental system for curriculum matters. Indeed, this was reinforced by the authority, who insisted that all heads of houses should be appointed on a scale 5 salary[11] which gave them seniority compared with departmental staff and automatically influenced the head's staffing strategy.

In 1973–4 there were sixty-nine full-time and six part-time teachers at McGregor. All teachers worked simultaneously in houses and departments (except the headmaster, deputy head and senior mistress). Bishop McGregor School had a young staff. Even the heads of houses and heads of departments who were the senior teachers were, with a few exceptions, in their mid-thirties.[12] Some teachers had been recruited from other schools to take up higher posts, as was the case with Gillian Davies, who became a head of house at McGregor having been head of a geography department in a secondary modern school, and George Jackson who came to be head of the English department at McGregor where he had more staff, more facilities and a more highly paid post than in his previous school. Several other teachers had been promoted internally, particularly from the post of head of department to that of head of house. When this study was conducted there were five basic positions of assistant teacher. Each of the positions from scale 2 to scale 5 represented a stage of promotion, an increased level of responsibility and a higher salary. At McGregor, forty-three of the sixty-nine full-time staff were given scale posts of responsibility that attracted an additional salary above the basic payment on scale 1. The scale posts that were held are shown in table 3.1.

Table 3.1   Scale post holders in Bishop McGregor School, 1973–4

Scale	Salary range (£)	Number of staff
1	1306–2406	26
2	1446–2533	12
3	1718–2658	13
4	2143–3083	9
5	2556–3404	9
Total		69

Source: Headmaster's documents and the National Union of Teachers' salaries card for 1973–4.

Each post above scale 1 carried with it extra duties as shown by the following examples of actual posts at Bishop McGregor School.[13]

Scale 1   Probationary teachers or assistant teachers with no special or additional responsibility.

Scale 2   Don Williams, who was in charge of resources in the religious education department.

Scale 3   Mollie Richards, head of the music department. A small department with only two teachers.

Scale 4   David Gray, head of the modern languages department. A medium-size department with four teachers.

Scale 5   George Jackson, head of the English department. A large department with six full-time teachers and several part-time teachers. All the heads of houses with responsibility for some 200 pupils and ten to a dozen staff.

In general, the higher the post the greater the responsibility that individual teachers exercised for their subject or area of the school. All the positions in the houses carried higher posts of responsibility than those in the departments, the only exception being in the English, science and technical departments where the heads of departments had to co-ordinate the work of as many other teachers as the heads of houses, and were rewarded with a similar salary.

At Bishop McGregor School there were various formal hierarchies among teachers which were based upon age, teaching experience and administrative position in the school. Most teachers used scale posts and salaries to allocate their colleagues to the formal hierarchical structure in the school. The most common hierarchy that was established among teachers is shown in figure 3.1.

Figure 3.1   A pattern of formal organization at Bishop McGregor School

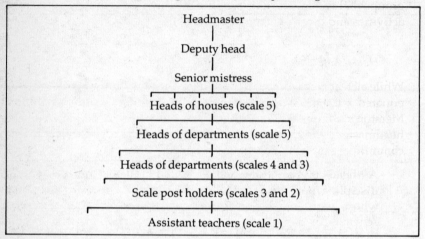

Note: Some staff considered that the deputy head and the senior mistress were equals, but the majority considered that the senior mistress was subordinate to the deputy head.

However, as Watson (1973, 411) has remarked:

> To speak of a single hierarchy of formal authority in the secondary school staff is to oversimplify the picture. Rather we must have in mind a structure of triangles each having at its apex the headmaster, who is usually the formal superordinate of each authority system.

Certainly, at McGregor there were other hierarchies. On some occasions teachers used administrative criteria to establish a hierarchy. As Easthope (1975, 88) indicates, this was based upon control of the pastoral system. Here, the heads of houses appeared at the apex of the triangle and in particular, Gillian Davies, head of Hexham House, was ranked first as most teachers considered that the head would always do what she wanted. In these circumstances, he was subordinate to her.

Many teachers thought in terms of formal ranking within the house and departmental systems. Here, distinctions were made in terms of the effectiveness of heads of houses on discipline, each house head's position being based on this criterion. Among heads of departments, however, the criterion used was academic/non-academic, which in turn was linked to results in public examinations. In addition, the heads of departments were also ranked in terms of departmental resources, the size of their staff and the children they taught. In these terms, heads of houses and heads of departments could be allocated to different formal positions in the school hierarchy depending on the criteria that were employed in any particular discussion. But no matter what criteria were used, a basic distinction was drawn between house staff and department staff. It is therefore to these groups that we now turn to examine the way in which they defined their activities and those of other members of the school.

House staff

While all teachers worked in the houses, the term 'house staff' was usually equated with the heads of houses. The importance of house heads in Merston's comprehensive schools was indicated in a letter which one headmaster (who chaired the local comprehensive schools' headteachers' committee) sent to his colleagues, when he stated:

> As heads we certainly cannot shoulder all the responsibility [for discipline and good order]: in house heads we have lieutenants whose work can be of crucial importance and help. Clearly, no schemes of curriculum development, no new teaching methods involving pupil enquiry and movement will stand a chance if our discipline and organization are not strong.

In these terms, house heads were to maintain standards of discipline in order that curriculum development and other departmental activities could take place successfully. They were seen as essential if heads of departments were to work effectively.

At McGregor, the duties of a house head were defined by Mr Goddard in the first copy of further particulars for potential staff. He expected them to 'play a very important part in the moral and social education of their house pupils'.[14] Their duties were therefore defined in social terms, which corresponded with the expectations of the authority and other head-teachers in the city. However, in a Catholic school a further dimension was added to the job as house heads were to be responsible for the moral development of their pupils. When the school first opened four house heads were appointed.[15] Each house head had to take responsibility for a subject, because few heads of departments had been appointed[16] and several departments were staffed with probationary teachers.

After five years, Mr Goddard found that he had to appoint a second generation of house heads, as several members of the first group had obtained deputy headships in other schools. When he wrote job descriptions for his second group of house heads he defined their role in greater detail. A set of further particulars for a house head in 1973–4 stated that the job involved:

> responsibility for the pastoral care, social and academic welfare and discipline of each child within the house. He [the head of house] is expected to be involved in the implementation of agreed school policy and play a major role in helping to plan future school policy.

As far as Goddard was concerned, house heads were responsible for welfare, attendance, discipline, uniform and progress.[17] In short, they were responsible for a range of activities similar to those of a headteacher in a small school. Many of them therefore saw their houses as 'mini-schools' and organized them accordingly – a move which acknowledged structural divisions in the school.

At McGregor, house heads were to interpret and implement school policy. Each head of house was given a degree of autonomy to develop his or her position and house. However, individual house heads defined the school's activities in different ways. When the school opened, house heads had taken the opportunity to establish their own distinctive pattern of work and routine. In letters that were sent to parents, house heads did not merely identify their house colours but indicated differences in their aims, objectives and activities. In Westminster House, the aim was simply to form a link between the home and the school. Meanwhile, in Southwark House, it was emphasized that there would be social, educational and fund-raising activities. In Arundel House and Hexham House, the differences were apparent in terms of the activities which were established. In Arundel there were to be regular house Masses together with a variety of clubs and societies for house pupils. But in Hexham the emphasis was different. Parents were told that the house was named after the Diocese of Hexham and it was intended that direct links should be established with this diocese. Furthermore, there were also house patrons and it was the intention of the house head to involve the pupils in the fund-raising activities of these patrons. Hexham, unlike any other house, also had a house motto which was the word 'endeavour'. The selection of this motto was explained by the head of house in a letter to Hexham House parents when she said:

> As our House motto we have a single word 'Endeavour' and this, I hope, will be the keynote of our efforts. I should like to feel that every boy and girl in Hexham will at all times give of his or her best in whatever circumstances they find themselves.

Each house therefore developed a distinct set of aims, routines, practices and activities. The result was a group of discrete units which related to the whole school. This was summed up by Gillian Davies who said that her house was 'beginning to develop into a community within the school', a point that was confirmed on ceremonial occasions such as sports days as well as in daily routines. Individual developments in the houses were supported by the headmaster, who stated in a letter to the director of education that 'the strongest form of house system comes when each head of house is set free to create his or her own thing'.[18] In these terms the house system at McGregor was close to the model that had been established in the public schools.[19]

Each house had a different ethos. Maggie Rolls, who was head of Clifton House, followed the 'mini-school' model as she considered that her post was 'the equivalent of a headteacher in a small junior school'. She considered that pastoral work was more important than class teaching and much more interesting than working in a department. She saw her task in social terms: discovering children's backgrounds, visiting pupils' homes, meeting parents, and interviewing pupils who were particular problems to other teachers or in 'trouble' inside or outside the school. She therefore defined 'pastoral work' in terms of administrative tasks: in the sense of gathering information on pupils and their families and maintaining social control.[20]

Many house heads interpreted their task in similar terms – by distinguishing between the pastoral and academic aspects of the school.[21] The head of Hexham House wrote several memoranda to the headmaster in which she stressed the importance of social rather than academic standards in the school. In one memorandum she stated:

> If the pupils are given frequent 'chances' we shall lose our hold over them and the rot will set in. If we are to set any kind of standard for the fifth year now is the time to do it. Academic ability is not really important, it is the willingness to accept that the staff are right to demand certain standards from pupils.[22]

This house head not only emphasized the importance of pastoral work over academic work by means of private communications but also by the way in which she handled day-to-day activities. Her time was devoted to interviewing pupils, issuing orders to staff and pupils and administering punishments. In this respect, her version of pastoral care was defined in terms of social control: routine, discipline, rules, moral standards and achieving compliance from pupils.[23]

Eileen Marsh, who was head of Arundel House, considered it her job to set standards among staff and pupils. On an occasion when a uniform check was taken among all pupils, she did not merely send the headmaster comments about her pupils' style of dress but also commented on the teachers' clothing as she considered that 'McGregor must have the most unprofessionally dressed staff in the city'. But the head did not do anything about her comments or for that matter about the jeans, sweaters and lack of ties about which she had complained.

In their study of a comprehensive school Mays, Quine and Pickett (1968, 31) concluded that house staff were 'child-centred' while academic staff were 'subject-centred'. This dichotomy was too simple for McGregor where house heads defined their duties in social rather than academic terms, and in many respects were surrogate headteachers.[24] However, they defined school routine in at least six different ways, social standards were presented from different perspectives and different ideas were transmitted about the school and the education it provided.

When the heads of houses were criticized by the heads of departments, the criticisms related to the fact that their job did not involve 'real' teaching. David Peel (head of the geography department) summed it up by saying, 'If you're a head of house you just check to see that all your kids are in uniform and that you have enough chairs for dinner sittings and your job's done'. George Jackson considered the job involved 'looking after the children of Mary'. These views were shared by other heads of departments and many subject teachers who thought the house heads were paid large allowances for doing very little. For them, 'real teaching' involved introducing pupils to subjects, getting them to work and obtaining examination successes. In short, the departmental staff considered that the 'real' work of the school was done in subject departments.

Departmental staff

Heads of departments were appointed to develop a curriculum area within the school, to develop the syllabus and teaching methods and to initiate curriculum development. Unlike the heads of houses who had a dozen or so teachers who were not paid special allowances for their duties in the house, each head of department had a team of specialists, many of whom were paid additional allowances for their special duties. The differences between houses and departments and between the departments themselves existed along a number of dimensions. The status of the departments depended on their physical resources, the size of their staff, and the scale posts given to their teachers. In addition, departments were designated *academic* or *non-academic, examination* or *non-examination*, and this influenced the way in which they defined their work. The English department with a suite of rooms, six staff, ten points for scale posts, a scale 5 head of department and an impressive examination record was held in greater esteem by most staff than the mathematics department which had a similar number of rooms, five scale points, a scale 4 head of department and a poor examination record.

While each of the houses had a base on the ground floor in each of the house blocks, the facilities of the departments varied. The facilities which each department held during 1973–4 are shown in table 3.2. The physical resources that were allocated to departments resulted in a hierarchy being established among them. Academic subjects such as English, mathematics, modern languages and the sciences were given suites of rooms. Other academic subjects such as history and geography were given only half of that allocation. Practical subjects such as physical education, home economics and technical activities were given specialist facilities in blocks or parts of blocks. However, the remedial department and the Newsom department were given only one room each. For the remedial department it was their second move in two years. They were established in a

Table 3.2   Facilities for departments in Bishop McGregor School, 1973–4

Department	Facilities
Mathematics	First floor of Arundel/Westminster
English	First floor of Hexham/Southwark
Modern languages	First floor of Clifton/Lancaster
History	First floor of Ampleforth
Geography	First floor of Campion
Sixth form	Ground floor of Ampleforth
Remedial	Ground floor of Campion
Science	First floor of Newton
Art	Ground floor of Newton
Technical activities	Burnham and Tyson blocks
Physical education	The sports complex
Home economics	First floor of Nunhead
Needlework	Ground floor of Nunhead
Music	Rooms in Ushaw
Newsom	A room in Ushaw
Religious education	No specific rooms

Note: The facilities for religious education reflected the staffing pattern in the school; that is, the subject was taught by several heads of houses who used the facilities in their house blocks.

redundant house hall with an assortment of furniture that was no longer required by other departments. Even these facilities had been obtained only after members of the department had made numerous requests to the headmaster for improved facilities. The Newsom department was in a similar situation. Its room was fitted out for science and technical activities and housed items of furniture which were surplus to requirements in other parts of the school, resulting in an assortment of desks, tables, chairs and stools.

The differences between departments were also evident in terms of the number of staff allocated to them (see table 3.3), and the seniority of their teachers in the school. All the departments except for the Newsom

Table 3.3   Numbers of full-time teachers in each department in Bishop McGregor School, 1973–4

Department	Number of staff
Mathematics	7
Science	7
Technical (woodwork, metalwork, technical drawing)	6
English	6
Physical education	5
Modern languages	4
Home economics	4
Religious education	4
Art	3
Geography	3
History	3
Music	2
Commerce	2
Remedial	2
Careers	1
Newsom	0
Total	59

Note: The staff numbers do not include heads of houses or teachers who worked in more than one department.

department had at least one teacher who worked in only one department. However, a different number of teachers were allocated to each department. Just as the basic academic departments (English and mathematics) had the largest number of rooms, together with the practical subjects they had the greatest number of full-time staff. The same pattern was true of academic subjects which became optional in the upper school, such as geography, history and music, and those which were only taken in the upper school, e.g. commerce. Finally, some departments, like careers and Newsom, had few teachers who worked within them on a full-time basis.

Each department had a number of teachers with scale posts. The number of scale posts that were held within the departments depended on the number of points (above scale 1) with which they were allocated (see table 3.4). The main distinction was between houses and other groups within the school. As a group, the houses were given more points than any department. Among the departments, however, the subjects which commanded most resources held the most points, while those departments which only provided courses in the upper school held the least number of points. The result was that some of the large subject

Table 3.4 The distribution of points for scale posts (above scale 1) at Bishop McGregor School, 1973–4

Houses, departments and general duties	Total allocation of points
Houses	20
English	10
Technical	9
Science	7
Mathematics	5
Modern languages	5
Sixth-form tutors	4
History	4
Art	4
Physical education	4
Religious education	3
Geography	3
Newsom	3
Careers	3
Remedial	3
Music	2
Audio-visual aids	1
Humanities and recreational activities	1
Hospitality	1

Note: During this academic year there was only a head of religious education for years one to three.

departments had teachers at different stages in their careers. In the English department a scale 2 post was given for responsibility for

1 the departmental library
2 courses for non-academic fifth formers
3 students' teaching practices
4 stock control
5 internal examinations for middle-school forms
6 records of pupils' progress[25]

while a scale 3 post was given for

1 the running of the department in the absence of the head, and
2 first- and second-year English throughout the school.[26]

These middle-range posts in large departments not only provided teachers with higher salaries but also provided experience that would help the individual to gain a higher post in the career structure. In the case of the holders of these posts, Stuart Mills (on scale 2) became the deputy head of an English department in another school, while Jane Adams (on scale 3) became the next head of the English department at McGregor. But departments with few points for scale posts had very few experienced teachers other than the head of the department. This was the case in commerce and music where only the heads of departments had scale posts, while the other teachers were either assistants, or probationers or part-time staff.

Table 3.5   Scale posts held by heads of departments at Bishop McGregor School, 1973–4

Heads of departments	Scale post held
English	5
Science	5
Technical activities	5
Mathematics	4
Geography	4
History	4
Modern languages	4
Careers	4
Home economics	4
Commerce	3
Art	3
Music	3
Physical education: boys	3
Physical education: girls	3
Remedial	3
Religious education	3

Note: This table excludes heads of houses who held scale 5 posts.

Each department (except for the Newsom department)[27] had a head of department who held a scale post. However, different scale posts were held by different heads of departments as shown in table 3.5. The highest posts were held in those departments which represented the basic subjects taken by all pupils throughout the school. Of the subject departments which were responsible for pupils in the whole school, only the head of the mathematics department did not hold a scale 5 post. Current gossip among the staff attributed this to the fact that he was not a Catholic and because the department had some very poor examination results.[28] The criteria that were used by the headmaster to appoint teachers to senior posts of responsibility in departments included: personal academic achievement, and proven teaching ability in a range of schools. The scale 5 posts in the academic subject departments attracted teachers who had wide experience as shown by the following example:

George Jackson, head of English
1936–44	St James's College, Cork
1945–6	Bank clerk
1947–53	Assistant manager in a restaurant
1954–5	Trained teachers' certificate (Canada)
1954–7	BA degree obtained (Canada)
1957–8	Assistant teacher in Canada
1959	Supply teacher, Durham
1959–60	MA degree obtained (Ireland)
1960	Supply teacher, Durham
1961–4	Assistant lecturer grade B in a college of further education
1964–6	Assistant master scale 3 (Catholic direct grant school)
1966–9	Assistant master scale 3 (direct grant school)
1969	Appointed head of English scale 5 at Bishop McGregor School.

This head of department had obtained several qualifications (a teachers' certificate, a first degree and a higher degree), had work experience outside education together with a range of teaching experience and posts of responsibility in different schools and colleges.

Heads of departments who held scale posts at a lower level tended to be in departments that provided options in a particular area of the school or who taught practical subjects. Also, their qualifications and range of experience suggested a lower post as shown by the following examples:

Head of history	*Head of art*
Educated in direct grant school	Educated in a grammar school
BA degree	BEd degree
Trainee accountant	Vacation work experience
Assistant teacher (3 years)	Assistant teacher at a comprehensive school (3 years)
Scale post holder (3 years)	Head of art at Bishop McGregor
Head of history at Bishop McGregor	

Alongside scale post holders and the heads of departments were eleven staff who were in only their second year of teaching, and fifteen probationary teachers who were new to the school and the teaching profession. These teachers were appointed to work within a department, and, like all other departmental staff, were attached to a house, where the vast majority had responsibility for a tutorial group.

Among the departments there were several differences based on resources, number of teaching staff, and posts of responsibility. These structural differences provided a background to the relationships which existed among teachers and between teachers and pupils and influenced the way in which they defined their work.

Relationships among teachers

The times when teachers can meet together on a formal and informal basis are defined by the school timetable. At McGregor, teachers came together in house and department meetings, and they also met each other before school, at break time and lunch time, in 'free' lessons and after school. Each of these meetings gave me an opportunity to see the way in which teachers defined their daily activities.

Formal meetings among teachers

At McGregor, there was no single place for teachers and pupils to gather in the early morning. Before the first bell was rung teachers went to the working staff rooms in the house blocks. A quick conversation, a cigarette, and a glance at the morning paper preceded the routine of the day. Once the bell was rung, they reported to their head of house so that the deputy head could be informed of any teachers who were absent and whose lessons needed to be 'subbed'[29] by another teacher.

When the teachers met in house heads' studies, it was a time for gossip to be exchanged about children, about fellow teachers and about the headmaster and his views on school routine. It was also a time when the house heads passed on messages about school activities, duties and changes to the daily programme. The house heads occupied a key role in the communication system, as they transmitted school policy from the headmaster and his senior colleagues to other teachers. They, in turn, were supposed either to relay this information to pupils in their tutorial groups or implement this policy in their daily activities in the house and, to some extent, in the departments in which they worked.

An early morning meeting in a house, therefore, contained several elements which I recorded in my fieldnotes one morning in Westminster House:

> About ten minutes before the bell was rung, I went into Ron Ward's study where many of the staff had already gathered. The staff were sitting around in the positions shown in figure 3.2.
>
> Ron talked about his study and said how dull he thought it was. Sue and Terry disagreed with him and said that it was much brighter

Figure 3.2   Seating arrangements in Ron Ward's study

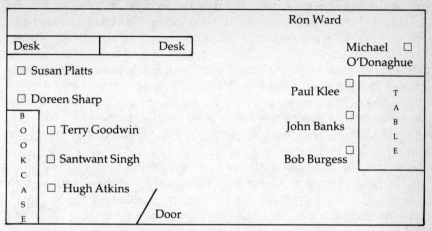

than in the past as the former head of house used to sit in there with the blinds down and the light on. A joke was made by Terry about the sexual significance of drawn blinds. Ron brought some order to the scene and started to make some announcements. He told the staff that the headmaster's advisory committee on social policy had produced a series of plans for activities that could be followed by the fifth year when they finished their examinations. These included: sports, building an adventure playground, social work, camping and teaching English to immigrants. Staff laughed about the last suggestion and Doreen Sharp commented, 'They need someone to teach them English!' Most people laughed and several agreed with this remark. Ron continued to read through the list and suggested that other ideas and observations should be given to Terry Goodwin who was a member of this committee.

Ron then went on to talk about a note that the headmaster had produced on emergencies in relation to dealing with epileptics. He explained that this had been produced because a child had an epileptic fit in a lesson earlier that week. However, he did not agree with the suggestions that were given for dealing with such a situation. Ron asked the members of staff for information about one or two families of pupils in the house. When no information was forthcoming, Ron said that he would go and have a snoop around at the weekend to see where they lived. Ron then continued by reminding us that third-year option forms had to be completed by 1 March. Finally, he told us that as the period after half term would be Lent he had arranged with Eileen Marsh (head of Arundel House) that tutorial groups from Arundel and Westminster would combine on Thursday mornings for a series of Masses. He said that those

Catholic teachers who wished to attend the masses should arrange to have their tutorials covered by other teachers. He then said it was time that the pupils were registered so that tutorials could arrive on time in the hall for assembly.

This illustrates the type of activities that took place in house heads' studies before the teachers met the pupils and will be used to examine the importance of the house system in the school, the position of house head and the teachers' perspectives of the school and its pupils.

All teachers, regardless of their position in the school, had to report to their head of house each day before school started. In this respect, the importance of the house system and the head of house was emphasized to each teacher. House heads were an essential link in the chain of school administration, responsible for passing on messages from the headmaster, reading out notices and keeping registers up to date. They were gatekeepers between the headmaster and other teachers.

House heads were responsible for communicating school policy. In Westminster House (in common with other houses) it was this activity that structured the early morning meeting; a situation where the house head made announcements and the teachers listened, because it was rare for them to discuss formally any points that Ron made. Instead, comments were kept to jokes, gossip, and answers to questions that were directed at individuals by the house head. As Ron communicated messages and school routines to the staff he had an opportunity to define and redefine school policy and promote activities that he considered important for the pupils. In short, house heads were powerful reality definers in the day-to-day activities of teachers and pupils. In this particular meeting we have two examples of the way in which information is redefined and the activities of the school are changed. Firstly, when staff were told about the headmaster's proposed procedure for dealing with epileptics, Ron discussed the information with them, and worked out an alternative procedure. Secondly, when he told the staff about the activities in which Westminster House were to engage during Lent, he explained that they were not merely to observe Lent through the Lenten charities which had been suggested by the headmaster but also through a series of house Masses which he had arranged with another house head. Ron had, therefore, redefined the headmaster's suggestions and added to the range of activities in which his house engaged.

In common with other early morning meetings with the house head, no teacher disagreed with any of Ron's proposals or suggestions, which indicated that they formally and publicly recognized his position. However, outside these meetings it was usual for some discussion and private dissension to take place among teachers in the working staff room, who would modify Ron's suggestions about routines to be adopted with pupils. In some cases, modifications were involved, while in other situations teachers would claim that they were not going to implement particular aspects of school policy. This occurred at the end of the spring term when Paul Klee announced to several of us that he was no longer going to ask his tutor group to collect or contribute to a charity, because he considered that too many collections had taken place during Lent.

While school routine was the main topic of conversation in these meetings, particular pupils came a close second. On the subject of pupils, teachers contributed freely to the discussions. They taught the children and were, therefore, ready to contribute comments on an individual pupil's ability, behaviour and potential. Often pupils and pupil behaviour were typed[30] by teachers on the basis of slight information. At the beginning of the autumn term, when Terry Goodwin saw the surname McNab in her first-form register she announced to the rest of us, 'Oh my God, we've another McNab!' Other members of the house who also recognized the surname talked about the misbehaviour of several other McNabs who they automatically assumed were older brothers and sisters, and without any evidence imputed similar behaviour to this child before they had seen him. Automatically this gossip established an identity for the pupil that had the potential to structure the early stages of his career in the house and his relationships with teachers.[31]

These regular daily meetings with house heads had no direct equivalent in the departments. While heads of houses met their staff at a set time each day, heads of departments held such meetings on only two or three occasions during each term. Department meetings were opportunities for the staff to discuss departmental policy, teaching methods, curriculum content and the progress of individual children. Unlike house meetings, department meetings usually had a formal agenda which was drawn up by the head of the department. However, within the meetings, discussion took place between all teachers as shown by the minutes of a staff meeting in the religious education department.

Present: headmaster, Father Mooney (school chaplain and local parish priest), Miss Marsh, Miss Davies, Mr Williams, Miss Robinson, Mr Ryan, Mr Dunphy, Mrs Ryan.

The agenda
1 Requisition
2 List of resources
3 Years 1–3 progress, comments on syllabus
4 AOB

Minutes
1 Sheila Ryan apologized for not circulating the agenda previous to the meeting.
2 Discussion on requisition and resources

(i) Don Williams stressed the need for text books with a definite doctrinal content. Asked if there were any known titles.

(ii) Sheila suggested spending the £90 on Bibles, maps, a few recommended texts for use with Konstant[32] or building up existing sets of books.

(iii) Richard Dunphy – concerned with having films – cash has to come from the department.

(iv) Gillian Davies mentioned the service run by the museums for free loan but this may be of little value for religious education.

(v) Headmaster said that he is circulating lists to all departments for lists of religious education material and their own resources, which may be of interest to members of the religious education department for short-term loans.

(vi) Don said that single copies of the Gospels may be obtained for 1p each from the cathedral.

(vii) Sheila Ryan offered to circulate the timetable showing when she is in room 23 for the distribution of resources, and she asked if people would tell her of any suggestions for their own requisition requirements before Friday, 21 September.

3 Comments on Konstant's syllabus

(i) Don asked if we could undertake as a priority of value, an examination of the syllabus as he has reservations about the adequacy of treatment of doctrine.

(ii) The headmaster replied that this syllabus was a rather dry-boned skeleton and it was a matter for individual staff to supply the doctrine.[33]

This set of minutes (in common with others) highlights the difference between teacher relationships and the content of discussion in formal meetings within departments compared with houses.[34]

In the religious education department, Sheila Ryan was in charge of work with pupils in the first three years. While Sheila drew up the agenda for the meeting she did not 'hold the floor'. The meeting was an opportunity for all members of the department, regardless of their seniority, to express their views on the department's work. In this context, the headmaster, heads of houses and assistant teachers who worked in the religious education department were all theoretically 'equal'. However, it was usual for junior staff to look towards the headmaster and the house heads for direction and for points of information concerning resources and school organization. Within this meeting, items of business were devoted to departmental organization and the content of the curriculum which was discussed by all teachers – a distinct contrast to the practice which was followed in the houses.

Another formal occasion when teachers had an opportunity to discuss the curriculum was at open forum meetings held once a month after school. These meetings were designed by the headmaster, not for particular segments of the school, but for all staff. Here, the head wanted to provide a venue in which junior teachers could debate issues that affected the school with senior staff. Despite this attempt to get some dialogue beween senior and junior teachers, there were few signs of success. At most meetings the heads of houses were conspicuous by their absence, a situation which thwarted the head's aims. Indeed, Mr Goddard told me that he thought heads of houses would not attend these meetings because they did not want to debate issues concerning school routine with junior teachers.[35] Certainly, of all the senior teachers at McGregor only the house heads were often absent; a situation that emphasized their separation from departmental staff in general and junior teachers in particular.

Nevertheless, at open forum meetings that I attended, the subjects discussed included school organization and the content of the curriculum, as sessions were devoted to the form of the annual prize-giving ceremony and the organization of the sixth-form curriculum. At the meeting when the prize-giving was debated, there were twenty-two teachers; two heads of houses, four heads of departments and sixteen assistant and probationary teachers. The headmaster opened the discussion by explaining that he wanted to see a prize-giving which rewarded academic achievement. But he was quickly reminded by Terry Goodwin that McGregor was a comprehensive school, and that it should be possible to create a new form of prize-giving which rewarded elements of schooling other than just academic work. This point was taken up by other junior teachers who remembered their own school prize-givings as formal speech days when teachers wore gowns, school choirs sang and individuals collected prizes while the vast majority sat bored.[36] The heads of the English and modern languages departments disagreed with these views and recommended that a conventional pattern should be followed. However, by sheer force of numbers the junior staff were able to discuss and design, with the support of each other, a new-style prize-giving with a distribution of prizes, a short period for an address and discussion followed by an evening 'disco'. The headmaster supported the two heads of department who expressed their reservations about this form of prize-giving and who, like the head, were concerned that academic worth should be honoured. Indeed, the headmaster told me afterwards that he had definitely wanted the meeting to recommend a formal prize-giving with gowns and speeches. The recommendation of the majority of staff at the meeting was instead for an informal evening and prize-giving – a recommendation which was later implemented by the headmaster. In this context, junior teachers were able to advance their ideas about school organization which in turn led to a redefinition of the head's view of prize-giving. The structure of some events at Bishop McGregor School was therefore not merely based on the ideas of senior staff but involved the participation of everyone. However, junior staff were only able to define school activities in any sense when their numbers at meetings outweighed senior staff, a situation which was rare beyond the open forum.

These formal meetings between teachers highlighted divisions between house staff and departmental staff and between senior staff and junior staff. They were often reinforced by the structure and content of meetings. Firstly, house staff were formally distinguished from departmental staff. The house heads were senior to the departmental staff and they considered it their job to implement some of the headmaster's ideas about school organization. In turn, heads of houses also established their own routines which added to the complexity of school organization and in some cases changed its direction. Secondly, the approach adopted towards the implementation of house and departmental policy was somewhat different. In each house, it was the head of house who defined the situation by advancing his or her point of view, whereas points of practice in departments were worked out by discussion among members of staff. There were also occasions when the heads of houses and heads of departments joined forces against attempts by junior teachers to change school policy. However, the failure of some house heads to attend meetings on school policy where junior staff were present led to situations such as the prize-giving meeting when junior staff could take decisions. Alliances between houses and departments were rare as they were interested in different aspects of education. While the houses focused on social aspects of education, the departments focused on the curriculum. The result was that house heads concentrated on pastoral activities which they interpreted predominantly in terms of administration and social control, while departmental staff were concerned with class teaching. However, as all departmental staff were required to be members of a house and take some part in pastoral work there was an undercurrent of continual conflict between house and departmental duties. In addition to differences between the formal activities of houses and departments, informal relationships between staff were also influenced by the terms of their appointment. It is therefore to the pattern of informal relationships among teachers that we now turn.

Informal relationships among teachers

Each day I joined the teachers in the main common room which was located up two flights of stairs in the administrative block, beyond which the children were not allowed. The headmaster had made it a practice at the school for all teachers, except those who were on duty, to go to the main common room for their morning coffee-break. This was a voluntary arrangement but it was the only regular time when teachers could gather together.

The main common room was very large and took up the whole of the top floor of one block (equivalent to three classrooms). It was brightly decorated with a mural at the far end, opposite the entrance, and contained carpets and easy chairs. From this room it was possible for teachers to survey the whole school. The common room and the main groups that I observed are shown in figure 3.3.

Figure 3.3   Informal groups in the staff common room during morning breaks

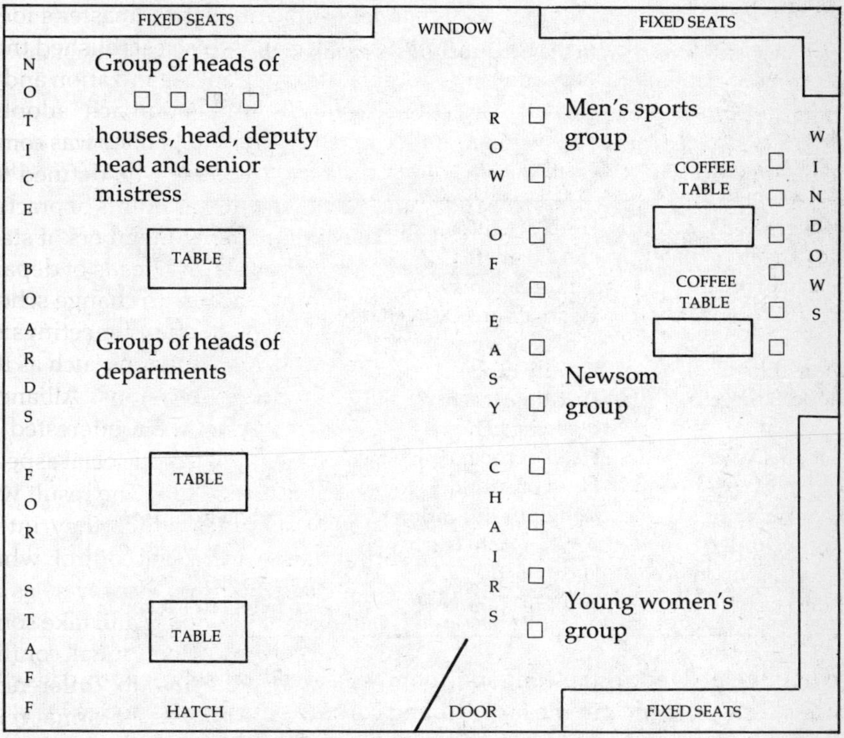

It appeared to me that there were five major groups that formed in the common room during the morning breaks: the heads of houses, heads of departments,[37] men's sports group, Newsom group and young women's group.[38] I recognized that many of these groups were formed on the basis of the members holding similar positions in the formal organization of the school. None of these groups had an exclusive membership, that is, not all those who sat in the young women's group were either young or female and, likewise, not all those who sat in the heads of houses group were house heads. However, I have given titles to these groups on the basis of their main members and their recognition by other teachers.

While I was at the school, I joined three of these groups which helped me to recognize the various informal divisions that occurred among the staff. At various times, I sat with the heads of houses group, the men's sports group and the Newsom group. I often sat on the edge of the women's group and I also mixed occasionally with heads of departments who tended to meet around the coffee-tables.

When I started my research, my key informants[39] on the staff were also my initial contacts: Sylvia Robinson, at that time head of careers and in charge of Newsom, and Maggie Rolls, the head of Clifton House. The first morning that I was in the school I was taken to the staff common room by Maggie.

Table 3.6   Staff who sat in the heads of houses group in the first half of the summer term, 1973

Staff member	Position in the school	Member of staff who brought individual to the group (if any)
Maggie Rolls	Head of Clifton House	
Roy Carey	Head of maths	
Jean Chapman	Senior mistress	
Sylvia Robinson	Head of careers/in charge of Newsom	
Frank Lloyd	Deputy head	
Robert Burgess	Part-time teacher/ researcher	Maggie Rolls and Sylvia Robinson
Gillian Davies	Head of Hexham House	
Eileen Marsh	Head of Arundel House	
Don Williams	Religious education teacher	Sylvia Robinson
Keith Dryden	Art/Newsom teacher	
Geoffrey Goddard	Headmaster	
June Harper	Head of commerce	Sylvia Robinson

When we arrived in the common room we served ourselves with coffee and sat on the bench in the far left-hand corner of the room. I noticed that during break we were joined by Sylvia Robinson, Roy Carey (the head of the mathematics department) and by Jean Chapman (the senior mistress). On my second day in the school, Sylvia Robinson took me to the common room and we sat in the same corner of the room. As these teachers were my initial informants I continued to join them in this particular area of the common room during breaks in the first half of the summer term.[40] The staff who sat in the group during this period are shown in table 3.6. This group consisted of the heads of houses, the headmaster and his senior colleagues: the people who held power in the school. In addition, the group was usually joined by Roy Carey and Sylvia Robinson. It was generally agreed by members of staff that Roy Carey always sat in this group because he was friendly with several of the house heads. Meanwhile, many teachers considered that Sylvia Robinson sat there in an attempt to gain membership of the group who helped to run the school, and in the hope that she might one day take up a senior appointment. Sylvia usually brought her friends from Clifton House (Don and June) to sit among this group. Added to this she always brought visitors such as the careers officers and potential employers to sit in this corner of the common room.

After I had stopped sitting with this group, I continued to make systematic observations of those individuals who sat together. I found that when new heads of houses were appointed they tended to go and sit among the group during the mid-morning break. On one occasion when interviews were taking place for the position of head of house, one candidate asked a group of teachers if the far left-hand corner of the common room was where the heads of houses always sat. The teachers automatically confirmed that this area of the common room was the daily meeting place for house heads.

While membership of this group was dominated by the heads of houses, I also found that the conversation was predominantly between them and the headmaster and his senior colleagues. During the time I sat in this group, the topics that were discussed included points of school routine which had been recommended by the headmaster and the way in which they were to be implemented. Comments were also made upon individuals and their attendance or lack of attendance at school and at lessons. In short, the group used the mid-morning break as a time for an informal meeting when they could discuss aspects of their work and take decisions about how they would implement school policy.

One morning in the summer term I arrived in the common room only to find that all the seats were taken in the corner in which the heads of houses sat. I decided to go and join a group of young men who sat on the opposite side of the room. The members of this group were drawn from various departments: physical education, technical activities, and science together with the heads of the geography and history departments. Several of these teachers taught some games lessons. The conversation in this group was based on sports matches in which individuals participated in the evenings and weekends, while others discussed sports programmes which they had seen on the television. As I had neither an interest in nor a knowledge of sport, I was unable to participate directly in the conversation of this group. However, I was able to use this opportunity to observe the common room and verify my initial observations about the groups within it.

In the autumn term, new members of staff joined some of the established groups in the staff common room. However, one new group was also established. Several young men had been appointed to work in the

Newsom department or to work with Newsom pupils in other depart-ments. On the basis of their common work situation, a further mid-morning group was established. This group of male Newsom teachers consisted of Tony Davis and Keith Dryden from the Newsom department, Paul Klee from the English department, and Gerry Cochrane from the religious education department. This group met around the edge of one of the small coffee-tables near the window. One person would usually perch on the edge of the coffee-table and the others would sit around nearby. As I was a part-time teacher who worked in the Newsom department I decided that it was appropriate for me to join this group. I found their main topics of conversation related to the pupils they taught, the organization of the Newsom department and the topics which they attempted to teach. The favourite topic of conversation was the pupils. Individual teachers had particular 'favourites' as Tony Davis would report on Peter Vincent, Keith Dryden on John Slattery and Paul Klee about Terry Nicholls. Usually the conversation consisted of 'news from the front' and referred to pupil behaviour that morning. This information was exchanged so that those of us who were to teach these pupils later in the day could make preparations for the 'battle'. Paul would come in some days with the news that Terry was 'on form', which indicated that Terry Nicholls was acting the fool and set on a course of maximum disruption in lessons. Meanwhile, Tony Davis would arrive and tell me about the kind of mood Peter Vincent was in that day and then suggest ways in which I might handle him. The group also spent some time exchanging the current school gossip. But the main topics of conversation related to their pupils and their work within the school. In this respect, typifications[41] of Newsom pupils were updated on a daily basis.

The main informal groups that existed in the staff common room during the mid-morning break appeared to be based on the formal groups and formal roles which individuals held in the school.[42] On the basis of my participation in some of these groups, I found that the conversations related to the formal activities in which the individuals were engaged. In this sense, the informal relationships among the teachers seemed to rein-force the basic divisions and duties which I had already recognized in the formal organization of the school, that is, the division between house and department among members of the school.

Teachers' relationships with pupils

The role of the teacher is such that it is not usual for a teacher to observe colleagues working with pupils.[43] The exceptions to this are when teachers engage in team teaching situations or when they take assembly. In Bishop McGregor School, I had the opportunity to observe the heads of houses as they conducted morning assembly. During the period I was in the school, I belonged to two houses (Clifton in the first term and Westminster for a period of one year). Over this period, I saw two heads of houses and one acting head of house conducting assembly. A similar procedure was used in each house where religious worship was followed by a series of house and school notices.[44]

In house assemblies where all the staff and pupils from one house gathered together, the situation was used by the head of house to talk about Catholicism, about school rules and routines, and the rules and routines which were special to that house. House assembly was, there-fore, used to reinforce much of what had been said by the headmaster about the school. However, it was evident that heads of houses modified some of the head's arrangements with the result that different rules and routines existed in different houses.

On some occasions I found that an assembly taken by the head of house was mainly devoted to prayers, as I recorded in my fieldnotes one morning when Ron Ward took assembly:

When I went into the house hall many of the children were being put into straight lines by Susan Platts (the deputy head of house) who was shouting to pupils, 'Stand up straight, take off your coats and face the front'.

When all the tutorial groups had arrived, Ron Ward began the assembly by asking pupils to say together the Hail Mary and the Lord's Prayer. The staff and pupils recited both prayers in unison. This was followed by further prayers that were read aloud by Ron. The first prayer thanked God for allowing pupils to be at school, this was followed by a prayer that emphasized that shoddy work should not be given in. Finally, there was a prayer asking God to help those pupils who were at present taking mock examinations. The assembly closed with the Grace.

On another morning, Ron used the assembly to talk to his pupils as I recorded:

Ron began the assembly by talking to the pupils about time and the way in which pupils can use their time usefully in school. He read a poem which was based on a conversation with God about how differ-ent people use their time. Ron said, 'I want you to ask yourselves, at the end of each day, "What have I achieved in school today? What knowledge or skill have I got today? What have I found out today that I did not know yesterday?"' Ron continued by saying that it was important that all of us should ask social questions such as 'Have I been pleasant to those around me? Have I been friendly to those who I am with? Have I helped people who are lonely?'

On both occasions, the assembly was used by this house head to talk about school activities. Catholicism and religion were used in this context to talk about school-wide norms.[45] Religion was therefore used as a focus for school and house activities and also to present ideas about the school, standards of work and relationships with fellow pupils. The head of house thus presented a series of norms which reinforced what the headmaster considered important in the school.

Each assembly was designed to promote and encourage good habits of work among the pupils. Whenever a talk was given in assembly, it was usual for religion to be linked to the values which the school held. In the second house assembly quoted above, the head of house emphasized two aspects of the school: the academic and the social. The school was portrayed as a place where pupils came to achieve, to learn, to acquire knowledge or skills and to find things out for themselves as well as a place where individuals had social obligations to fellow pupils.

The heads of houses also had an opportunity to discuss further aspects of the school and the house when they announced various notices after religious worship. House heads often took the opportunity to talk about 'school rules' which once again emphasized their role in maintaining standards of behaviour. In one term, Ron Ward reminded his pupils that they should not leave the school site without his permission, that school property should not be vandalized, that school uniform should be worn and that money for the school fund should be paid to support school activities. Here, pupils were given these instructions without any reason being provided about why they should be followed. In this instance the house head was reinforcing the instructions which the head had given to all pupils at the beginning of the year.

Alongside support for these school routines, practices and norms, some time was also devoted to an expression of the qualities which the house wished to encouraged. During the summer term all house heads emphasized the importance of winning the sports trophy. Similarly, Ron Ward also told his pupils that it was important to produce work of very high quality in order that they could win the Tyson trophy (for good work) during the spring term.

Each house also had distinct characteristics and qualities which were established by the house head. In Westminster House, Ron Ward established special routines for movement within the house and for school lunches. When members of the house came into Westminster he wanted them to remove their outdoor jackets. He wanted Westminster to be a house which was clean and tidy, so pupils were told that litter must not be dropped in the house hall. He once announced in assembly, 'We don't want you bringing the playground into the house'.[46] Ron also encouraged his pupils to attend the regular Wednesday morning mass which took place before the start of school, as he said that it was important for the house to be represented. Westminster House also had a number of prefects who were selected from members of the fifth form, who Ron said should be obeyed in the same way in which obedience was shown towards him. Westminster House therefore had a separate image and separate routines. While many of these routines related to the practice of the school, they were nevertheless distinct in their own right.

My relations with teachers and pupils highlighted some of the differences between houses. Some houses, like Lancaster House under the leadership of Alan James, were regarded as 'hopeless' by the departmental staff as no support was given on discipline. Hexham, under the leadership of Gillian Davies, was regarded as a 'strong' house as it supported the staff against the pupils. Members of staff therefore advised me that it was wise to find out which houses the pupils belonged to before sending them to a house head. It was considered that a teacher could always select pupils from Hexham or Westminster (another house noted for its strong discipline) to be sent to their house heads for disciplinary action as it could be guaranteed that the individual would be 'dealt with', and this would act as a salutary warning to other members of the class. In contrast, I was advised not to send pupils to Lancaster House as this would be treated as a joke by the class, especially when pupils were sent back without being seen[47] or after being told not to play around.

This difference in standards of discipline maintained by the houses was also recognized by the pupils.[48] One teacher told me that when he sent a child out of his lesson to see Gill Davies the pupils had said that he would be caned – a prophecy that came true! I also found that during lessons which I took, the pupils knew that if they got sent to Mr James nothing would happen to them. Some pupils considered this was 'unfair' because if you truanted from a lesson or from school and you were in Lancaster House nothing happened other than a letter being sent home. One boy explained that if you were in Southwark House (as he was) then truancy resulted in corporal punishment and a letter being sent home. The houses did therefore exhibit distinct characteristics which were highlighted in their dealings with pupils. It was this aspect of school organization which pupils were most critical of; especially when different punishments were given by different house heads for the same 'crime'.

The departments, like the houses, also upheld distinct routines and practices. However, these routines were not so public as those in houses. Unlike the houses, the departments did not see pupils *en masse*, but instead saw them in small option groups and classes. The headmaster distinguished between academic and non-academic departments and in the upper school between examination and non-examination courses. These distinctions were taken up and used by teachers and pupils to define the role of a particular department and its staff.

In the English department, teachers agreed upon certain policies which should be followed concerning the way in which children should behave, the standard of work which they should do and the way in which they should present their work.[49] The result was that in this particular department the pupils were acquainted with the teachers' expectations. In this respect, any child who caused problems for staff in the English department was made to spend all of his or her English lesson time with the head of the department. In contrast to several other departments (such as mathematics) the English department would only enter pupils for public examinations whom they considered had worked reasonably hard and had produced work which would give them a chance of obtaining a pass. This set of practices, together with particular requirements about the way in which work should be completed and corrected, earned the department a reputation among some pupils as being 'tough' and 'mean'.

Several children distinguished between teachers who taught 'proper' subjects like history, geography and science, where it was possible to learn, and those who taught courses that did not involve 'proper' subjects and where 'nothing' was learned. One boy took this a stage further when he claimed that as Newsom was not a proper subject, teachers did not have to hold qualifications to teach in this department as they did not need to know very much.[50]

The teachers in different houses and departments emphasized some school routines but also individual practices which characterized their relationships with pupils. So it was in this respect that the pupils while being members of the same school encountered different aims, objectives, routines and practices that were defined by the heads of houses and heads of departments in the areas in which they worked.

Summary and conclusion

Earlier chapters have drawn attention to the major physical division of the school into houses and departments. This chapter has continued this theme by focusing on the teachers. The characteristics of house and department staff have been examined together with the formal and informal relationships that existed between them. Finally, the relationships between staff and their pupils have been briefly examined but will be taken up in more detail in subsequent chapters.

Each house and department held a position in the school which had initially been defined by the headmaster. However, the staff in these houses and departments quickly established their own patterns of activity, their own characteristics, their own standards of acceptable work and conduct and their own relationships with each other and with pupils. The teachers' membership of houses and departments influenced the way in which they worked and defined their relationships with colleagues and with pupils. The result was a basic division of the staff into those who were concerned with pastoral work and those concerned with departmental work.

The school was therefore defined, divided and subdivided into a number of distinct units by social and academic criteria used by teachers. However, each teacher and pupil simultaneously belonged to the school, a house and a department. The result was that each member of the school was exposed to different definitions about the institution and the education it provided. There were a number of potentially conflicting accounts of the school which teachers and pupils had to resolve in their day-to-day lives at Bishop McGregor School. In the next chapter we turn to looking at actual situations in order to identify the ways in which individuals handled the divisions and definitions of their school lives.

Notes

1 Various methods of internal organization used in comprehensive schools are reported in National Union of Teachers (1958) and Department of Education and Science (1979). For discussions of methods of school organization in individual schools see, for example, Boyson (1974) and Davies (1976).

2 See Benn and Simon (1972, 328). Compare Pedley (1978, 118–23) in which he points out that the weaknesses of the house system have resulted in fewer schools using houses.

3 For an example of a school that uses a house and departmental system see Richardson (1973). For a critique of this form of organization see, for example, Richardson (1975, 60–9).

4 'Memorandum on comprehensive schools', a report by the director of education, Mr C. D. Bridges, presented to the education committee, 9 February 1949, p.2.

5 Interview with Charles Bridges.

6 For a critique of this type of system see Boyson (1974, 45) where he argues that a fusion of academic and pastoral positions would create difficulties for post holders, because they would find it problematic to assign their time and loyalties between the two roles.

7 This committee was composed of teachers who were drawn from every sector of education in the city.

8 'An address by the director of education to the housemasters' and housemistresses' meeting', 5 February 1958.

9 ibid.

10 For a discussion of some difficulties involved in transferring the house system into state schools see, for example, Lacey (1970, 162), Lambert (1966, xi–xxxii) and Pedley (1978, 119–20).

11 At the time, this was the highest scale post available for an assistant teacher in any school.

12 By summer 1981 only one teacher had retired from the school.

13 These examples of posts are for Bishop McGregor School. As heads are free to decide on duties, posts may vary between schools.

14 First set of further particulars for posts at Bishop McGregor School, spring 1969.

15 The house staff appointed included two men and two women who were later joined by a further man and woman.

16 This was because the authority provided few scale posts of responsibility for subject staff.

17 Cf. King (1973a, 70–1) who discusses his findings on houses and houseteachers in comprehensive schools. He found that the duties consisted of pastoral care, discipline, careers advice and parental contact. For further accounts on the role of house staff in state schools see Boyson (1974, 35–44), Lacey (1970, 155–85) and Chetwynd (1960, 90–109).

18 Letter to the director of education, 1 May 1974.

19 Compare the model established by Arnold at Rugby School, where Dean Stanley writing of Arnold states:

> Every house was thus to be, as it were, an epitome of the whole school. On the one hand, every master was to have, as he used to say, 'each a horse of his own to ride' . . . and on the other hand, the boys would thus have someone at hand to consult in difficulties, to explain their case if they got into trouble with the headmaster, or the other masters, to send a report of their characters home, to prepare them for confirmation, and in general to stand to them in relation of a pastor to his flock. 'No parochial ministry', he would say to them, 'can be more properly a cure of souls than yours.' (Stanley 1903, 70)

20 For a discussion of pastoral care that highlights these dimensions of the concept see Best, Jarvis and Ribbins (1977).

21 Cf. Bazalgette (1978, 62–3).

22 Extract from note by Gillian Davies written to the headmaster in 1970.

23 Cf. Best, Jarvis and Ribbins (1977).

24 Cf. King (1973a, 71).

25 Further particulars for posts in the English department, February 1973.

26 ibid.

27 The Newsom department staff were supposed to work as a team with no individual in overall charge. However, this created competition between individual members of the department (see chapter seven).

28 In summer 1973 no candidate who entered for Ordinary-level mathematics achieved a pass and the fail grades that were obtained were the lowest possible. When the headmaster talked about public examination results at the first staff meeting for the academic year 1973–4, he said that while the results in Ordinary-level English were among the best he had ever seen (95 per cent of the candidates entered had passed – many with high grades) the mathematics results were the worst he had ever seen in any school.

29 When a lesson was 'subbed' in the school it meant that another teacher took the lesson with the class in the absence of the teacher who had been scheduled for it. For a discussion of 'subbing' in another school see Mays, Quine and Pickett (1968, 37).

30 The concept of 'typification' is drawn from the work of Schutz (1972) and Schutz and Luckmann (1973). In the sociology of education it has been applied to teacher–pupil interaction and social relations. See, for example, Hargreaves, Hester and Mellor (1975) and Hargreaves (1977).

31 For a further discussion of the ways in which teachers typify pupil behaviour through speculation see Hargreaves, Hester and Mellor (1975, 140–70).

32 A religious education syllabus for Catholic schools named after the author. See Konstant (1967).

33 Minutes taken of the religious education department meeting on Wednesday, 12 September 1973, by the head of the department for years one to three.

34 This meeting was similar in terms of structure and content to Newsom meetings that I attended and which are discussed in later chapters.

35 For a discussion of a similar type of meeting that encountered similar problems see Berg (1968, 68–9).

36 For a discussion and description of such prize-givings see, for example, King (1973a, 62–3).

37 The existence of this group was confirmed for me by Dick Wilkinson, who when in conversation with various people in the common room one day mentioned how it was the usual practice for heads of departments to gather around the centre tables at break to talk to each other.

38 The existence of this group was reinforced during one lunch hour when a man went and sat in this part of the common room. He was ridiculed by the women who claimed that he was in their part of the common room.

39 For discussion of key informants see, for example, Burgess (1982a, 39–40, 98–104) and for their use in this study, see Burgess (1982b; 1984a).

40 For a discussion of some of the problems and implications of gaining access to this group for fieldwork in the school see Burgess (1979; 1984a).

41 For a further discussion of this concept and its use in the sociology of education see, for example, Hargreaves, Hester and Mellor (1975, 140–70).

42 For a further discussion of social interaction in a common room see, for example, Hargreaves (1972, 403–7) and Hammersley (1981). In addition, see Partridge (1968, 35) where he discusses how seniority influenced discussions in a staff room. For a similar point of view see Lacey (1970, 165) where he shows that seniority and membership of departments were the criteria for seating arrangements in the staff room.

43 For a further discussion of this point see, for example, Shaw (1969).

44 For a description of school assembly see King (1973a, 52) and Waller (1967, 122).

45 For a discussion of the way in which religion is used to discuss school activities see Mays, Quine and Pickett (1968, 30) and chapter two.

46 This statement might well have referred to behaviour as well as litter; Webb (1962) argues that teachers wished to keep the activities of the playground and the classroom very separate.

47 Alan James (head of Lancaster House) would often refuse to see pupils who were sent to him in the middle of classes. This practice helped to establish his reputation for weakness among the staff.

48 For a discussion of the way in which pupils make distinctions between teachers see, for example, Partridge (1968, 121) who notes that the teachers were distinguished as 'softies' and 'bastards'. For a discussion of the way in which pupils evaluate teachers, see Gannaway (1976), especially p.60. For further pupil typifications of teachers see Furlong (1976) and Woods (1976b, 132–5).

49 The head of the English department had, in fact, established a file of information on the routines that were to be followed in the department. A copy of this information was provided for all teachers who worked in the English department.

50 Cf. Blackie (1977) and Burgess (1984b).

4

SOCIAL PROCESSES IN THE SCHOOL: AN ANALYSIS OF THREE SOCIAL SITUATIONS

The previous chapters have focused on the structure of the school, especially the social structure and social relationships among teachers. The evidence suggests that the positions which individual teachers held in the school structure influenced the pattern of their relationships with other teachers, the ways in which they defined their work, and the conceptions which they held of the school. Different conceptions of the school were transmitted by the headmaster, the heads of houses, the heads of departments and the assistant teachers. These different conceptions appeared to influence the way in which reality was defined for both teachers and pupils. Each had to accommodate different ideas about activities, routines, practices and rules within the school.

During my fieldwork I examined how different conceptions of the school were employed in social situations. In particular, I was interested to see the way the school *actually* worked in contrast to the ways different teachers thought the school *should* work. The questions that were posed included: were there distinctions between the way the headmaster considered the school should work and the way it actually worked? What were the differences between the work of house staff and departmental staff? How did the social structure operate? Why did conflict occur? How did conflict occur? How was conflict handled? On what norms and values was the conflict based? How was conflict reconciled? This chapter will, therefore, focus on the social structure of the school in operation and the ways in which seemingly different accounts were handled by its members.

While earlier chapters have used isolated case materials to illustrate the ways in which individuals established definitions of situations, this chapter uses a series of connecting cases involving the same persons or groups over a period of time.[1] A key exponent of this approach has been Victor Turner who suggests that the unit of analysis should be a situation, event, or crisis that he terms a social drama (Turner 1957, 82–130). Turner (1971, 352) considers that the specific aim of the social drama is

> not to present a reputedly objective recital of a series of events; it is concerned, rather, with the different interpretations put upon these events, and the way in which they express nuanced shifts or switches in the balances of power or ventilate divergent interests within common concerns.

In this way, the social drama may help us to look at the social processes involved in the operation of social structure; the ways in which people actually live and pursue particular objectives.

In this chapter I examine three social situations or social dramas to see the social processes that are involved when conflict occurs, how it is handled and on what basis it is handled. The first situation took place in my first term in the school and is an analysis of the events surrounding a bomb scare. Secondly, a mass walk-out of pupils in the autumn term and, finally, the events surrounding the end-of-year activities in the summer term. Each situation appears to be an isolated incident, yet all three are linked together as they were defined by the teachers as major crises. Furthermore, they all took place on a school-wide basis and could not be handled by any one group alone. Each situation also involved the same teachers: the headmaster, heads of houses, heads of departments and assistant teachers. As a consequence, they can be used to examine the ways in which teachers attempted to maintain their definitions of orderly conduct in the school and the way in which the school worked. Each situation will be described and related to the pattern of social relationships that occurred among the teachers and will be used to present a picture of the ways in which norms were put into effect within the school.

The case of the bomb scare

The late summer of 1973 saw a bombing campaign launched on public buildings in mainland Britain. These attacks had a series of common features: anonymous telephone calls, bombs reported to be in buildings and timed to explode within half an hour of the call being made. As these bomb attacks were related to the events in Northern Ireland it meant that towns, cities and public buildings with an Irish connection were on constant alert. Merston with its large Irish population was considered a possible target. Similarly, pubs, clubs, schools and organizations with an Irish connection were regarded by the police and the public as highly vulnerable. In these circumstances, McGregor possessed all the characteristics of a possible target, especially as it was housed in separate buildings on a thirty-four-acre site where access was relatively easy. This situation also made the school a ripe target for hoaxes from pupils who appreciated its vulnerability. It is against this background that a series of bomb scares at the school have to be considered.

One Thursday morning in early June I arrived at the school and found everyone busily talking in the common room about a school bomb scare that had occurred on the previous day. Dorothy Gilmore told me that the bomb scare had started early in the afternoon. The first she knew of the situation was when she was told to take her class on to the sports field. She explained that teachers and pupils had waited around on the field, while the buildings were searched by several male teachers assisted by two policemen. However, after an hour's search, the police had decided it was a hoax and the deputy head had allowed everyone to return to the buildings.

On this particular day, she explained, the headmaster had been absent from school. As a result, all the organization had fallen to his deputy, Frank Lloyd. Some teachers had found an article in a daily newspaper with the headline, *Lloyd is the man for the crisis* and this was now pinned in a prominent position in the administrative block for all to see. The concept of 'crisis' was central to the teachers' conception of the situation as it was taken up and employed by staff in discussions throughout the morning break. I was sitting with the 'corner group' which consisted of the heads of houses together with Roy Carey and Sylvia Robinson. Several members of the group considered that the deputy head had managed the crisis very well in the head's absence. However, alongside their praise for the deputy head was some criticism of the head. Roy Carey was quick to use this situation to criticize the head as he remarked, 'It's just typical of the boss to be away when there's a crisis'. He complained bitterly that they had had to face this situation without any ideas from the head about how such a situation could be handled.

These comments in themselves highlighted Roy Carey's ignorance of the way Mr Goddard worked and the pattern of school organization. We have already seen how Mr Goddard considered the craft of being a headmaster involved direct participation in the life of the school and the management of crisis. One of the ways in which Goddard provided a framework in which his staff could work was through the advice, information and routines which he circulated at the start of each academic year. Among the memoranda issued was a collection of notes on wise and effective action which could be taken in an emergency.

In this respect, Mr Goddard had already thought out a contingency plan if a fire should break out, if there should be an explosion or a bomb scare. The result was that the headmaster could guide such situations even in his absence, as he had provided a framework which teachers could use to take effective action. The general principles embodied in his memorandum on emergencies indicated the way in which he expected teachers to work. The memorandum stated:

   (i) Each teacher will be responsible for checking their group and getting the children in his or her care to either their house block or a place of safety.

  (ii) If teachers are injured the nearest teacher/responsible adult conducts unharmed children to a place of safety.

 (iii) At the same time the head and deputy head are to be informed. The head will get to the scene of the accident, the deputy head will go to the administration block to take charge of organizing outside help and receiving reports from the rest of the site. Mr Jackson (teacher in charge of safety) will join the deputy head.

 (iv) As soon as possible after delivering children to a safe place and handing them over to a responsible adult, heads of houses will conduct a register check and at the earliest opportunity will notify the deputy head of any missing children. They will remain with the children of their house until further instructions are given.

  (v) Other teachers will, when practical, join their head of house. Assistant heads of house will inform the deputy head of any staff missing.

The reporting to the deputy head in (iv) and (v) is *essential*.

 (vi) Mr Penfold and Mr Dare will, as soon as they have handed over their children, report to the head at the scene of the accident.

(vii) All roads and paths must be kept clear for emergency service vehicles.

Action by secretaries

(a) care of those sent to rest room
(b) phoning for ambulances, etc.
(c) contacting parents whenever a child is going to hospital
(d) collecting, issuing information under the guidance of headmaster/deputy head

(e) ensuring that accident reports are completed and appropriately distributed.

To assist in (c) it is very helpful if telephone numbers for contacting parents are available not only at house level but also in the main office, and heads of house are asked to ensure that as many phone numbers as possible are given to the secretary.

This document outlined the routine which the headmaster expected his staff to follow. Here, he utilized the basic structure of the teaching staff and gave particular emphasis to ways in which teachers were expected to work. While the house heads rather than the departmental staff were to play an important part, it was evident that the headmaster was to be the key participant in any emergency. He would be at the scene of any incident. While the head, deputy head, senior mistress and the house heads were responsible for general organization, the assistant teachers – including the heads of department – were to be responsible for the pupils. It was evident that this was an ideal plan which the staff had failed to put into effect in the bomb scare on the previous day.

During Thursday lunch hour the staff continued to go over the incidents of the previous day. Many teachers posed questions about the situation: 'Will there be more bomb scares? Will the next bomb scare be for real? Will there be a bomb scare this afternoon? What will happen today?' These questions together with the associated gossip created an air of expectancy among the staff. Several teachers half expected some incident that afternoon, yet no individual in the common room went to check on the routine outlined by the headmaster. In fact, the conversation indicated that many teachers were still unaware of his plans for handling emergencies.

By the start of afternoon school, many staff expected a further bomb scare. I went over to Clifton House for afternoon registration. When I arrived with Sylvia Robinson and Sally Clarke, we found that Maggie Rolls (our head of house) and Roy Carey had spent the lunch hour in the house. They were not in such a serious mood as the other teachers and were unconcerned about bomb scares. They both laughed as Maggie explained that they had spent the whole of the lunch hour marking all the Clifton House registers. The rest of us were puzzled about her reasons for marking these registers. Maggie explained that as the coming Friday was a Catholic holiday it meant that Thursday was technically the last day of the week when all the registers had to be totalled and sent into the office. Maggie said that she had completed all the registers this week so that they could be sent quickly to the office. This should ensure that she would win first place in the register race that the school secretary promoted among the heads of houses.

The teachers were amused. Those who had tutor groups asked what they were to do with the children at registration that afternoon. Maggie suggested that the tutors should just go quickly to see if most children were present and then return with their registers. She added: 'We've marked all the registers "blind" and so we must just hope that nobody has appeared or disappeared since this morning'. Despite the fact that many tutors expected an emergency that afternoon, not one of them challenged Maggie's instructions. The bell rang for registration and the tutors went to their classes. A few minutes elapsed and they returned with their 'marked' registers. Maggie did not ask if pupils were absent and no tutor reported that any pupils had returned to school since morning registration, nor were absentees mentioned. The registers were quickly collected and we all went to our first afternoon lesson.

As I had a 'free' period I went to the Clifton/Lancaster working staff room. No other member of staff was 'free' at the time and I therefore corrected some work which my class had completed that morning. About half an hour after the lesson had started Maggie Rolls came into the working staff room. She looked very worried. She had been asked to search her house base for any suspicious object as the school secretary had received another telephone call to say that there was a bomb in the school.

A thorough search of the working staff room would have been a formidable task. There was little furniture: a table, some chairs and a few lockers, but the room contained piles of books, a few cases, dirty games kit and old exercise books together with some remnants of the stalls which had been assembled for the school fête in the previous year. Maggie did not attempt to go through all the things in the room. She opened a few lockers, looked inside them and then pushed them shut. She picked up a few of the books on top of the lockers, looked behind them and then returned everything to its original place. Finally, she took one quick look round the room, grinned nervously at me and went out.

I went to the staff-room window to see if there was any increased activity on the site. There were few people around other than two pupils crossing the lawns. Twenty minutes after Maggie Rolls had gone, Sally Clarke came into the working staff room and talked about the bomb scare. She was quite alarmed. She wondered if it was another hoax or whether this time it was for real. She thought it could be just another hoax but, she explained, the deputy head was taking it all seriously as he had sent a note round to all the staff, with the instruction that tutor groups were to be assembled on the sports field at 2.50 p.m. It was already twenty minutes to three o'clock and this was the first I had heard of this arrangement.

Ten minutes before three o'clock a short bell was rung and I packed up my things to go on to the field. When I got outside the staff room I found the corridor jammed with pupils from various tutor groups. Teachers were taking their tutor groups on to the field but the movement was not organized. Eventually I reached the sports field where I found the deputy head, assisted by several heads of houses, attempting to keep the tutor groups in areas which were occupied by each house. Each house had a different idea about methods of assembly. Hexham House had all its pupils assembled in straight lines and staff were busy checking children against their names in registers. Meanwhile, Clifton House pupils were standing in lines but no register check was taken; in any event this exercise would have been useless as the registers had not been properly marked that afternoon. Some houses neither had their children in ranks nor took register checks and as a result many pupils were wandering around in small groups, attempting to break into the lines of other houses and playing around near the buildings. There was chaos.

An attempt to bring some order to the proceedings was made by the deputy head. He was assisted by Roy Carey, Dick Wilkinson and Keith Dryden who were bawling out instructions and attempting to get pupils to stand still. But for most staff the exercise was just part of another hoax as they stood around talking to one another. Shortly after 3.10 p.m. when the bomb was supposed to explode, the deputy head announced that the police had declared the buildings safe. A huge roar went up from the children. The pupils in lines began to disperse as their teachers walked back towards the buildings. The crisis was over. I joined a group of Clifton staff as they made their way towards the school. They thought the event had been staged by a pupil who had decided to play this trick, having seen the chaos that the hoax had created on the previous day.[2]

However, hoax or not, this crisis and its unfolding did reveal several aspects of school structure and the way in which it actually operated. The headmaster's document provided some guidance about procedures. Indeed, although Goddard had been absent from school he had 'participated' in the events, because elements of his plan had been used by the deputy head. The staff who were supposed to be responsible for this situation were the house heads, assisted by other teachers. In practice, the situation operated somewhat differently as house heads interpreted their responsibilities in different ways. There was a stark contrast between the way in which teachers were supposed to work and the way they actually worked.

One of the interesting features of the afternoon was the diverse way in which the house heads interpreted their work. Each head of house was responsible for a similar number of pupils. Some made a careful check of all their pupils, while others allowed their pupils to wander around unchecked. Furthermore, one head of house had jeopardized the welfare of her pupils by completing all her registers so that she could be 'first past the post' in the register race with her colleagues. Finally, it was rumoured that other teachers who assisted the deputy head and the heads of houses to ensure the safety of the pupils had only participated to secure advantages for themselves.[3] This situation therefore revealed a series of events which were defined and redefined by different teachers depending on their positions and the way in which they worked through this crisis.

Originally, the normal routine of the school had been breached by the telephone call announcing the bomb scare that had started the crisis. The crisis itself highlighted the way in which house heads in particular managed affairs within their houses. There were not merely differences in the way in which they handled the crisis, but also differences between their actions and those of heads of departments and most assistant teachers who did not consider that they had a central role in the situation. Several of these themes occur once more when we turn to our second situation. Here, we shall see how the same individuals and groups handled another school-wide crisis. In particular, it highlights the different actions, activities, norms and values of teachers, especially house heads and departmental staff.

The case of the royal wedding: the Princess Anne affair

During my fieldwork, it was announced that Princess Anne was to be married in London on Wednesday, 14 November 1973. To mark this royal occasion most local education authorities decided that children within their areas would receive a one-day holiday. Only a few local authorities did not follow this practice, among which was Merston. A meeting of the local Labour Party and in turn the city education committee and the council decided that there were other ways of celebrating the royal wedding without any loss of education to the city's children. As a result no special holiday was given to Merston children. It was this decision that influenced events at Bishop McGregor School on 14 and 15 November 1973.

During the weeks before the wedding, several teachers wondered whether the city council would reverse its decision about 14 November. However, very few were hopeful. As the school returned from the October break we realized that our pessimism was well founded. On several mornings in early November teachers discussed the situation. Some teachers thought the decision was unfair since they would miss the television broadcast of the wedding, others were sorry that they were not getting a day off school. Several women in my house started to make plans for 14 November. Mollie Richards announced that she was not going to miss the television broadcast and would be getting all her classes to go to the audio-visual aids room where they could watch television. The pupils were not so vocal on the subject. A few thought it unfair that they were not given a holiday for the wedding. But only one or two girls mentioned that they would like to see the wedding on the television and indicated that they would have to be 'ill' that day so that they could stay at home.

The day before the royal wedding, conversations turned to 'wedding plans'. Mollie Richards, Doreen Sharp and several other women made plans to watch the television broadcast with their classes. Meanwhile, other pupils were taking active notice of the absence of a holiday. In one of my Newsom classes on the Tuesday afternoon, several pupils considered they had been robbed of a holiday. However, when I asked one boy why he should get a holiday he grinned and replied: 'I'm always ready for a day off'. But he admitted that he was unaware of the royal wedding until he had been told about it by some other pupils that morning. Nevertheless, at the end of the lesson some of the girls left me in no doubt that they would be absent on Wednesday as one girl shouted out, 'Cheerio sir, I'll be in again on Thursday as I shall be ill tomorrow'.

As I only worked part-time in the school, I was not at Bishop McGregor on Wednesday, 14 November. The day following the wedding I went into school. As usual, I caught the bus from the centre of Merston which was packed with McGregor pupils. While I was reading the newspaper, a group of boys who were sitting behind me started to talk about school the previous day. They caught my attention when one boy said, 'It was great to see all those kids walk out'. I continued to pretend to read the paper and listened to their conversation. As far as I could understand it, a large number of pupils (600 – at least half the school) had walked out of McGregor the previous day because they had not been given a special holiday.

The boys considered that they had acted as a group and that most teachers had supported them. As far as they were concerned, the teachers had made little attempt to get the pupils back into school and in some cases encouraged those in school to join those who had walked out. A fifth-year boy, whom I recognized as a member of Arundel House, said he had gone into Miss Gilmore's lesson and she had asked, 'What are you doing here? I thought you would have gone off with the rest.' The boys interpreted this statement as positive encouragement to walk out of school. Another boy commented, 'You ought to have seen Goddard's face when he saw us all out there, he was really amused by it'. Yet a further boy remarked, 'This is the start of action' which implied that there was more to come.

As I entered the school, I overheard several pupils talking to each other as they walked towards their houses. One girl said to her friend, 'All the older ones were out yesterday. Didn't you see it in the *Advertiser* last night?' These were my initial contacts with the events of the previous day. At this stage, I thought I would have to find out about it – instead I discovered that I became very much a part of the actions which followed throughout the day.

When I went into the Westminster/Arundel working staff room, I found Doreen Sharp and Mollie Richards talking about the royal wedding. Doreen turned to me and said, 'Did you see our report in last night's

Evening Advertiser?' When I replied that I had not, both of them proceeded to tell me how half the pupils had walked out of school the previous day and Doreen commented, 'We [the staff] didn't do anything to stop them. We just let them get on with it.' Susan Platts arrived and joined in the conversation. She did not discuss her actions but reported on the events. She estimated that about 600 pupils had gone out of school, because in some of her classes only two pupils were present. She told me that some parents had brought their children back to school in the afternoon. She also explained that not all the staff had taken things so easily. Gillian Davies, the head of Hexham House, had told her pupils that if they went off the site they would be punished when they returned to school.

As other staff arrived, the conversation continued and I began to build up an intricate picture of the events which had taken place and the positions that had been adopted by various teachers. Several staff expressed the view that it would probably all 'blow over' now. However, this idea was soon dispelled when John McGuire arrived and told us that an emergency heads of houses meeting was being held in the head-master's office. At this news, the staff began to speculate on what would happen. Several teachers were concerned about the action which the headmaster might take against the staff, as he might feel they had supported the pupils. However, the general feeling was that the head-master only had himself to blame for what had happened. They thought he should have put a stop to everything rather than 'play it cool'. John McGuire commented, 'It's all very well for the boss to say that the staff should have done something but he should have decided what he wanted the staff to do'. Michael O'Donaghue added that the headmaster could have encouraged the pupils to leave the site. Mike said that he had walked up to the science laboratories with the head just after nine o'clock when several pupils were wandering around the school, either uninvolved with those who were going out of school, or not at lessons. At that time, he recalled, the head had shouted at them, 'Either join them or go to lessons' which he considered could have been interpreted as an invitation to leave the site.

The staff agreed that the pupils were undecided about what they should do. Gerry Cochrane told me he had a good view of everything that happened as he had been teaching in Westminster House hall which overlooked the sports field where the pupils had gathered. He thought the whole thing had been started by pupils from Westminster and Arundel who had called out to pupils from other houses to join them in the walk-out. He said that most pupils were just wandering around and appeared uncertain about what they should do. Gerry considered that the real organization took place at break time when the pupils had gathered on the mound outside Westminster House before leaving the site. However, according to Gerry (and other staff supported his story), the headmaster had watched the pupils from the common-room window and had said that he was not going to take any action. Gerry added that very few teachers had done anything at this stage except the house staff, who had issued threats to their pupils, and individual teachers such as Stuart Mills, Michael O'Donaghue and Keith Dryden who had been outside attempting to get the pupils back into school.

These accounts of the previous day helped me to analyse the situation. It appeared that the pupils had staged a walk-out which was unorganized and spontaneous,[4] because at the time it occurred, pupils were still encouraging others to leave the site. The reactions by the staff suggested a distinct division between the house staff who had discouraged the pupils from leaving the school and many teachers in the departments who had encouraged pupils to leave. Meanwhile, the accounts about the headmaster varied. Some teachers said that he acted passively while others claimed that he encouraged pupils to leave the site. Many teachers used the latter account as this helped them to rationalize their own activities. These accounts provided a background to the events that followed.

When the bell rang at 8.35 a.m. all of us who were in Westminster House left the working staff room and went to our house head's study. When we arrived we were greeted by Susan Platts, the deputy head of house, who told us that Dick Wilkinson (the acting head of house) was at an emergency heads of houses' meeting. When the staff heard this news some of them became very agitated but eventually they decided that nothing very much would happen. Susan Platts made arrangements for assembly and for teachers to go and mark registers while I returned to the working staff room. At about 8.45 a.m. John McGuire came in and told those of us there that we had to go back to the house head's study for an emergency house meeting.

I went into Dick Wilkinson's study. Several staff were already there looking at a sheet which each of them had been given. One or two looked up as I went in. They seemed agitated and annoyed. Dick was quiet but appeared bad-tempered. He gave me a sheet which had been written by the headmaster. When all the house staff returned from their tutorial groups, Dick announced that he was going to read through the sheet to clarify any points that were not clear. There was silence as he began reading:

ACTION TO BE TAKEN ON THURSDAY, 15 NOVEMBER 1973

From 8.35–9.40 there will be house and tutorial time

1 For any child absent from school all day Wednesday the normal procedure of notes will be followed.

2 For any child who was present at morning registration, who ordered a dinner but did not eat it, that child must be charged the cost of the dinner.

3 For any pupils who went off site but later returned . . . an apology in writing to those teachers whose classes were missed will suffice.

4 For any pupils who went off site and who did not return I want
   (a) a written explanation of why they did as they did and
   (b) a written account of what they did, and at what time they reached home.
I then want these letters scanned for the excuses used and a check made into the validity of any excuse.

At this point, Dick broke off from reading. He looked up and said, 'The headmaster is particularly interested in names being named of members of staff who encouraged the pupils to leave the site'. Nobody replied to this remark. Terry Goodwin went red in the face and several staff stared at the sheet or at the floor. Dick continued to read:

5 These pupils are then to write letters of apology to each teacher whose lessons were missed, to the head of house and to the head.

6 All the work they should have done yesterday is to be made up by Monday and the level at which this is to be done is to be determined by the heads of departments, each for his or her own department.

7 In addition essays are to be written on the following scale:
1st year 200 words 2nd year 300 words 3rd year 400 words by Friday a.m. on The Royal Wedding. An alternative for those whose writing capacities are limited will be 50, 100 and 200 times the phrase Princess Anne and Captain Mark Phillips.
For fourth year and for fifth year an essay of 800 words or 350 times the phrase. The staff are to determine for each pupil which punishment is imposed.

8 I want to see each member of the sixth form starting at nine a.m. in the office in Campion.
I may want to see each member of the fifth but if I do so then I shall make the arrangements at break this a.m.

9 Any refusals to do work set are to come to Miss Chapman, Mr Lloyd or myself.

10 Any additional punishments may be imposed by heads of house to implement promises they made individually yesterday.

G. Goddard

When Dick had finished reading, Terry Goodwin asked meekly, 'How does the headmaster view the situation today?' Dick replied that he was not exactly pleased as he had heard that some teachers encouraged pupils to leave the site and, therefore, he wanted specific details and names named. Terry immediately responded by saying, 'Well, I don't think it's bloody fair. I think he ought to consider his own actions. After all, it's his responsibility and he should bloody well look to himself. He didn't do anything yesterday. It's only because of this report in the evening paper that he's so concerned now.' Other members of staff asked Terry if she had encouraged the pupils to leave the school. She replied that while she had not encouraged them neither had she discouraged them. Dick still seemed rather gruff. He shrugged his shoulders and said, 'Well, that's the way Mr Goddard wants it, so it's now tutorial time'. There was to be no assembly that day and therefore the staff went to their tutorial groups and I returned to the working staff room.

Gerry Cochrane came into the room looking troubled. He wandered over and started to tell me what he had said to the pupils the previous day. It was evident that he wanted to talk to someone about his part in the business. He said that he had been asked by pupils for advice on what they should do and that he had told them, 'It's up to you to make your own decision but these are some of the things which you can do'. He had told them that they could stay at school, go home or walk out with the other pupils. He asked if I thought this could be interpreted as positive encouragement to leave school and seemed relieved when I gave a negative response. He told me that Paul Klee had used the situation to lead a class discussion on democracy but he said that Paul was now concerned about how this would be interpreted.

Gerry thought that several staff must now be in a difficult position as it could appear that they encouraged pupils to leave the site. He considered that the 'witch hunt' that was now taking place was not the headmaster's idea but the brain-child of the heads of houses who wanted teachers as well as pupils reprimanded for their actions. His views were based on the house heads' activities of the previous day. He explained that Gillian Davies had put up two notices in Hexham House, saying that she did not want Hexham pupils to leave the site otherwise she would be forced to punish them. While we were in the working staff room several tutors from Westminster and Arundel came in and talked. One tutor said the first year were scared as they had been encouraged to leave the site by their older brothers and sisters. A third-year tutor said that several pupils had named the headmaster as the person who had encouraged them to leave the site when he had remarked, 'Either you go or you go back to lessons'. The tutor remarked that this phrase had been quoted by several pupils.

At the end of the tutorial period, I went to the main office to see the school secretary who told me that the headmaster was out in the school. She considered that Mr Goddard's absence from the office was part of his strategy to avoid talking to local newspaper reporters. When I went upstairs to the common room I found several teachers lounging in easy chairs, talking about the situation. One teacher said that she had asked one boy why he was not out of school on the previous day and he replied, 'I don't want to get expelled and anyway Miss Davies already has enough against me'. She then read out another fifth-form boy's excuse for being out of school which said, 'Sorry I missed lessons. It was silly but it's done now.' This amused the staff and helped to relieve the tension.

When I went to my class, the Newsom pupils gave me their account of Wednesday's events and the first two lessons that morning. The pupils were excited about what had occurred. One of the pupils, Jim Green, spoke for the rest of the class. He explained that it was not an organized walk-out as there had been no leaders. He said 'It was just an idea that thirty or forty kids should come out'. Jim said that they had as good a reason to walk out as the teachers who had been out of school on the Monday.[5] Furthermore, he considered that they had been encouraged to leave school by several teachers, including the headmaster who had said to them, 'If you want to go, then go, otherwise go to your classes'. The other pupils agreed with Jim, since all of those who had been out of school considered they had received some encouragement from their teachers. I enquired what they had done on Wednesday. Some had gone to find their friends at other schools, some had gone home or into the city centre, while only a few had watched the television presentation of the wedding. The pupils who had stayed away from school and produced a note to cover their absence said that they were sorry to have missed the fun but were glad that they did not have any writing to do.

At the mention of writing there was uproar. I quietened the class and we continued to talk. Another pupil, Patrick McConnell, said that he did not mind writing letters to apologize for what had happened but he objected to the essays. Several others agreed with him. Diane Lane, an obstreperous member of the class, said that she thought the essays were a punishment and as they had not done anything to be punished she would refuse to do them. Other pupils nodded in agreement. Even Nigel Rogers who was usually very quiet said that this was how most of the fifth year felt and therefore the teachers were unlikely to get their essays. At this the subject seemed closed for the moment, but it did reveal the pupils' perspective of the walk-out and the way in which they intended to deal with the headmaster's impositions.

At lunch time, Gerry Cochrane and Paul Klee came to talk to me about the situation. Like me, both teachers had spent part of their lessons analysing the current situation with pupils. They had heard that the headmaster was using the letters the pupils had written to discover which teachers had encouraged the situation to develop. They enquired again if I considered their activities warranted any action being taken against them. When I said that I thought this unlikely, it seemed to ease their minds. During the lunch hour the headmaster came to the common room to fetch

Don Williams. When Don returned he looked annoyed. Gerry decided to join him to find out what was happening. He discovered that Don had just had an argument with the headmaster who accused him of encouraging pupils to leave the site. As Don explained to me later that day, it seemed that Mr Goddard was set on using some teachers as scapegoats for his own actions.

Paul Klee told me about the headmaster's actions on the previous day. He said that the head had ordered register checks to be taken at mid-morning break and at lunch time. During the lunch hour Goddard announced that he had sent a telegram on behalf of all staff and pupils to Princess Anne and Captain Mark Phillips, congratulating them on their marriage. Paul interpreted this action as an attempt by the headmaster to cover his tracks. However, he objected to the telegram as he did not think Goddard had any right to assume that all teachers and pupils shared his sentiments.

By the end of the day, rumours were still circulating. John McGuire and the school chaplain talked to me about the activities surrounding this event. The priest remarked that he was 'rather surprised by Geoff's reaction . . . I thought he would let it all blow over'. We sat and talked about the reactions of various house heads. John McGuire was critical of their activities. He said he had heard that in Clifton House the house head had marked 'truant' on the record cards of those pupils who walked out of school. Meanwhile, he claimed that in Lancaster House the house head had caned both boys and girls. We all agreed that these punishments highlighted the major differences between the houses and the various ways in which the heads of houses worked. The priest considered that there was a major difference between the heads of houses and other teachers, remarking 'Eileen [head of Arundel House] and the others have a particular attitude towards the kids which sets them against the house heads before they start'. It was also his opinion that the action taken against the pupils had been suggested by the heads of houses, although it had gone out as instructions from the headmaster.

At the end of the day, there was a Newsom department meeting which I attended with several staff, including the headmaster. Mr Goddard appeared quite cheerful but it seemed that this covered his concern over the day's activities. At the start of the meeting, we all discussed the day's events. The headmaster made no mention of staff involvement in the activities but talked about the pupils. He said that he had been told that some pupils might refuse to write essays. However, he claimed that he would insist that these were written as he wanted the pupils to realize that if anything similar happened again he would 'kill them for it'. But at this late stage on Thursday he was optimistic that his instructions would be obeyed.

I collected information about these events from a variety of sources:

the headmaster, heads of houses, departmental staff and pupils. It appeared that the pupils had staged the walk-out as an unplanned, unorganized, spontaneous action which would provide them with a day off school regardless of the royal wedding. In addition, the events suggested that Goddard had misread the seriousness of the situation early on the Wednesday morning. The result was that he used Wednesday afternoon and the whole of Thursday to manoeuvre his way out of the situation and to redefine his authority which had been visibly challenged by collective action.

The pupils' activities highlighted two groups on the staff: those who belonged to houses and those who belonged to departments. These groups were not mutually exclusive because heads of houses were assisted by other teachers. However, while the heads of houses attempted to discourage pupils from leaving the site and to uphold school rules on obedience and order, several departmental staff were busy encouraging pupils to leave school. In this situation, it appeared that while departmental staff had a nominal membership of the house system, they did not help to implement the behavioural norms which the house heads attempted to establish. Instead, they made themselves quite distinct from the implementation of 'discipline' in the school which they regarded as a duty of the house heads. This situation made the differences between houses and departments apparent to the pupils who were now ready to disobey house heads implementing different scales of punishment for the same 'crime'. The walk-out had, therefore, created disorder in the school as it highlighted the way in which different teachers worked and the loyalties which different groups upheld.

It was this disunity which led to a 'cooling out' process[6] over the next few days. During the autumn term there were periods when the head found it difficult to obtain supplies of oil as part of the nationwide fuel shortage. Usually the school worked on, or oil was obtained from other sources. However, on the Friday of 'wedding week', Mr Goddard informed the staff that there was no oil to heat the school, none could be obtained and as a result the school would be closed until the following Tuesday. Several teachers were suspicious as it had always been possible to obtain fuel in the past. A few teachers discussed this situation with me. They considered that this was a way in which the headmaster was buying time; he had identified the disarray in the school and was now using the oil crisis to 'cool out' the Princess Anne affair.

McGregor was closed for four days. This period allowed staff and pupils to forget many of the events associated with the Princess Anne affair with which they had been so concerned the previous week. When I went into the Westminster/Arundel working staff room on the Tuesday morning, I found that staff were not even talking about the Princess Anne affair because they were so pleased to discuss all the things they had done in their extended break from school. When I received my copy of the weekly news sheet I saw that the headmaster was taking school assembly that week on the theme *collective action*. I thought it was probable that he would talk about the Princess Anne affair because he usually related his central theme to day-to-day events in the school (see chapter two).

School assembly that morning followed the traditional pattern. The headmaster started by leading prayers which staff and pupils recited together: the Lord's Prayer, a prayer for the Souls in Purgatory, the Hail Mary and the Grace. He followed this by saying, 'We've just taken part in what could be described as collective action'. He remarked that it was collective action because we did it together, we did it for ourselves but you did not necessarily do it for yourself. He went on to explain that when individuals did things for themselves they had to take decisions, just as some people had to take decisions last week. At this point, he remarked that he was not going to have much to say about last week. Nevertheless, he went on to talk about aspects of the Princess Anne affair from his perspective.

He stated that last week was history, but it was history that we should not forget. He cast his eyes round the house halls and said that there was just one thing he would like to comment upon. 'I'm told by my spies that I'm in serious danger of being removed by the local education authority for encouraging you to leave the site.' But he continued, 'that's one version of what happened but it's not true. I never encouraged anyone to leave the site.' There was no visible reaction from the pupils but one or two staff looked at each other and grinned.

The head continued to explain how the school had already established ways in which pupils could engage in collective action through their elected representatives on the school council. He explained that this group provided contact between teachers and pupils where matters of current interest could be discussed. At this point he announced that the school council would meet during the week to see what could be done about the current situation. He closed the assembly by saying that he was pleased to see that everyone was now back in school and he hoped that the buildings would be warm enough 'for us to educate you and you to educate yourselves. I hope we can now go on to meet your educational needs.' With this remark the assembly closed and with it the last 'official' public comment had been made on the Princess Anne affair.

In the days that followed, few remarks were made by staff or pupils about the Princess Anne affair other than by pupils who refused to do essays and by staff about the absence of essays. The headmaster appeared to do nothing to recover the missing essays. He had played out his part in the assembly. Firstly, he had developed a strategy which would 'cool out' the teachers and pupils so that some semblance of order and unity could be restored to the school. Secondly, he had used a school assembly to bring together teachers and pupils and to discuss his own position which involved a redefinition of the events in the previous week. In this way he had attempted to re-establish his position and his authority in the school.

Overall, the events in this situation cast light on the way in which the school operated. Firstly, it illustrated the roles of headmaster, head of house and departmental staff. Secondly, it revealed the way in which staff worked in groups and, finally, the way in which these groups upheld different norms and loyalties within the school. As far as the headmaster was concerned we have seen the way in which he participated in the events and was one of the most powerful definers of reality in the school. He not only defined the situation but also redefined it when he discovered that his earlier strategies had failed; a point which was criticized by many departmental staff. The heads of houses operated as a distinct group. Although all staff were supposedly responsible for behavioural norms, it was only the heads of houses and a few assistant teachers (rumoured to have career motives) who attempted to discourage pupils from leaving the school. While all the heads of houses were united in their attempt to establish order, it was evident that they did so in different ways. The result was that children from different houses were punished in different ways.

The departmental staff formed another broad, if not exclusive group. They disassociated themselves from preventing the walk-out and punishing pupils. However, the way in which they did this took different forms. Some junior teachers actively encouraged pupils to leave the school as a holiday for the pupils meant a holiday for them. Meanwhile, some heads of departments stood apart from the situation, doing nothing to promote or prevent the walk-out or to punish children when they returned to school. In short, while departmental staff held different positions in this situation, they were united in their belief that it was not their job to intervene in these events.

This situation reinforced the idea that there were two major groups of teachers: house heads and departmental staff.[7] While each group was unified on some issues they were polarized on others. The result was that each major group had a number of subgroups who performed their duties in different ways. The ideas about the school, its norms and the work of teachers were therefore presented to the pupils in different ways. Some of these themes recurred once again in the situation in which I became involved during the last week of the summer term 1974 and which involved a series of crises.

The case of the secret document

It was usual for secondary school pupils in Merston to spend their last day at school participating in various traditions and ritual ceremonies: saying goodbye to teachers, collecting autographs, returning school books, and taking part in the Leavers' Service. Alongside these traditions were a variety of informal activities which included tearing each other's uniforms to shreds, throwing flour and eggs at other leavers and going into 'town' to dance in the fountain with pupils from other schools.[8]

At the end of the spring term 1974, I witnessed the end-of-term ceremony at Bishop McGregor School. In the early morning, many of the leavers were visiting teachers in their classrooms to say their goodbyes and to collect autographs. At break time the pupils took coffee (and, it was rumoured, a cigarette) with the headmaster and after break attended the Leavers' Service in the school chapel. The main thing which struck me about these pupils was their school uniform. Some leavers whom I had never seen in uniform or anything that resembled it were now almost completely attired, in fact some of the uniform looked quite new.

The Leavers' Service was taken by the school chaplain and lasted for about half an hour. I was aware that the service was over when the silence in the school was broken by shouts from several leavers as they rushed out of the chapel block on to the lawns. I was in the staff common room with several other teachers. When we heard the noise several of us went to look out of the window. 'Now the fun will begin', said David Peel with a grin. He had hardly made this remark when another boy came rushing out of the block. Suddenly, two boys pounced on another and began to pull at the sleeve of his blazer. A blazer arm disappeared and then a pocket. Meanwhile, the others were throwing flour at the rest of the group. Soon other leavers joined in, girls' tights were ripped, skirts were torn and blazers shredded. The leavers ran across the lawns throwing flour over each other, smashing eggs down their school clothes and pulling uniforms to shreds.[9] The 'spectators' in the common room were highly amused but nobody went out to stop the 'fun'. These activities continued throughout the day so that by the early afternoon those leavers who had come to school in uniform looked more like tramps whereas those in everyday clothes were dirty but still had their garments intact.

The teachers in the common room regarded this behaviour as 'normal' for the last day of term. But they disliked the whole process as they thought it degraded the individuals and the school, especially when it was taken on to the streets at the end of the day.[10] Nevertheless, those teachers who criticized this behaviour indicated that they would not attempt to go and stop these activities as they might get covered with flour and eggs for their trouble.

While the departmental staff sat and watched from the safety of the common room or retreated to the local pub for an end-of-term drink, the house heads remained in the school to handle the situation. Ron Ward from Westminster House went among the leavers and asked them either to stop their 'antics' or leave the school grounds. Meanwhile, Gillian Davies of Hexham House told other pupils (who were to return to school in the summer term) that they would be caned if they participated in these activities. This situation, in common with several others, divided the staff. In this case, the house heads attempted to maintain order and discipline while the majority of teachers in the departments ignored what had occurred. These reactions might partly be expected. House heads, as we have seen, were responsible for order and discipline and for seeing that their pupils were in uniform. The pupils were, therefore, attacking the symbols of the house heads' authority and departmental staff saw no reason why they should assist the house heads; it was beyond their jurisdiction.

This was not the end of the matter. The end-of-term activities were discussed at the first house heads' meeting at the beginning of the summer term. The members of this meeting were unanimous that they all wanted this Merston practice stopped at Bishop McGregor School. The house heads put forward different strategies to 'solve' the problem involving different punishments. Some suggested caning offenders, while others proposed instant expulsion from the school together with a refusal to provide the offender with a reference. Despite the different approaches, they were all agreed that they could only stop this situation developing if they had co-operation from the whole staff. It was in this context that the events which took place during the last week of the summer term 1974 have to be seen.

During that week I went into school on the Tuesday morning. At the start of the day I joined a small number of Westminster House staff in Ron Ward's study. Many teachers were out of school that day visiting places of interest with their classes. Ron told us that these visits made the school difficult to organize, added to which, he explained, there was a special routine for the whole week which had been worked out by the head-master. He told us that this routine had been circulated on printed sheets and he would be telling us about the programme each day. However, he said that because Jean O'Rourke and I were both part-time staff, we should spend some time reading the sheets, otherwise he thought we would find it difficult to understand what was going on when we came into school. Ron told us that these sheets were highly confidential and therefore, when we had read them, they should be returned to the back of his file.

While the other teachers went away to mark registers, Jean and I stayed in Ron's study and read the following information:[11]

NOTES FOR STAFF DEPLOYMENT DURING THE LAST
WEEK OF THE YEAR

Two objectives underlie these notes. The first is that we should end this year in as pleasant and as dignified a way as is practical. The second is like the first but is expressed negatively . . . it is that we should not have the sorts of 'leavers' displays that we have endured for the last three leavers' dates.

I am, therefore, asking heads of houses to keep staff posted on what is to happen. I am also extremely grateful not only that no one has been to see me to opt out of the tasks involved but that so many have gone out of their way to say positively that they would do whatever is required.[12]

MONDAY AND TUESDAY
There will be normal timetable but special substitution lists will be prepared because of trips and these may well involve the collapse of classes, but not, we hope, the collapse of staff.

WEDNESDAY
Until 10.40 a.m.	Normal timetable.
10.40–11.40	Period 3 normal timetable.
	Period 4 will be abandoned.
11.40–1.00	Lunch hour.
1.00	800 m and 1500 m will be run, physical education staff to organize.
1.10, 1.15 and 1.20	Normal three bells after which the school will go up to the sports field. Disposition of staff will be according to instructions issued for that day.

I would be grateful if those remaining on the site at lunch time would take a 'constitutional' around the ground at some time during the lunch hour.

If in the view of the deputy head the weather is too bad to allow the sports to take place then normal Wednesday afternoon timetable will follow and the sports will be held on Thursday afternoon, these arrangements taking the place of those detailed for Thursday.

THURSDAY
Objectives: to bid farewell to the leavers and to contain those elements in the fifth who feel that a 'rave-up' is necessary.

8.35–9.00	Normal house assemblies.
9.00–12.00	Years 1 to 4 . . . Normal timetable. Additional staff on duty at break. 3 from each house, designated by head of house – 1 to stay in the house area while the other 2 patrol the areas indicated below:

Arundel	Grassed areas in centre of site.
Westminster	Cinder path and areas adjacent to this.
Hexham	Top fence bordering church, cemetery and public footpath.

Southwark	Areas round Ushaw, craft block, home economics block and gate.
Clifton	Rough play area near Gardener's House and up to Rosemary Lane.
Lancaster	Rough area bordering North Road.

9.00 onwards for 5th year

| 9.00–9.35 | Headmaster, heads of house and fifth-form tutors. A coffee morning for the fifth will be held in Arundel House hall. |
| 9.35–10.10 | Fifth year with their tutors (initials given below) in the following rooms, or rooms agreed as suitable alternatives: SG 125; SP 18; JA 32; TP 35; BD 55; KS 130; SJ 6th; DE 124. |

At this stage tutors are asked to collect books from their fifth form inserting in each book a slip of paper with the name of the borrower and the department to which it is to be returned.

10.10–10.45	Leavers' mass in Hexham House hall. Headmaster and heads of houses to attend. Other staff who are free are most welcome to attend at this time.
10.50	Leavers leave and during the subsequent hour sixth form will be available to stay with classes left untaught because of the supervisory tasks being undertaken. Deputy head will remain in Main Office to act as liaison with various groups.
	HM and SM will patrol the area of the shops.
	RW and EM to supervise the 19 bus stop.
	AJ and DW to supervise the area of the Bull by car.
	GD and JB St Columba's by car.
	SP and RR South Road towards Locksley.
	ST and SR South Road towards town.
	BD and KS cinder path and Cedars Hotel.

We hope that by playing it in strength but cool we can avoid any form of confrontation. However, we must make it quite clear that all the fifth are to depart and are not to return without written consent signed by HM, DH or SM.

By 11.50 we should all be back on the site and ready to take an early lunch at that time, when the bells will go.

Staff who need cover in order to undertake these duties are asked to put in their requirements to Mrs Jacques who will send two sixth-formers to any group on request.

We hope that lunch time will be quiet, but I would again welcome partners in a saunter round the site.

P.M.   Period 5 Normal timetable.

2.00–3.20   House tutorial time.

        Staff *v.* pupils cricket match. Pupils <u>may be taken</u> to watch this. They are not to be sent to watch it.

        This match will be followed by the staff final between Team A and Team B

FRIDAY

8.35–9.10   Normal house assemblies, etc. plus a special check on flour, eggs and other missiles. All ammunition can be handed in and no punishment will be meted out. Any pupils found thereafter to have any such ammo on them will be punished and taken home. A note will also be made of the name so that we can reinforce our action in the autumn. Tutors should also use the time to warn their charges about the illegality of tights' ripping, etc. Anyone who finds this stage amusing should be sent to the head of house. Heads of house can send specials on to me.

9.10–9.45   Period 1 Normal timetable.

9.45–10.20   Period 2 Normal timetable.

10.20–10.55   Break.

<u>All non-house blocks to be secured, windows shut by teachers and doors locked by head of department in charge of block.</u>

During first fifteen minutes Arundel, Hexham and Clifton staff are asked to take break duty while Westminster, Lancaster and Southwark staff take coffee.

During the next five minutes, those taking coffee should come out and relieve those on duty.

During the final fifteen minutes Westminster, Lancaster and Southwark should be on duty while Arundel, Hexham and Clifton staff take a break.

Division of labour. Two staff from each house on house blocks, cinder paths and approach to shops, grassed central areas, tennis courts and round pond and boiler house, Tyson, Burnham – behind Ushaw and on rough play area. Field watch perimeter near church and cemetery.

10.55–11.30   House time for assemblies, as decided by head of house.

11.30–12.15	Lunch time and again I would be most grateful if those not leaving the site could 'show the flag' a little round the site. I shall be in Rosemary Lane for much of this time and around the shops.
12.15	First p.m. bell
12.20	Second p.m. bell
12.25	Third p.m. bell and groups go to tutorials from which they should be dismissed as follows:

Those taking the No. 11 bus to the Beacon at 12.25 and these go to the middle road of the site.

The No. 11 bus will leave at 12.30 with GD and PL on board and with HA following by car.

At 12.30 first and second year travelling by the No. 19 bus will leave classrooms as will those travelling on the No. 12 and No. 21 special buses.

The No. 12 bus will have on board KD and SP and will be followed by JB as chauffeur.

The No. 21 bus will have DW and DS on board and will be followed by JH.

By this time most classes will be down to halves and I am leaving it to houses to arrange the necessary cover for staff departing to supervise bus loads.

At 12.40 those taking the No. 18 bus will leave their tutorials as will those taking the No. 16 and No. 14 bus.

However, the pupils on the 14 and 16 buses will travel in one bus the No. 16 and both passes will be acceptable on this bus.

On board the combined bus load No. 16 will be TP and BD with TD as chauffeur.

On board the No. 18 will be JS and PB acting as chauffeur.

At 12.45 the remainder of the pupils will be dismissed, those travelling on the No. 13 leaving at 12.55. On the No. 12 will be KS and SR acting as chauffeur.

On the 12.30 dismissals of pupils for the 19, HM and RW should go to the No. 19 bus stop in South Road and they will travel to town on the first No. 19 to arrive.

AJ and DG are asked to perform in a similar fashion for the second No. 19 which should come through at about 1.00 and should travel with that bus. EM is asked to act as chauffeur for them and to arrange a suitable rendezvous in town since Westgate is banned for private cars.

Do please convince the children of the importance of good behaviour on the buses. Many schools notified them of their needs in mid-June. We only talked to them last week and are in fact getting rather special treatment.

Corner shops: PH South Road towards Locksley, DE and SR South Road towards town RR and PK.

The Bull DW and SC.

St Columba's SG by car.

Grassed area opposite shops SM.

Rosemary Lane SL and RD.

North Road Baptist Church and Cemetery MD and JM.

Cinder path TG and GJ.

Will all other members of staff not allocated, please make themselves available to the deputy head for covering for absences and for preparing the staffroom for the return of the rest of the staff. I expect we should all be able to relax from about 1.45 onwards.

It must seem slightly hysterical after all this, but I would also like to thank you for all the support and help you have provided during the last four or five weeks. If I have appeared snarly, then I am sorry. Anno Domini, I think!

G. Goddard

By the time we had read half-way down page two, Jean O'Rourke looked up. She was shocked. 'It's absolutely unbelievable', she remarked, 'It's just like preparations for a battle'. I agreed. We continued reading and found the plans for Friday were even more detailed than for Thursday and involved almost every member of staff.

When we had finished reading, we sat and talked. We were amazed. Jean had taught in schools for many years but had never seen anything so detailed. She said that it almost made her think that the education which the school provided must be pointless if these were the lengths to which teachers had to go to enforce order. Neither of us could really believe what we had just read. We returned the instructions to the back of Ron's file and went into assembly. In the house hall, the assembly had not begun as tutor groups were still filing in. We joined Paul Klee in the back corner where we discussed the document we had just read. Jean explained that the document was a plan to stop any trouble at the end of term, but she said that it looked as if it could resemble a battle. I thought it involved all the staff in an attempt to stop the end-of-term ritual. However, Paul, who had trained as a sociologist, commented that if the headmaster thought that he was going to stop the end-of-term activities he must be mistaken. Paul analysed the end-of-term events in Merston's secondary schools as an institutionalized ritual that was backed by the force of tradition and as such would be difficult to fight.[13] At this point our conversation was temporarily interrupted as it was time for prayers.

After assembly, Paul had a 'free' lesson and joined me in the Arundel/ Westminster working staff room. In the course of our conversation, he raised the subject of the document that we had talked about shortly before assembly. He remarked that if, as we had thought, there might be a battle it could be that 'the staff will win the battle but not the war'. He considered that the action which was planned could change the attitude of the pupils towards the staff. But he acknowledged that there were house heads who would be prepared to jeopardize pupil–teacher relations at any price for obedience and order.

I found Jean's and Paul's reactions to Goddard's document not atypical. Their remarks were echoed by many department staff who considered the plan incredible, ridiculous and untenable. Like Jean and Paul, they agreed to go along with it, but were very sceptical about its viability. In this respect, they held very different views from the headmaster and heads of houses, who appeared to believe that misbehaviour could be eradicated.

Each week, I always went to the office to obtain copies of all the documents that were issued to staff. Later that morning I went to get a copy of the document I had been shown by Ron Ward. When I went into the office I asked Mrs Watson, the headmaster's secretary, if I could have 'one of the sheets that went out to the heads of houses about the end-of-term arrangements'. Mrs Watson looked up from her typewriter and demanded, 'Who told you about that?' I replied that Ron Ward had shown it to me. I did not mention that he had left it in his file for any Westminster staff to consult, as I could see that there was something 'special' about this document. Mrs Watson was red in the face by this time and replied, 'I'm sorry but that's it!' Evelyn (the other secretary who shared the office) looked puzzled. Mrs Watson got up and stomped off down the corridor to the deputy head's study. On his door was a large notice which read, 'Do not disturb under any circumstances'. However, she just tapped on the door and went in, so I realized that there must be something extra-special about this particular document. Mrs Watson was gone for two or three minutes while I stood waiting in the corridor.

Frank Lloyd appeared from his office. He said that he was sorry he could not give me one of the sets of notes I had seen, but they were only produced for the heads of houses, the headmaster, the senior mistress, George Jackson (the new director of studies) and himself. Frank told me that the headmaster had stressed at the house heads' meeting that these sheets were highly confidential and should not be shown to other teachers. However, he said that I could have a copy of the document when the exercise was over on Friday. I apologized for my error and the confusion I had caused, but Frank just laughed as he returned to his study.

I went back to see Mrs Watson to apologize for the trouble that I had caused her. She did not seem to mind as she said I was not to blame. She blamed Ron Ward as she thought he should not have told me about it. She remarked, 'It just proves he can't keep anything quiet. I always thought he talked too much.' She was obviously pleased to have caught Ron out. She continued, 'I wonder who else he has told'. I did not say that I had read the document with another teacher. Despite the fact that the document was supposed to be secret, Mrs Watson proceeded to tell me the background to it. She explained that she had received instructions from the headmaster that none of the other office staff was to know what she had typed. She remarked that the head had taken all the rough copies and spare copies home with him and he had given her strict instructions that the stencil was to be shredded when she had run off the number of copies that were required. Mrs Watson now wanted to get even with Ron Ward. She suggested that I should tell him that I got into trouble when I asked for a copy of the document. 'It would do him good to have a fright', she said. 'He should be much more careful about what he tells members of staff.' When I left the office I went up to the common room to consider the situation. I realized that I had better see Paul Klee and tell him not to mention the document, as Jean O'Rourke and I had told him of its contents immediately we had read it. I thought that if he mentioned it to anyone it would create trouble for him and in turn for Ron and me. I went up to Paul's room at lunch time and told him the difficulties which I had got into that morning. He agreed it was best to keep quiet about what we knew, although the incident amused him.

I thought this would be the last I would hear of the document and the arrangements for the end of term. However, in the early part of the afternoon I was in the common room when Don Williams came in. He came over and asked if I had heard anything about the arrangements for the end of term. I replied that I did not know what was happening as everything was in a state of flux during the last week.[14] He laughed as he told me that there was to be a special system for dismissing the pupils this term with many of the staff travelling on the buses. Don said he was surprised I did not know about these arrangements as he had heard that Eileen Marsh had read out a whole list of instructions to Arundel House staff, and his head of house, Maggie Rolls,[15] had told him that he was 'riding shot-gun on the number twenty-one bus'. He explained that this was only a small part of the plan which he understood was designed to overcome the problems associated with the end of term.

These events helped me to identify some of the social processes involved in the working life of the school. The headmaster had devised a plan to deal with the problems which surrounded the end of term. However, despite the fact that all the staff were to be involved in the implementation of this plan, only the heads of houses were provided with its details. This indicated the seniority of the house staff in the school structure, the extent to which the headmaster relied on their loyalty and the way in which he saw their duties with respect to the maintenance of order and discipline. Nevertheless, although the headmaster regarded his plans as confidential to heads of houses, many of them had other ideas. Ron Ward had given staff access to the plan, Eileen Marsh had read it out to her staff and Maggie Rolls had divulged some of the contents. It was evident that the house heads did not give complete allegiance to the headmaster in this instance.[16] I was therefore interested in how the end-of-term events would operate on the Thursday and Friday.

When I went to McGregor on Thursday I found that the activities outlined in the document were in operation. In the Westminster House staff meeting Ron Ward read out the major objectives for the day which, according to the headmaster's document, were: 'to bid farewell to the leavers and to contain those elements in the fifth who feel that a "rave-up" is necessary'. Having read this, Ron outlined the timetable for the day so that we would know about the special arrangements for the fifth-year leavers. These events, he explained, were to take place alongside the normal timetable for other classes. When Ron Ward took the house assembly he carried out the headmaster's instructions; in the course of the notices he reminded pupils about their behaviour. He said, 'As tomorrow is the last day of term we want a reasonable day and we, therefore, do not want any ammunition brought to school'. At this point several pupils laughed.[17] Ron ignored the laughter and repeated the statement that no ammunition was to be brought into school which he said meant, 'no flour and no eggs or anything'. He then told the fifth year that they were to meet in Arundel House hall after assembly.

I went to the fifth-year meeting in Arundel which was attended by house heads and fifth-year tutors. I found that only 55 fifth-year pupils were in school out of a total pupil population of 228. The staff and pupils mingled together. When the pupils were told that they were to leave school that day they were puzzled, but many were pleased by the additional holiday. To begin with, the teachers served the pupils with coffee[18] and everyone stood around chatting in groups. The headmaster then stood up and addressed us. He explained that the leavers would be going to their tutor groups to make arrangements about returning books, obtaining examination results and keeping in touch. He said that we would gather together at 10.10 a.m. for Mass and for an opportunity to say a formal goodbye. The teachers and pupils were then dismissed to their tutorial groups.

Just after ten o'clock I went to the leavers' Mass in Hexham House hall. As the school chaplain was on holiday the Mass was celebrated by another priest. He addressed the pupils during the Mass, reminding them of three things. Firstly, that Sunday Mass was vital, for if they gave up the Mass then he considered that they would give up the Catholic faith. Secondly, that they should give thanks to God for all the teachers who had taught them in the past five years, and finally, he wished them well for the future, with their examination results and with their jobs.

After the communion, the headmaster spoke to the leavers. He said, 'Five years ago we all started life in the school by saying Mass together in these two house halls. It was, therefore, only fitting and right that your school life should end here.' He remarked that the previous five years had gone very quickly for him but now it was over. 'You are the first group to have completed five years in the school,' he said, 'and I wouldn't mind being judged on you people as the products of this school.' He said that he always thought of Bishop McGregor School as a family where you could have your rows and certainly, he commented, 'We've had our ups and downs'. However, he added, we have all come through it and, 'I hope that you will regard McGregor as your second family'. He looked forward to the times when some of them would return to the school as married men and women with their own families. He also remarked, 'Even if you never come back I hope that you will, at least, remember your days at McGregor as happy days'. Finally, he said, 'I come from the north where boys and girls wear their best clothes to school when they leave'. He added that he would like to remember them all as the smart, well-dressed young men and women that they obviously were. He said that they should be proud as pupils of Bishop McGregor School, as Catholics and as members of Merston and of England. He finished by saying that it was now time for them to leave and he would like to take the opportunity to speak to each person individually. Here, the head was still attempting to reinforce school rules.

The pupils sat straight-faced and silent throughout this address. As they each went forward to speak to Mr Goddard and some of the other teachers it was evident that they had very mixed feelings about leaving school, especially as they had not expected all this to happen until the following day. Eventually, staff and pupils moved outside the block and on outside the school. Several pupils looked stunned. They had left school almost without knowing it had happened. Soon there was no sign of either teachers or pupils as they all moved off the site. When the teachers returned at lunch time they were very pleased with themselves that the unpleasant scenes they had witnessed in the spring term had not been repeated. However, they still wondered if Mr Goddard's strategy would keep them out of trouble on Friday.

Eventually, the last day of term arrived, and as I went through the school gates I saw a group of fifth-year leavers sitting astride motor cycles at the corner of the lane. In the staff room several others remarked that they had also seen these pupils and wondered if they would influence the activities that day. When we went into Ron Ward's office before assembly, he said that he would go through the plans for that day. As he read them out the staff sat and laughed. One teacher remarked, 'The boss must be mad', but he continued to read amidst all the laughter. Some of the teachers said they did not like searching pupils for ammunition, but Susan Platts who had been taking the whole affair very seriously remarked that she would be delighted to assist anyone who wanted pupils searched. The teachers went away, conducted their searches and reported back that all was quiet.

Since assembly and break time had been changed the school settled down to classes. At break, the staff were divided into two groups. While the first group patrolled the grounds the second group had coffee. On the sound of a short bell the groups changed. I went outside with Paul Klee in the second half of break. It was obvious to anyone, especially the children, that something was happening as so many teachers were outside. The pupils looked puzzled but amused. I walked around the perimeter of the sports field with Paul. We could see that a group of ten to fifteen teachers had gathered on the far side of the field so we made our way towards this group. When we got there we found that David Peel had spotted one of the Easter leavers attempting to get through the hedge. It was Sean Kelly and he was loaded up with ammunition. The sight of so many teachers sent him scurrying back to the corner café with the result that break time passed off without incident.

Break was followed by the end-of-year assembly in the houses and an early lunch. By noon, lunch was over and after a further short break the pupils were sent back to their tutor groups. At twelve-thirty many of the pupils were out by the school gates climbing aboard buses. The scene was very calm. The revised pattern for the school day appeared to have mystified the children.

As the pupils boarded their buses, the staff assembled in cars. I joined Paul Klee and Roger Ryan as we had been asked to follow the pupils towards town. As the number 16 bus pulled away from the school we followed. There were staff on board and all looked quiet. Pupils alighted at the terminus and we drove around the nearby streets. A few pupils were wandering along each street but there appeared to be no reason for us to wait around and so we returned to school. Back at McGregor I saw the headmaster who was delighted with the fact that the whole week had passed off without incident. He laughed and said, 'You didn't half cause a stir among some people when you asked for this' as he gave me a copy of the secret document.

The headmaster had successfully defused a potential crisis. This particular situation highlighted the structure of the staff and the way in which teachers operated in distinct groups. In addition, it also revealed the way in which Mr Goddard worked as a headmaster. An earlier chapter has indicated how he saw himself as a headmaster participating in the day-to-day activities of the school. In the end-of-term situation he had planned the whole programme. However, in order successfully to implement his plan he had to obtain the co-operation of the heads of houses, departmental staff and the pupils. The house heads had agreed to such a plan as it upheld the norms and values which they maintained throughout the year. Meanwhile, the departmental staff who had normally remained inactive at the end of term agreed to co-operate, because in return the head had agreed to suspend the Friday afternoon timetable. Finally, he had obtained compliance from the pupils when he took the opportunity to remind them of school norms and values. His skill in manipulating the situation and the sheer show of strength from the staff had defused the situation. The end-of-term incident, therefore, not only revealed the way in which the school operated but the way in which Mr Goddard managed its members and their daily activities.

Summary and conclusion

The events that have been presented in these three social situations were unique and dramatic. They took place over one year and brought together the same groups of people. For the purposes of analysis I have chosen to focus in particular on the headmaster, the heads of houses and a range of staff drawn from departments. Although these teachers participated in all three events it may appear that there was little in common between the events. However, if these three cases are examined in the light of criteria that have been used by Turner (1957) in the analysis of social drama, definite linking themes emerge.

In the course of his studies Turner[19] has isolated four phases in the social drama. These phases may be summarized as follows:

1 A breach of norm-governed social relations between persons in the same system of social relations.   (BREACH)
2 A phase of mounting crisis. The breach may widen and become co-extensive with some dominant cleavage in the widest set of social relations to which the parties belong. Here the patterns of social relationships among members of the group may be identified during the period of crisis.   (CRISIS)
3 To limit the crisis both formal and informal redressive mechanisms

Table 4.1 Phases in the three social dramas

	PHASES			
	Breach	Crisis	Redressive mechanisms	Re-integration
Bomb scare	External threat to the school with report that a bomb has been planted in buildings.	Early search of buildings and movement of pupils out of buildings. Division of staff work.	Action by headmaster previously planned and carried out by deputy head and heads of houses.	Bringing school back after a holiday.
Princess Anne affair	Decision taken by LEA not to grant school holiday.	Walk-out by 600 pupils. Divisions of house and department staff.	Action by headmaster and heads of houses.	'Cooling out' period by granting holiday and using school assembly.
Secret document	Merston city-wide ritual of uniform-tearing transferred into school.	Easter leavers enact ritual of uniform-tearing – highlights problem, especially for house heads.	Action by headmaster and heads of houses with co-operation from other teachers.	'Cooling out' through staff social and main holiday.

are used by leading members of the social group to limit the spread of the crisis.   (REDRESSIVE ACTION)

4 Re-integration of the disturbed social group or social recognition and legitimation of schism between the parties.   (RE-INTEGRATION)

While Turner indicates that these are the main phases of the social drama, he suggests that not all social dramas proceed through these four phases and in fact if re-integration does not occur, further crises may follow. The four phases which I have summarized as breach, crisis, redressive mechanisms and re-integration can be identified in the three social dramas as shown in table 4.1. The phases which Turner identified can be seen within these three social dramas.

Breach

In all cases the breach of the 'normal' pattern of social relationships was internal to the school. However, the origin of the breach was external to the school in each situation: an anonymous telephone call, a decision taken by Merston city council, and the traditional leavers' ceremonies that had been enacted in Merston long before Bishop McGregor School was built. In short, external factors influenced the pattern of social relationships that occurred within the school.

Crisis

In the second phase the term 'crisis' has been used to cover the period when most activity takes place. In each situation the time period varies: the bomb scare covered a crisis period of approximately two hours, and there was a crisis period to the Princess Anne affair of two days. The secret document plan was much more drawn out, as planning had taken place 'behind closed doors' for one term with public elements of the crisis covering a whole week. Each of these crises exposed the patterns by which teachers worked. In particular, each of the crises drew attention to the central role of the headmaster, the way in which heads of houses gave him general support and the broad division that could be identified between house heads and departmental staff. The divisions between the teachers who worked in houses and departments were also highlighted by the norms and values that they each employed.

Redressive mechanisms

Each of the crises involved redressive mechanisms being used by both the headmaster and the house heads when they attempted to define the situation to prevent crises from escalating. In each case, there were not only divisions between house heads and departmental staff, but also between house heads, and between house heads and the headmaster. This, in itself, gives force to the notion that different versions of the school were presented to the pupils. Finally, in the case of the secret document, the classic division of house and departmental staff was not maintained. However, in this instance the support of departmental staff had to be 'bought' in exchange for a staff social on the last afternoon of the summer term.

Re-integration

All the crises exhibit a phase of re-integration. In some cases, the events that surround re-integration might be termed fortuitous, while in others they were consciously planned and used by the headmaster. All of the crises were followed by a holiday; in two cases (the bomb scare and the secret document) these holidays were pre-set by the local education authority, while in the Princess Anne affair the headmaster used the fuel shortage to grant two days' holiday. In each case, the holiday 'cooled out' teachers and pupils. The head also used other mechanisms to 'cool out' situations. In the Princess Anne affair a school assembly was used to redefine the situation, while in the case of the secret document the head-master was involved in bargaining with departmental staff to gain their co-operation.

Links can also be made concerning the positions of the key partici-pants in all three cases. In each case, the headmaster was the most powerful definer of social reality. He imposed a framework on the situation that told teachers and pupils how he expected them to operate and the norms and values to which he expected them to subscribe. In addition, the crises also demonstrated the way in which Mr Goddard took a participant role in the school.

Earlier chapters have outlined the way in which the staff at Bishop McGregor School could be subdivided into house heads and departmental staff. This formal subdivision appeared to override all other sub-divisions of young, old, male and female among teachers. Certainly, in the three cases which have been examined, the house heads supported the headmaster and attempted to uphold the behavioural norms and values of the school, while the departmental staff did little, as they considered that these responsibilities lay with house staff. However, there were excep-tions to this division of staff. In each of the cases examined, the house heads were assisted by a small group of departmental staff who, it was rumoured, had career motives. Certainly, if they did participate for career reasons it has paid handsome dividends as all these individuals have gone on to higher posts, within or beyond the school.

Further subdivisions could also be identified among the teaching staff. There were distinctions between house heads especially in the way in which they defined norms, routines and practices, and administered punishments. Nor did all departmental staff interpret their duties in a similar way: differences could be attributed to teachers from particular departments and between those who were newly qualified or experienced, male or female and at different points on the salary scale.

In this respect, the social drama which is 'a limited area of transparency on the otherwise opaque surface of regular uneventful social life'[20] helped to identify the social processes involved in the operation of the school. I was therefore able to consider the ways in which school activities were defined and redefined by different teachers and the ways in which pupils reconciled different conceptions of the school to which they were exposed. The following chapters look at the teachers and pupils in the Newsom department and focus on some of these themes.

Notes

1 For a discussion of this approach see Gluckman (1961; 1967) and for another point of view see Van Velsen (1967). For its use in empirical studies see, for example, Gluckman (1942), Mitchell (1956), Loudon (1961), Bell (1968, 147–58), Morgan (1972, esp. 201–4) and Cohen (1982).

2 Some teachers jokingly suggested that I had staged this situation as an 'experiment' for my study. For a similar view on crises see Morgan (1972, 203).

3 A year later Roy Carey obtained a higher graded post in another school, while Dick Wilkinson and Keith Dryden obtained higher posts at McGregor the following academic year.

4 The characteristics of this walk-out can be compared to a wild-cat strike as discussed in Scott and Homans (1947) and Gouldner (1965).

5 This was a reference to the previous Monday when members of the National Association of Schoolmasters went on strike for half a day over pension rights with the result that the school had to be closed.

6 For a discussion of this concept see Goffman (1952).

7 For a comparable analysis based on two small groups see Pons (1961).

8 The deputy director of education in Merston recalled that this first occurred in the late 1950s when girls from Lady Rigby's Grammar School enacted this ceremony which was later taken up by pupils from other schools.

9 The pupils were destroying elements of school authority. At McGregor this was the province of the house heads so it was evident that they, in particular, felt threatened. For a similar analysis see Woods (1976a, 185).

10 Such events involving pupils from other schools were frequently reported in the local newspaper.

11 These sheets of information, as the analysis indicates, were not obtained until the last day of term because of their secret status.

12 This comment was puzzling as these tasks had only been discussed with house heads and not with other teachers.

13 Paul Klee followed Van Gennep (1960) for his analysis. Meanwhile Scharff (1976, 235–54) analyses the end of term as a period of mourning in contrast to Willis (1977) who considers that pupils are pleased to leave school.

14 This was untrue and raises questions about truth-telling and deceit in field-work. It has been argued by Barnes (1979) that compromise is essential in this context. For a discussion of this situation see Burgess (1984a; 1984c).

15 It was evident from this remark that Maggie Rolls, the head of Clifton House, had told staff about all the end-of-term arrangements. It seemed that Maggie had told members of staff far more than Ron Ward, even though Maggie, like Ron, had been told that the document was confidential. However, this might partly be explained by the fact that during the summer term she had been in dispute with the headmaster and the deputy head.

16 The headmaster considered that the house heads did not give him complete support for fear that his plan would not work.

17 The laughter had been predicted by the headmaster in his document. He had indicated that action was to be taken against the offenders, but Ron Ward did not do anything about this misbehaviour.

18 Similar arrangements have been discussed by Shipman (1968, 173–4) which he considers to be an element of role reversal.

19 See, for example, Turner (1957, 91–2) reprinted in Burgess (1982a, 231–3) and Turner (1974, 37–42).

20 See Turner (1957, 93).

PART 2

NEWSOM PUPILS

AND THEIR TEACHERS

5
FIRST DAYS IN THE
NEWSOM DEPARTMENT

Large-scale studies of comprehensive schools (Benn and Simon 1972; Department of Education and Science 1979; Monks 1968) have found that different strategies are used for grouping pupils within departments. Monks (1970, 60–99) found that departments in comprehensive schools adopted different patterns of pupil grouping in the first to third years, in the fourth and fifth years and in the sixth form respectively. In the fourth and fifth years, the survey revealed that pupils were grouped by:

1 streaming and banding on ability
2 setting on ability in separate subjects
3 choices of subjects from option blocks
4 division into leavers and non-leavers
5 division into courses of a vocational nature
6 various combinations of these.[1]

At Bishop McGregor a combination of all these principles was used to group pupils in the fourth and fifth years. All pupils had to follow a core course (see chapter one), while the remainder of their timetable involved options subdivided into examination and non-examination courses. In examination courses, pupils were grouped by ability, whereas non-examination courses involved small numbers of pupils covering a wide range of ability.[2]

As Tibble (1970), Lawton (1975) and White and Brockington (1978) have shown, teachers encounter difficulties when designing non-examination courses, because they have to be 'interesting' and 'relevant' to maintain the interest of pupils who have a reputation for being unwilling to co-operate with schools.[3] The problems that these pupils pose for teachers were recognized by the Newsom committee (1963) who recommended that better provision could be made for pupils between the ages thirteen and sixteen who were average or below-average ability. It suggested raising the school-leaving age to sixteen, providing a curriculum relating to pupils' occupational interests and providing for personal, social and emotional development while recognizing the pupils' status in society.[4] In short, the report recommended that teachers in individual schools should devise special programmes for school leavers.

Since the publication of the Newsom Report, many schools have devised leavers' courses which are vocational and practical and contain an element of local studies.[5] These courses have been organized in separate departments which take their name from the report. However, this pattern of school organization together with its associated curriculum has been the subject of much criticism from curriculum theorists such as Lawton (1973, 155) and from sociologists such as Eggleston (1977, 115), who maintain that this type of arrangement establishes deep divisions within the school and the curriculum.

When I began my fieldwork there were few sociological studies on teachers and pupils involved in non-examination courses,[6] although they had been the subjects of several novels.[7] (However, some accounts are now available on the classroom experience of school leavers in non-examination groups.)[8] I turned therefore to an analysis of life and work in the Newsom department. This chapter is based upon my early experiences in the department and follows up some of the themes that were raised in earlier chapters.

When I joined Bishop McGregor School, I began to gather basic data on the Newsom department and other teachers' views of Newsom pupils, Newsom work and Newsom teachers. On many occasions, teachers freely talked about their early experiences in the Newsom department and their knowledge of Newsom courses. Furthermore, Newsom pupils regularly figured in staff-room gossip without prompting from me. It was on the basis of these discussions together with documents obtained from the headmaster's files that I was able to contextualize my school experience.

The development of the Newsom department

The headmaster was crucial to the development of programmes for less-able pupils which he considered one of his special interests. Goddard had achieved considerable success in teaching less-able pupils in secondary modern schools, had initiated a successful leavers' course in his previous school, and had, at one time, considered writing a thesis on courses for less-able secondary school pupils. At McGregor, he realized it was essential to establish non-examination courses for non-academic pupils in the fourth and fifth year as he wanted to 'keep them interested and do something for them'.[9] However, he explained that this course was also introduced because 'I realized that if we did not do something for them [the non-academic, non-examination pupils] they would destroy the rest of us'.[10] This indicated that Newsom courses were not merely planned for the pupils involved in them but were also designed to allow other members of the school to continue with their work. Implicit within this statement was the idea that Newsom pupils did not regard the 'normal' school programme as something for them.

Goddard considered that Newsom pupils had little success in the academic areas of the school and therefore required an alternative programme. Indeed, he indicated that Newsom pupils not only failed to meet the academic expectations of their teachers but also failed to meet their behavioural expectations as they were 'the less able, the less willing, the most severely handicapped in terms of social handicaps and learning handicaps'.[11] Newsom pupils were described in negative terms. They were pupils who deviated from the academic and behavioural patterns of 'normal' fourth- and fifth-year pupils, who took public examinations and upheld their teachers' expectations.

According to Mr Goddard, Newsom pupils required a special programme which 'is designed to develop and strengthen those talents in the non-academic which will be most useful to that youngster in society – job-wise, marriage-wise, recreation-wise'.[12] However, he recognized that this programme would be based on common-sense, everyday knowledge which would distinguish it from the academically based examination courses. In this sense, the course carried the stigma that it was designed for pupils who had 'failed' the conventional school programme in the first three years. This was summarized by the headmaster's definition of 'Newsom' as 'work on non-examination material designed for pupils for whom the maximum expectation of success in public examinations seems likely to be three CSE grade 5s or less'.[13]

The first Newsom group at McGregor had consisted of thirty pupils who followed a programme that, according to the headmaster, consisted of 'core courses in English and maths (setted), in PE and games and in RE (open choice of courses) with their fellows' and they also 'took their tutorial period with the rest of the tutorial group they had joined on arriving in the school'.[14] This statement, in common with many of Goddard's remarks, presented an ideal situation. In practice, Newsom pupils took core courses at the same time as pupils in their year. But teachers found to their cost that the bottom two sets in English and mathematics were heavily populated with Newsom pupils allocated to these groups on the basis of their limited academic ability or lack of application to academic work, or both.

Newsom pupils also took options with Newsom department staff. The headmaster summarized the first scheme by saying:

> The options for the year were arranged in 5 pools and these youngsters were able to choose CSE or non-examination subjects from pools A and B. While pools C, D and E were operating (12 periods a week) they took a series of specially designed courses staffed on average at a 1:12 ratio.
>
> After six weeks the composition of the groups and the content of some of the courses were substantially altered. A total of ten staff (two of whom were probationers) shared the work which produced courses of success varying from very high to almost nil. Small success courses have been dropped or heavily modified, staffing ratio for this year for the fourth year moved to 1:14/15. We know that staff ought to be volunteers. We also think that one, two or three teachers with a fairly large number of Newsom periods plus 6–10 others with a 2–4 period allocation weekly has a high chance of success.[15]

The Newsom department therefore had a somewhat chequered start at Bishop McGregor School. The course was experimental, had experienced some failure and was subject to changes in content and staffing. Yet in some respects it had been planned that way as Goddard had wanted to see if his teachers could cope with Newsom work. For a small number of teachers it had been an enjoyable experience with its own rewards, but for the majority it held bitter memories of noise, disorder, distraction and disruption. After this, most teachers no longer wished to teach Newsom pupils. One teacher who had worked with Newsom pupils summed this up by saying: 'I neither know nor care about the Newsom department and its pupils'. Other teachers who continued working with these pupils exchanged 'war stories'[16] with their colleagues who found many of their tales horrific. They considered that classrooms should be quiet, orderly places where pupils came to work. In contrast, those who worked with Newsom pupils found it difficult to keep them quiet and almost impossible to get them to work. It was common for teachers to describe situations where pupils went to sleep, swore at them, made paper aeroplanes and floated them around the room, looked at comic books and smoked or asked to smoke in stock cupboards. These experiences or knowledge of such experiences led many staff to conclude that they would not want to teach Newsom pupils.[17] Goddard considered that it was better for pupils and teachers alike if only those members of the staff who really wanted to teach Newsom pupils participated in the Newsom courses. Accordingly, in 1973–4 all Newsom teachers were volunteers.

When the second group of Newsom pupils entered the fourth year in September 1972 they numbered forty-two. Sylvia Robinson (the head of careers and teacher in charge of Newsom in that year) thought at that time they were almost impossible to teach. She recalled situations where pupils were difficult, resentful and restless. She considered that they had failed in conventional school courses and had experienced poor relationships with their teachers, who had regarded them at best as pests and at worst as beasts whom they were determined to control. These earlier experiences with other teachers had made them suspicious of the Newsom department and its teachers. She told me that it had been necessary for teachers to suspend the official timetable and intersperse Newsom work with classes where pupils were allowed to play table tennis. These 'games' lessons became a point for discussion among teachers in other departments, as whenever these lessons occurred in rooms close to other classes the staff experienced constant noise. Pupils could be heard shouting, banging table-tennis bats on desks and, in some cases, slamming doors as they moved out into the corridors. These events confirmed for many teachers the unpleasant stories they had heard about Newsom courses and pupils.

Some Newsom pupils had extensive 'track records' as a result of their past misdemeanours. Among these pupils were Peter Vincent and John Slattery whose activities in the spring term convinced many staff that Newsom pupils were disorderly and disruptive 'beasts'. Peter Vincent had always had a reputation for bad behaviour. Even the toughest pupils would not challenge Peter, as in the past he had committed physical violence upon others. Teachers had been involved in a constant 'battle' with Peter who had been punished in numerous ways: detention, corporal punishment, placing on report and working with an individual teacher for a whole week. The failure of these punishments helped to establish Peter's reputation among teachers and pupils.

In the spring term of the fourth year, Peter was involved in a further attack on another pupil whom he had kicked to the ground. This incident resulted in suspension from school. The headmaster considered it of such importance that he produced a dossier containing letters to Peter's parents, to the chairman of the governors and the director of education about Peter's suspension which teachers could consult. In addition, a special notice was displayed in the common room which outlined what had happened and the headmaster's response. All the staff were therefore able to read the following account by the headmaster:

Account of an incident at Bishop McGregor School, Merston; Friday, 23 March 1973 – 9.00 a.m. Taking part – Peter Vincent, Mark Gibson, John Slattery and Mark Ball, all fourth formers in Hexham House. (All will be referred to by surnames since two have same Christian name.)

Immediately after Friday morning house assembly, Gibson and Ball were showing each other a 'faked blow'. Vincent asked to be shown. They refused. Vincent tried to get hold of Gibson's football badge at which point Ball thought Vincent was attacking Gibson. Ball then jumped on Vincent's back to pull him away from Gibson. Slattery pulled Ball by the hair and kicked him. Ball fell to the floor. Vincent turned round and he kicked Ball several times with considerable force. Slattery had also kicked Ball 'to make him let go of my sleeves'.

Ball went to hospital with Gibson.

Ball's parents informed.

All witnesses questioned and statements taken.

Vincent and Slattery questioned and statements taken.

Both kept on the site and given lunch at house expense.

Messages received from hospital. Ball bruised about body. No bones broken, no apparent serious internal injuries.

Action ordered by head.

Friday: Vincent and Slattery each to receive three strokes of the cane. This is to be the immediate punishment for the violence *after* Ball was on the floor.[18]

Slattery taken home by head of house and a verbal warning to be given to parent that any further involvement in violence will be met by the head with suspension.

When Slattery was taken home, parents were not in. Evidently, the father is in hospital and the mother was visiting him. Slattery was brought back to school and a note from head of house was sent home with him.

Note: this is being followed up by a formal letter from the head of confirmation to the parents.

Vincent will be suspended for the rest of this term as a punishment for disobedience to the head. On returning from his last suspension, the head laid it down as a condition of his return that if there was an episode of serious violence, suspension would be used for dis-obedience in addition to any punishment for the violence.

Action being taken on Monday, 26 March 1973, by head.

1   Letter to the LEA informing them and associated departments of action already taken by head.

2   Letter to the chairman of governors informing him of action taken by head.
3   Letter to Mr and Mrs Slattery confirming the warning already given about future violence offered by their son to others.
4   Letter to Mr and Mrs Vincent confirming present suspension and stating conditions for readmission after the Easter holiday.

(signed)   G. Goddard
Headmaster

This account of the activities of these two Newsom pupils reinforced their reputations among teachers with the result that they were often considered 'typical' members of the fourth-year Newsom group. This view was used by teachers to construct accounts of the Newsom pupils and their pattern of behaviour when talking among themselves and to new members of teaching staff.

Teachers' conceptions of the Newsom pupils

When Sylvia Robinson first took me to Clifton House she introduced me to the other teachers who worked in various departments by saying: 'This is Mr Burgess who has come to work with our Newsom pupils'. At this remark, several staff pulled faces while one teacher murmured 'You're welcome'. Maggie Rolls spoke first, saying, 'You've got my sympathy as staff dread taking fourth-year Newsom'. She explained that if any Newsom teachers were absent, their lessons had to be taken by other staff. She said that most teachers hated taking this group as they were a 'nasty lot', especially if Peter Vincent and John Slattery were in school. She told me that the group contained numerous troublemakers, including a boy who had been sent to Borstal: now back at school for a short period before going to a remand home for what he described as 'mugging a wog'. Then she started to describe Peter Vincent, who she claimed was taller than me and twice as broad.[19] She said that I would have the 'pleasure' of teaching Peter, as he was now back in school after his suspension. This account was supported by other teachers, who characterized Newsom pupils as nuisances, troublemakers, bullies and pests. Being a Newsom pupil carried a social stigma which was, in part, transferred to their courses and their teachers.

The labels that teachers applied to these pupils were not merely communicated to colleagues but were evidently transmitted to the pupils who were ready to tell new teachers, 'Other teachers don't like us'.[20] From their remarks it was evident that they appreciated teachers' conceptions of them as 'difficult to teach' which they were not slow to establish. Sylvia

Robinson told me that the pupils were quick to point out that Newsom meant non-examination, which in their view meant no written work and as little other work as possible. As a consequence, Sylvia explained 'the type of work which is usually done in the Newsom department does not involve writing. In fact, it's very doubtful if they do any writing for any other teachers in the school'. Several of her remarks were confirmed for me in my lessons and in a conversation with Jane Adams, who taught some Newsom pupils when they attended her fourth-year English set. Her lesson occurred at the end of the day and she was surprised that the Newsom pupils always arrived without books, pens, pencils or paper. She confessed that she was amazed how they had 'survived' the earlier part of the day. As a consequence, if she wanted these pupils to do any written work she had to supply all the materials.

As the Newsom department and pupils were common currency in staff-room gossip, I found they were used as the subjects of jokes which were told in the staff room at the end of the day. Newsom pupils were put into foolish situations: displayed in cages and put behind bars. In short, the Newsom pupils were subjects of local humour based on their own folly which was greatly exaggerated.[21] Here, the jokes contained stereotypical accounts of pupils' behaviour and incidents unlike real life, because the teachers were always in complete control of the pupils' actions. The jokes therefore helped the teachers to unwind and to restore their authority which had been attacked by Newsom pupils (among others) during the day.

These were some of the more popular accounts that I was told about Newsom pupils. The ideas which teachers had about 'Newsom' revealed several characteristics of the department and the pupils. Firstly, they saw the pupils and their work as different from the rest of the school – a point which the pupils were willing to acknowledge since it helped to fuel an ideology of non-work for them. Secondly, the teachers compared the pupils unfavourably – in terms of work and behaviour – with those pupils who followed examination courses. Newsom pupils were seen in negative terms. Thirdly, it appeared that these pupils attacked teachers' identities by redefining and manipulating classroom situations. This assault on the teacher role and on conventional ideas of schools and schooling earned these pupils their hatred; a hatred which was released in conversation and in jokes where the teachers could control the pupils.

This was the picture of the Newsom pupils and their activities which was created for me before I met my classes. However, these portraits of the pupils helped me to pose a number of questions: who were the Newsom pupils? What did they do in classes? What were their relationships with teachers in general and Newsom teachers in particular? Questions such as these were sharpened and focused on the basis of my early encounters with the Newsom pupils.

Meeting the Newsom pupils

The first day I was in the school, Sylvia Robinson suggested that I should go to see the room where I would be teaching the Newsom pupils. Late that morning I went to Ushaw block with the idea of having a look round. As soon as I was inside the block, Sylvia came out of a room (which I later learned was her 'office')[22] and invited me into the classroom where she was teaching. I soon realized that her invitation to come and see the block had been a cover to get me over to Ushaw for a chat. This was also my first encounter with the Newsom pupils.

As Newsom pupils were taught in very small groups, Sylvia had only twelve girls with her. My first impression was of a group of girls just sitting around a collection of tables. Some were talking to each other, others were standing beside the windows, another was reading a magazine, while two girls were writing in their exercise books. This scene was not reminiscent of my previous experience of secondary school class-rooms where it was usual for pupils to be sitting working at their desks or moving around in pursuit of some activity.[23]

The most striking feature of this group was their lack of school uniform. When I had attended school assembly earlier that morning, I had been surrounded by a sea of navy blue, gold and grey which were the school colours. Row after row of navy blue jackets could be seen. However, in this group only two girls were dressed in uniform. Several girls were sitting in the room in their outdoor coats – a habit which I later found was forbidden. One girl wore a brown coat while another was dressed in a multi-coloured coat of yellow, red and blue. Another wore a short, off-white outdoor coat with a distinguishing feature of large brown buttons, while a fourth was in a black sweater and grey skirt. Although these pupils did not wear school uniform, I still needed to discover whether they were representative of Newsom pupils.

When I met my Tuesday afternoon class for the first time, I took note of their appearance. I had a mixed group of boys and girls who were dressed in a variety of clothes and were distinguished by their lack of uniform. Some of the girls had been in the group I had met that morning. Only two boys had the navy blue blazer and grey trousers while the others wore a mixture of part uniform and part casual clothes, or no uniform at all. One boy was distinctive in blue jeans and faded denim jacket bearing 'I love Tessa' slogans marked on it in ink. Another boy had no jacket, while two more wore jackets but of the wrong colour. A further boy was dressed in a blue anorak while the others had a varied assortment of coloured sweaters, shirts and trousers. They had very little school uniform between them.

School uniforms are symbols of school and teacher authority.[24] The uniform is an expression of the teachers' concern for the neat, tidy appearance of their pupils, the symbol of an individual's membership of a particular school and an acceptance of its norms and values. It appeared to me that the Newsom pupils' lack of uniform was an attempt to deny membership of the corporate body and its associated norms and values.[25]

Another feature of the Newsom pupils which I quickly became acquainted with was their frequent absence from school. Sylvia Robinson told me that the pupils often took days off school and occasionally truanted from lessons. She considered it essential to keep a register of pupils attending classes as she thought this helped to reduce lesson truancy. I was therefore given the names of eighteen pupils in my Tuesday class and nineteen names for my Thursday group. However, the first time I attended my Tuesday class only twelve pupils were in school and at the first Thursday class only fourteen pupils were present. I found this sporadic pattern of school attendance to be a constant feature of life in the Newsom department.[26]

As I checked off the names in my first lessons, I became acquainted with further information about the Newsom pupils as individuals volunteered stories about their absent 'friends'. I was told that one girl was rarely present as her mother was regularly ill and kept her off school to look after the younger children in the family. When I called out the name 'Diane Lane', another girl cried out 'Diane's wagging it today, sir'. The girl who had shouted out had a broad grin on her face. For a moment I was puzzled. I had not come across the term 'wagging it' before. But the laughter that prevailed together with the accompanying remarks were sufficient to indicate that the pupils were openly discussing truancy. The girl who had originally spoken explained (without prompting from me) that Diane 'wagged it' from school most Tuesdays because she disliked English lessons.

I returned to my list of names. When I reached the name 'David Jones' there was further laughter. One boy shouted, 'Who's he?' Others giggled at this remark. Before I could ask what the class knew about this boy, I was told that several weeks could pass before anyone would see David. They explained that even when he came to school, he was only present for a day or two, after which he would be absent for several weeks. This pattern of irregular attendance characterized the Newsom pupils, because on each occasion I took the group I found some pupils who were in school the first week absent in the second week, while in the third week further pupils would be absent from school. The Newsom groups, although kept deliberately small by the school, were therefore usually made smaller by the pupils themselves. Sometimes pupils were legitimately absent, but they often 'wagged it' from school or from lessons. On several occasions pupils hinted to me that their friends were 'wagging it'. It was relatively easy for pupils to absent themselves from lessons as the school provided numerous hiding-places and exits through which they could disappear, unseen. I also found the school organization worked against teachers. As all the Newsom pupils were members of different houses and tutor groups, it meant that whenever I wanted to check which pupils were present at the start of the session I had to spend at least twenty minutes of the lesson collecting all the fifth-year registers. In similar circumstances, other teachers suspected pupils of 'wagging it' from their lessons but could do very little to check up as the process was too expensive in terms of lesson time. The pupils had therefore developed a strategy for lesson truancy which was based on manipulating the organizational structure of the school (see chapter eight).

I have already indicated that the first Newsom pupil whom I got to know by name was Peter Vincent. During my first week at McGregor I met Peter when he attended my Thursday morning class. The first sight I had of him was some minutes after the official start of the lesson when a tall, well-built boy came into the room. He was followed by a tall, thin boy. They walked across the room and sat down at a table, making as much noise as they could by dragging their chairs and the table across the tile floor. They ignored the other pupils in the room, but the bigger boy spent some time watching me. I guessed that he was sizing me up. He did this by staring at me, to ensure that I knew what he was doing. I assumed that this was Peter Vincent as he resembled the description that I had been given.

When about a dozen pupils were in the room I went through my list of names. I adopted this strategy to attempt to learn pupils' names and to let them know that I was aware of who should be in my group: a strategy which I thought would help discourage lesson truancy. On this occasion I went around the room asking each pupil his or her name. When I got to Peter I did not let him know I had already heard of him so I just asked his name. He replied, 'I'm John Slattery, sir'. I thought this could not be correct, especially as several pupils were now laughing. However, I was not prepared to challenge the answer, as I thought it would only provide the rest of the class with free 'entertainment'. I proceeded to ask the next boy (his friend) what his name was and he replied, 'Peter Vincent, sir'. This was greeted with shrieks of laughter from the other pupils who had obviously been treated to this 'act' before. Earlier that week I had heard that some staff were refusing to teach Peter and were sending him to work with the deputy head. I decided to use this knowledge to my advantage. I said to the boy who claimed he was Peter, 'I've heard that you're not to come to this lesson as you're working with Mr Lloyd'. Immediately, the boy who had claimed to be Peter Vincent exclaimed, 'I'm not Peter Vincent, sir, he's Peter' (pointing at the boy seated next to him), 'I'm John Slattery'. Peter did not look amused, his reputation had been dented and I was able to continue my class in relative order. This incident made it abundantly clear that these pupils were prepared to 'play up' a teacher or to 'try it on' at a first meeting in order to maintain their reputation in front of other pupils and to establish their reputation among new teachers. Certainly, this was an aspect of life with the Newsom pupils which was confirmed by other events in my early classes that are discussed in a later section of this chapter.

I could also observe the Newsom pupils around the school. When I was in assembly it was usual to see another of my pupils, Patrick McConnell, ambling his way across the sports field. He was never in a hurry, despite the fact that the school had officially started some twenty minutes earlier. Some mornings when I was not in assembly he would wave to me as he passed the staff-room window in which I was sitting. This pattern of 'late arrival' was also characteristic of other Newsom pupils. When I took a class at nine o'clock in the morning it was usual for pupils to arrive between 9.30 a.m. and 10.00 a.m. They were never sorry about being late. Usually they explained their late arrival with statements such as, 'I was out late last night' or 'I got up late' or 'I missed the bus', all of which were difficult to check.

Late arrival also spilled over into other lessons. When a bell signalled the start of a class, it was noticeable that most pupils came out of their house blocks and moved to the blocks in which they were to be taught in about five minutes. However, I noticed that anything up to twenty minutes after this period elapsed several Newsom pupils would still be wandering across the site or playing around on the grass before going to lessons in Ushaw block. It was quite usual to meet members of the group wandering around the site in the middle of lessons. One boy told me that whenever he was stopped by a teacher he would claim to be carrying a message to another teacher. This, he explained, would allow him to proceed unimpeded. On some occasions when I had a 'free' lesson I would find several Newsom pupils walking around the site. The pupils were always eager to stop and talk to me as this was a means of passing time and staying out of classes. They always started the conversation by asking me what we were going to do in our next lesson, which was a redundant question, as when the lesson arrived they rarely wished to follow the activities I had planned. One day I found that I had been talking to one group of boys for about ten minutes when they were supposed to be with another teacher. I told them they should get along to their lesson. However, I was quickly informed that they were with a Newsom teacher and that it would be perfectly all right for them to be out of the class talking to me. On another occasion I was outside talking to a house head (who worked in the Newsom department) when Terry Nicholls came out of Ushaw block and started to walk towards us. He came over to me and said, 'I've just told Miss Robinson that you wanted to see me, so she said I should come and see you now'. I replied, 'But I don't want to see you for anything'. Terry looked at me, somewhat amazed. 'Oh, I know that!' he said, 'It's just got me out of her boring lesson for a few minutes'. With that he stood and talked to us both about what they were supposed to be doing in the lesson and then returned to his class. Another pupil strategy for using time had been unveiled.

On the basis of my initial meetings with Newsom pupils several themes emerged that I wanted to follow up. Firstly, the way in which pupils defined situations. Secondly, the way in which they redefined and manipulated situations in the school and finally, the strategies which they employed. So I decided to concentrate my observations on these particular features of their life and work in the school. I also increased my knowledge of Newsom pupils through my lessons and other teachers' lessons – to which we now turn.

Newsom lessons

Early in the term Sylvia Robinson asked if I would take some of her lessons when she had to work with the careers officer. I only agreed to do this on an occasional basis as I did not want to be seen by the pupils as a teacher who just took other teachers' lessons.[27] However, I thought that if I took the occasional lesson it would put me in the position of a teacher taking substitution lessons. As Sylvia wanted me to take her class it provided an opportunity to visit her room when she was teaching and to observe her Newsom lessons.[28] When Sylvia asked if I would look after her Tuesday morning class I agreed to do this, but explained that I needed to go into the lesson prior to the one that I would be taking if I was to continue with whatever they had been doing. She thought this a good idea and asked me to attend the latter part of the previous lesson.

When I entered the classroom I saw that Sylvia had a group of a dozen girls. As on my first visit some were standing talking to each other, some were near the window, while others were wandering around the room. Sylvia was sitting among a small group of girls. She explained, 'This is our lesson when we just sit and talk quietly to each other'. Her definition of 'quiet' was obviously very different from mine, because the pupils were bellowing at each other rather than talking. She seemed to be oblivious to all the activities, continuing to talk to the girls immediately around her. One girl was reading a magazine that was spread out in front of her on one of the tables, some girls on another table were passing notes to the girls next to Sylvia, while two others were drawing on each other's hands with a ball-point pen. Soon this activity escalated into a 'pen fight' to see who could scribble most on another girl's hand. One of them then sat for some time colouring in the slogan 'I love Donny Osmond' which she had drawn on the back of her hand.

When the bell rang, signalling the end of the lesson, Sylvia said that she would be going but suggested that I leave the pupils to carry on with whatever 'work' they had done in the first lesson. I agreed, because if I had attempted anything else uproar would have followed. The second lesson took the same form as the first lesson. I compared this substitution lesson with others that I had taken at McGregor. The differences were striking. In other classes the pupils were often set work or were eager to get on with some particular task, whereas in this class the pupils did not want to do any work apart from flicking through the pages of a magazine. Here, the emphasis was not on using time but passing time.[29] However, the pupils' activities were broadly similar to those in my classes.

My first lesson was planned as a short statement about what we were going to do that term, followed by a film and a short written exercise based on some duplicated material related to the film. However, what transpired was very different. The first ten minutes of the lesson were spent learning pupils' names. After I had noted their names I started to talk about 'living in towns and cities', the main theme for that part of the term. I only intended to talk for five minutes but it took far longer because of interruptions. Some pupils started to talk while I was talking so I stopped and asked them to keep quiet. They looked slightly injured by my request, but silence reigned momentarily and then some murmuring started. I tried to ignore it but was greeted by several yawns and the sight of two boys putting their heads down on their desks as if they were going to sleep. They were evidently 'trying it on' to see how I would react.[30] I stopped the class again, told them to sit up straight and then continued. Several girls who were sitting near the windows were playing with the blinds but I decided to ignore them so that I could finish what I was saying and show the film. The layout of the classroom and the projection room was such that when I wanted to show the film I had to leave the classroom, go down the corridor and into the projection room.

I told the class to sit quietly while I went out to start the projector. As I closed the door there was shouting, banging and much movement. I shot my head back around the door and all went quiet for a moment. Then one girl shouted, 'Come on, I thought you were going to show us a film'. I said that there would be no film until they were quiet and returned to their original seats (they had all changed places while I was out of the room). Some minutes elapsed while I got them to return to their seats. I went out of the room. Again I could hear movement. I went back and found them all in the process of changing places. This time I threatened to remove individuals from the class if they did not remain in their seats. Back they went to their places and I went to start the film amidst more shouting.

As the film started the noise dropped. The pupils were now 'busy' watching the film. However, there was little concentration as some were talking to their friends while others chewed gum. Nevertheless, they seemed more attentive than when the lesson started. After half an hour the picture started to flicker on the screen and I went into the projection room to see what was happening. Here, I found the projector spewing film on to the floor. It was not possible to continue with the film. I switched off the projector. As soon as the picture disappeared there were shouts of 'What's on?' from the classroom. I returned to be faced with a yelling mob.

Amid the uproar I explained how the projector had broken down and that there was no alternative but for us to continue by discussing the film. I asked several questions but got no response except silence. The pupils looked sullen; I realized that I was getting nowhere so I asked for their opinions of the film. There was no lack of answers: I was greeted with shouts of 'rubbish', 'boring', 'old-fashioned' and 'not very interesting'. My question was used to generate further noise. I quietened the class and asked why they did not like the film. Again there was silence, then one boy said, 'Films aren't any good unless they're in colour' and a girl remarked, 'We thought that film would last the whole lesson!' The last remark indicated that the pupils had not expected to do anything in the lesson other than watch the film and even this had been redefined as 'entertainment'.

I found it impossible to talk about the film without a shouting match so I decided to get the class to write about it. I started to distribute the duplicated sheets that I had prepared but had to stop several times as some members of the group were licking the duplicating spirit off the paper while others were rolling the pages up and down their desks. Within the space of several minutes I had to ask the pupils to put the sheets down on their desks. I started to read through the sheet but the noise continued. I told the pupils that I wanted the questions answered. Several girls at the front laughed and the boys at the back of the room leaned back on their chairs and stared at me. Two began writing while others talked to their friends. When I told one boy to start, he replied, 'I don't have a pen'. I asked those pupils who were without pens to put their hands in the air. Ten hands shot up. I was foiled. I had come without a set of pens or pencils as the Newsom department did not issue teachers with stock. The pupils were delighted. They appreciated my problem and knew they had won this initial bout. It was impossible for them to do any writing so we had to return to a 'discussion' of the film in which they were unwilling participants. The result was a lesson which I had defined as a situation where we would start some work, and which the pupils had redefined as a non-work situation. They had manipulated the events which had taken place so that it was impossible for work to continue.

I came out of this lesson feeling tired, dejected, and slightly annoyed as I considered that this class had been a shambles. On my way to the common room I met Sylvia Robinson who asked, 'How did you get on?' I provided a vivid description of the lesson and told her that I was disappointed, but she replied, 'It sounds all right to me. It's a typical lesson with the Newsom pupils.' She explained that Newsom pupils usually made more noise than other pupils and often wandered around the room. Added to this, she explained that it was quite usual for the pupils to have no writing materials, because they would not expect to do any writing in a Newsom lesson. At this stage, I had doubts about whether this lesson could be described as a 'typical' Newsom class. However, this was a theme that was followed up in subsequent weeks on the basis of my own experience and that of other Newsom teachers.

I found that in Newsom lessons it was quite usual for the group to arrive several minutes late. When they arrived they were often noisy and did not want to work. If they did discuss things with each other it would be interspersed with individuals eating crisps, passing around cigarettes, cigarette coupons and matches, talking to each other and kicking each other under the desk. Nevertheless, I was still doubtful about how typical my lessons were. However, when I talked to Sylvia Robinson and other Newsom teachers about my lessons they assured me that this was not because I was new but because 'that's just Newsom', a phrase which was to occur regularly in conversations.

This comparison between the Newsom department and other departments and houses in the school did not just apply to the pupils and the classes, because I found that I made comparisons between the facilities in the Newsom department and other departments. In addition, my participation with teachers in the house system also allowed me to make comparisons between the Newsom teachers and teachers in other departments. It is to these issues that we now turn.

Resources for Newsom teaching

During my first term at McGregor I spent some time in various parts of the school. In addition to Newsom classes I also took substitution lessons in other departments. In these circumstances, it was possible to make comparisons between the facilities available in the Newsom department with those in other departments.

I took substitution lessons in a number of departments, including English, modern languages and science. In the English department there were rows of desks, filing cabinets and cupboards to house the stock. In the modern languages department there were similar facilities and one room had been adapted as a language laboratory. In the science department there were specialist laboratories equipped with benches, tables and stools. The art rooms were also similarly equipped. These departments, therefore, had resources that are traditionally associated with the modern classroom.[31]

In contrast, the Newsom department had one classroom: the technical activities room in Ushaw block which had originally been designed as a project area. The room had been equipped by the head of the materials and design department and contained specialist equipment: workbenches, tools, plugs, gas-points, cupboards, and some science equipment (see figure 5.1). However, much of the equipment, although seldom used, looked much the worse for wear. Doors were hanging off the glass-fronted cupboards, the workbenches were broken and some parts were missing from the machine tools. Added to this a noticeboard in a corner contained graffiti and a faded poster which was held up by one drawing-pin. The room was decorated in what had originally been brilliant yellow paint but by now had a liberal coating of dirt from its service in the previous four years.

The classroom furniture consisted of tables and chairs, but several chairs were now broken. The pupils remarked that their room was boring compared to other rooms in the school and pointed out that unlike most pupils they had nearly all their lessons in this room. The girls, in particular, complained about their drab surroundings. They did not like to be surrounded with equipment that was never used. Certainly, in the time I was at the school I never saw the equipment used apart from those occasions when the Newsom pupils played around with the loose parts on the heavy machines.

After the pupils complained to me about the state of this room, I kept a systematic record of its contents which fluctuated weekly. Over the summer term the furniture gradually deteriorated, as some chairs and tables got broken but were neither replaced nor repaired until some weeks had elapsed. Shortly before the main period of public examinations in June, I found part of this room had been commandeered by the caretaker to store examination desks. It was now impossible to get at any departmental materials in the store cupboard. However, with the start of examinations the desks were removed from the room, and so to my dismay were all the chairs. The result was that while examinations were held, the only chairs available were those that could be borrowed from neighbouring rooms. However, once the examinations were over the chairs reappeared.

When I was asked to talk to the staff about my research in the school I began by giving a description of the classroom in which most Newsom lessons were held. This was news to most teachers who had no reason to go into the room. Automatically they were aware that these facilities were below the standard of those provided in other departments. Even the headmaster commented, 'I don't like what I've heard but I'm afraid it's true'. After this meeting the headmaster told me that he had gone to have a look at the room. He commented, 'You were right. The room was in an awful state so I immediately ordered that it should be repaired and repainted'. He agreed that the department's facilities were less good than those available in other parts of the school as the main classroom used was not specifically equipped for Newsom work or for pupils to complete written work.[32]

Figure 5.1   A plan of the technical activities room in Ushaw block

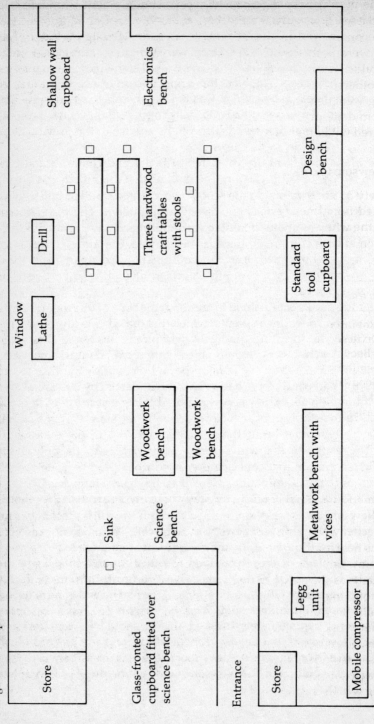

Note: This plan is not drawn to scale. Plan obtained from headmaster's files.

The pupils were also taught in rooms which their teachers used for other classes. Some classes were therefore held in science laboratories, the home economics block, the art room and house halls. In some cases, the rooms were used for the purpose for which they were intended, with practical science in the laboratories, cookery in the home economics rooms and mothercraft in the school flat. However, some courses such as wood-carving were designated classrooms which were totally inadequate. The Newsom department's facilities therefore indicated that it had low status compared with other departments.

Newsom teachers

A variety of teachers provided courses in the Newsom department. This stemmed from the headmaster's view that no individual teacher should spend the whole week teaching Newsom pupils because he thought this

Table 5.1 Newsom teachers at Bishop McGregor School in the summer term, 1973

Newsom teachers	Main subject work
Sylvia Robinson	Careers + general subjects
Keith Dryden	Art
Stanley Booth	Art (head of house)
David Smith	Art
Terry Goodwin	Home economics
Jim Parkes	Science (biology)
Headmaster	Variety of subjects – especially religious education and science

too demanding. As a result, no teachers were exclusively appointed to teach Newsom courses. When I joined the staff Sylvia Robinson was the only teacher who held a post of responsibility for Newsom work, and even this was held jointly with her work in careers.

In my first few weeks in the school Sylvia became one of my key informants as she was in charge of the Newsom department and a member of Clifton House. However, I also got to know Keith Dryden who had originally been appointed to teach art but now took a few periods of Newsom work. As the pupils frequently talked about other Newsom teachers, I was able to establish a list of staff who taught some Newsom work (see table 5.1). In addition to these teachers, I also met Tony Davis who was to join the Newsom team the following autumn and whose initial training was in craft subjects.

My initial contacts with the Newsom teachers were during breaks, lunch hours, 'free' periods and at departmental meetings. I gained several impressions on the basis of my observations and various remarks which they made and which were made by the pupils. It seemed to me that the Newsom teachers were distinctive in terms of their dress, their attitudes to the school, their approach to teaching, and their relationships with the children. Each Newsom teacher had one or more of these attributes which distinguished them from other teachers.

The most apparent distinction was in dress. David Smith who taught art and some Newsom work was most distinctive, because he usually wore blue cord trousers and a green-and-mauve-striped rugby shirt which he alternated with a similar blue-striped shirt. This action in itself delighted the Newsom pupils – here was a teacher who broke the conventions of staff dress just as they broke the rules concerning uniform. However, David's mode of dress was not approved by his house head who considered that this helped to make McGregor 'the school with the most unprofessionally dressed staff in the city'.[33]

David Smith also gained the pupils' approval as it was rumoured that he allowed them to smoke in his room during the lunch hours. They also approved of his lessons as it was possible to mess around and 'have a laugh' with him,[34] while doing some work. Two boys told me how they would have water fights in his art lessons. In one lesson a boy had soaked him with water. The result was that David had just picked the boy up and pushed him into a sink filled with water. Another example which the pupils gave of David's ability to 'have a laugh' with them was when he caught pupils eating sweets in his lessons. In these circumstances, he would demand a sweet from the offender in return for protection from the rest of the class, otherwise he would threaten to turn the rest of the class on that person for their sweets.

I learned more about the relationships that Newsom teachers had with their pupils during my time in the department. Keith Dryden treated the pupils as 'special friends' both in terms of the way he addressed them and the way they addressed him. Indeed, he considered that successful Newsom teaching was based on each teacher's relationship with their pupils. He thought that Sylvia's chatty manner contributed to her initial popularity, while Terry's friendliness and the head's ability to 'tell a good story' led to success with Newsom teaching. In another conversation with Terry Goodwin she told me how one boy regularly came into her room and put his arms around her saying, 'How are you getting on, miss?' and 'I hope your husband won't mind me doing this'. She only laughed about these incidents and remarked that at least you could be friendly with these pupils, which helped when teaching them.

The pupils often talked about their lessons with the headmaster who they thought was a good teacher. They considered that he went to a lot of trouble to make the lessons interesting and to organize visits for them. He also captured their interest and imagination by the stories he told and the different activities he planned. One boy said that the headmaster always told them that if they misbehaved he would make them stand up on the tables, or that he would twist their ears off. The boy found this highly amusing and remarked, 'We know that he doesn't mean it but we behave all the same'.

It appeared that the Newsom teachers were different from teachers in other departments. Some were different in terms of dress, others in their attitudes, teaching styles and relationships with pupils. When the pupils talked about teachers, the Newsom teachers were liked and respected for their good humour and consistency. While they required the pupils to do some work, they also took time out to 'have a laugh' and in so doing illustrated that they possessed human qualities despite being teachers. However, what the pupils liked most about the Newsom teachers were those qualities not usually associated with the teacher role. The Newsom teachers challenged established aspects of school life and teaching.

Summary and conclusion

This chapter provides an account of some of the major features of the Newsom department and its work as they struck me in the course of my first eight weeks in the school.[35] Newsom pupils and their teachers were simultaneously members of the Newsom department, other departments, houses and the school. Indeed, my work in these different settings helped me to appreciate the different structures and definitions of education to which these pupils were exposed. Life in the Newsom department therefore needs to be viewed alongside those aspects of school structure that have been discussed in earlier chapters.

My initial analysis indicated a need to compare the structures and definitions of houses and other departments with those in the Newsom department. The focus of my research was therefore directed towards the ways in which pupils and teachers in the Newsom department developed alternative definitions of the school through the strategies they employed in their work. In particular, I examined the ways in which elements of school routine were redefined within the Newsom department. My participation in the school, the house system and the department allowed me to unravel the sets of social interactions and social relationships occurring in different groups and the ways in which school policy was defined and redefined on a day-by-day basis. However, as I have shown in earlier chapters, different groups advanced different definitions of the situation and this appeared to take a particular form among Newsom teachers and pupils.

It appeared that most teachers' experiences with the first Newsom group had established an identity for Newsom pupils, Newsom work and the department. Added to this, the experience teachers had with individual Newsom pupils when they had been in lower forms in the school or within the Newsom department led to a situation whereby labels were attached to the pupils, and in turn to their teachers and the work of the department. The result was that teachers reconstructed the reality of the situation and advanced several myths about Newsom pupils. However, the only pupils in the Newsom department who appeared worthy of staff gossip were those who were labelled 'troublemakers'. An area that warranted investigation was, therefore, the way in which Newsom pupils were typified by teachers. In this context, a series of questions could be posed: who were the Newsom pupils? How did they become Newsom pupils? How were they typified by teachers in other departments, by the heads of houses and their own teachers? We shall turn to these questions in chapter six.

To complement my work on Newsom pupils I addressed similar questions on Newsom teachers. As far as staffing was concerned, all the teachers were 'on loan' from other departments because the number of lessons taken related to the time that teachers could be 'spared' from their work in subject areas. The Newsom teachers tended to be 'characters' in their own right who were regarded as 'good teachers' by the pupils because they modified the conventional definitions of school and teaching. Accordingly, a similar set of questions were used: what kind of teachers taught in the Newsom department? How did they become Newsom teachers? How did they teach? Why did they teach in the way they did? These questions will be followed up in chapter seven by examining the relationships I observed between teachers and between teachers and pupils.

Finally, I examine in chapter eight the character of 'work' and 'non-work' and the ways in which teachers and pupils developed strategies for their activities within the department. This analysis was based on the interactions and relationships among small groups of pupils and their teachers and takes us only part of the way towards understanding social relations in the school and classroom. It was, therefore, essential to pose questions about the Newsom curriculum and the ways in which it was adopted and adapted by Newsom pupils and their teachers in the Newsom department, in subject departments and in houses. In short, I wanted to examine the interplay between the members of the department and teachers in other parts of the school.

Notes

1 Monks (1970, 74).
2 The pupils whom I taught in the non-examination courses included a boy who had passed the eleven-plus examination and had been recommended for a

grammar school place, and several pupils who had been recommended for special school places.

3 For a discussion of such courses and the problems posed see, for example, Watson (1958).

4 For the main recommendations see Newsom (1963, xvi–xviii).

5 For a discussion of the types of Newsom courses which have been organized in schools see, for example, the reports by King (1973a, 115) and Benn and Simon (1972, 252).

6 An exception to this was Hargreaves (1967). However, Hargreaves does not discuss the school experience of the bottom stream 4E as he remarks on p.3:

> The pupils of 4E were excluded from special study, not only because of their severe difficulties in answering questionnaires without individual attention, but also because they tended to form a separate group in terms of friendship choices and the special teachers assigned to them.

7 For novels which discuss the position of non-examination pupils or school leavers see, for example, Braithwaite (1962), Hines (1969) and on pupils in a secondary modern school see Blishen (1971).

8 For complete monographs see, for example, Scharff (1976), Willis (1977) and White (1980). For discussions in papers see Furlong (1976), Woods (1976a) and Davies (1979).

9 Interview with the headmaster.

10 ibid.

11 ibid.

12 ibid.

13 Further particulars on Newsom work written by the headmaster.

14 ibid.

15 ibid.

16 For a discussion of the way in which 'war stories' are told by boys in street gangs see, for example, Patrick (1973). For a similar notion of the elaborate story see the discussion of 'bullshitting' in Mukerji (1978).

17 Compare the teachers' views of the boys in Hargreaves (1967, 83–107).

18 A report by the Society of Teachers Opposed to Physical Punishment has indicated that in many schools pupil violence is followed by corporal punishment which they regard as further violence. See Temperton (1981).

19 This was some achievement as I was almost six feet tall and weighed fourteen stone at the time.

20 Compare comments by the boys in Hargreaves (1967, 83–107) talking about teachers' opinions of pupils.

21 For a discussion of humour based on foolish actions see, for example, Fletcher (1974) and for an example of humour based on pupils in school see, for example, Woods (1979, 210–36).

22 Heads of departments generally compared the resources they commanded with those of house heads (cf. chapter three). In particular, they were critical of the fact that house heads had studies while they did not. However, the head of the English department and the head of the mathematics department managed to improvise and create 'offices' within large classrooms. The head of the English department had divided an area of his room using metal cupboards and had

equipped the 'office' with a table and easy chairs. Meanwhile, the room that was used for careers interviews was claimed and used by Sylvia Robinson as her 'office'.

23 If this scene is compared with Mannheim and Stewart's description of a class-room where they state, 'They sit in desks usually, often in rows, all facing one way' it is deviant. See Mannheim and Stewart (1962, 136).

24 Cf., for example, King (1973a, 46–52).

25 In this sense it might well be an expression of anti-school subculture as dis-cussed by Hargreaves (1967, 159–81).

26 Cf. White and Brockington (1978, 1–6).

27 At this early stage of the research I was establishing my role as a part-time teacher and I was afraid that if I took these lessons on a regular basis I would be regarded by the pupils as a student teacher – a role which I did not want to be given as I thought it held several problems among which was my impressions of the way in which pupils react to students (cf. Lacey 1977; Ball and Lacey 1980).

28 In such settings, researchers need to consider the extent to which this activity constitutes covert or semi-covert research. Certainly, I did not remind people each time I entered a classroom that I was doing research. For further discussion of the covert–overt debate see Homan (1980), Bulmer (1980), and in relation to this research see Burgess (1984c).

29 For a discussion of the use of time among boys outside school see Corrigan (1979, 119–41).

30 For an analysis of this process in early classroom encounters see Ball (1980).

31 Cf. Mannheim and Stewart (1962, 136).

32 Since the fieldwork was completed in July 1974 I have visited the school. Much new building has taken place including a new area for the Newsom department.

33 When a uniform check was conducted among the pupils the head of house in question returned a note to the headmaster about pupils without uniform and added:

> While enclosing my house report on uniform I feel that it is only fair to say that in my opinion the general appearance of the school pupils is only a reflection of the very poor standards set them by a fair number of the staff – some of them very senior members. I think that by comparison we must hold the record for the most casually and unprofessionally dressed staff in the city. I know no other school where lady teachers in trousers are tolerated, men teachers in pullovers with no shirts are accepted, together with a general air of grubbiness evident in some cases.
>
> I accept that the site and the geography of the buildings calls for warmth but do not feel that cleanliness and smartness need to be sacrificed. If you take a look around the staffroom there are few who consistently dress as professionals who are presumably setting an example.

34 Cf. Woods (1976a; 1976b).

35 For a similar approach see Geer (1964) and Pons (1969, 128–50) (reprinted in Burgess 1982a, 31–42).

6

THREE

NEWSOM PUPILS

Newsom pupils posed problems for teachers as they brought noise, disruption and misbehaviour into classes. As a consequence they were the subjects of many stories in which stereotypes were created of the group based on the misdemeanours of individuals like Peter Vincent and John Slattery to whom I had been 'introduced' on my first day at McGregor.[1] The teachers' stereotypes were based entirely on negative characteristics. They saw these pupils as apathetic, anti-school, awkward, unco-operative, idiotic and 'a waste of time'.[2] Furthermore, Newsom pupils were considered by many teachers to be of limited ability.

These views were not shared by Newsom teachers who considered it impossible to discuss Newsom pupils in terms of a narrow range of stereotypes. As far as they were concerned their pupils shared several problems, at the centre of which was school attendance.[3] Furthermore, some pupils did not meet the behavioural expectations of house staff, while others did not meet the academic expectations of subject teachers. However, Newsom teachers thought that some of their pupils had the ability to take examinations but lacked sufficient motivation, while others had alienated particular teachers, especially the heads of houses. They argued that Newsom pupils had a range of experiences of teachers, school and school work with the result that the pupils were not a simple, homogeneous group who disliked school.

Twenty years ago, the Newsom committee (Newsom 1963, 10) warned that it was too easy to see Newsom pupils as a single group when they remarked: 'We must not lose sight of the differences in trying to discover what they [the pupils] have in common'. The committee managed to reduce 6000 boys and girls (the subjects of a survey of fourteen-year-old secondary modern school pupils) to 6 pupil stereotypes.[4] The report focused on portraits of 3 imaginary boys and 3 imaginary girls.[5] Those boys and girls who were representative of the upper ability groups were the 'Browns', those representing the middle groups of ability the 'Joneses' and those representing the lower ability groups the 'Robinsons'. The Newsom committee (Newsom 1963, 194) reported that:

> The information that we have about the boys and girls in the sample is limited to certain questions of fact. We know a little about their physique, their family background, where they live, their school work and their social life. We know nothing about the imponderables which are ultimately much more important – the personal characteristics which make them happy or discontented, loved or disliked, useful members of the community or a drag on society.

This evidence provided little beyond the descriptive characteristics of some pupils who would be regarded by teachers as potential candidates for a Newsom course. There were no portraits of real pupils and very little was known about the social processes that influenced their school lives and experiences.[6]

With this lack of real information in mind, I orientated my study towards providing a detailed portrait of Newsom pupils in Bishop McGregor School. I was particularly interested in the processes involved in their schooling, their relationships with teachers and the way in which they became Newsom pupils. I also wanted to examine the implications of teacher–pupil relationships for pupil careers and the extent to which a theory of typing could be used to help understand how pupils became members of the Newsom course. This also allowed me to continue looking at the way in which situations were defined and redefined by members of the school.

There were 42 pupils in the fifth-year Newsom group: 18 boys and 24 girls. I taught 25 pupils, most of whom were boys since it was the policy of the head of department to allocate boys to male teachers and girls to female teachers.[7] I got to know the pupils within my groups with different degrees of familiarity depending on their attendance, participation, and involvement in my course and in the school. It was soon apparent that these pupils could not be seen as one group.

I established a composite picture of several pupils' school experience using their personal files,[8] accounts that pupils and teachers provided of their experiences and my own observations of individuals in my classes. Thus, a brief life-history approach was used to gather data on the pupils' school careers.[9] This chapter focuses on three pupils whom I got to know with differing degrees of profundity. These cases are used to extend my analyses of house and departmental staff by considering how they defined these pupils' school situations and how they processed them into the Newsom department. There is a consideration of home–school relations and a brief discussion of relationships between these pupils and their Newsom teachers (see also chapters seven and eight). Finally, this material is considered in relation to a theory of pupil typing. The three cases include two boys (David Jones and Sean Kelly) and one girl (Mary Rushton). In their own ways each of these cases might be regarded as 'extreme' or exceptional, but as Pons (1969, 176) has argued such cases exhibit social participation and relationships in a more pronounced form. They allow us to examine in greater depth social relations among teachers and between teachers and pupils in the school.

The case of David Jones

David Jones was among the first Newsom pupils I got to hear about when I started my research in Bishop McGregor School. The pupils themselves told me that David was frequently absent from school – a point which I was able to verify on countless occasions during my first term. David's attendance was very sporadic. Often some weeks would elapse before I saw him either in my lessons or in school. For David this was 'normal', because he had started to 'wag' lessons when he attended St Columba's junior school: a story which was verified by several other pupils who had attended that school.

David was fifteen when I first met him. He was unlike other Newsom pupils being small, clean, tidy and smartly dressed. He was also well spoken and eager to enter into discussion with me. I was interested to find out why David was in the Newsom group so I talked to teachers and pupils about him, consulted his personal file and talked to the boy himself. This led me to construct an account which took up questions of home–school relations and the way house heads and departmental staff processed pupils into the Newsom department.

It was evident that David did not like school, not only because of his periods of absence but also from the comments that he made about the teachers, the daily routine and school buildings. All this was summed up in his favourite phrase, 'This school's like a prison, only it's got windows instead of bars'.[10] One day, I questioned him further on this remark to see if there was anything he liked about the school, but I received a very definite response when he replied 'I'm not very keen on any of this school'.[11] This in itself seemed strange as I knew from reading David's

First-year report on David Jones

Date 10.vi.70   Age 12 years 3 months
Attendance D   Tutor group 1HB Hexham

| Subject | Grade | | Comment |
	Effort	Attainment	
French	A−	B	David is a good steady worker.
English	A−	B+	Always works well and has produced some very good poetry.
Religious education	A−	B	David is interested and gives of his best.
Geography	B	B−	David has tried hard: he must try to keep his mind on the job in hand though.
Music	B	B	Good standard of work.
Maths	B	A ⎫	Very good worker.
Technical drawing	B	B ⎭	
Art	C	C	Satisfactory.
History	C+	C+	Works well.
Drama			Fair effort shown.
Technical	C	C	Quite consistent in his work.
Science	C+	B−	Has worked very well throughout the year.
Physical education	C+	C+	Generally does quite well.

Grades: A = Excellent, B = Good, C = Average, D = Poor, E = Unsatisfactory

Group tutor: A very helpful and reliable member of the class.

R. Passmore

Head of house: A very pleasing report. David has worked hard and behaved well.

G. Davies
Head of Hexham

Headmaster: This is a very good start in a new school which should encourage David to try still harder next year.

G. Goddard
Headmaster

Note: All teachers' initials have been removed.

school reports and records that when he joined McGregor he had been considered 'intelligent' and eager to work for teachers. The question therefore remained: what accounted for the change in his attitude towards school?

David told me he had never really wanted to attend McGregor. At eleven he had passed the selection examination[12] with a verbal reasoning quotient of 124 but he did not want to attend grammar school, claiming 'I didn't want to be a swot'. Instead he wanted to follow his brother to a neighbouring comprehensive school. David considered that it was possible to do well at Ecclesfield Comprehensive when he explained:

> I didn't really mind the idea of going to Ecclesfield. They weren't swots or anything, but they knew a good bit. Me brother's come away from there now and he's got two 'A' levels and I don't know how many 'O' levels he's got.[13]

However, David could not attend this school as by the time he was eleven years of age his family no longer resided in that school's catchment area. David claimed that he would have preferred to go to Clayhill School – a local comprehensive which many of his non-Catholic friends attended. However, as a Catholic pupil living on the southern side of Merston he was automatically allocated to McGregor.

David joined Bishop McGregor School when it first opened and was allocated to Hexham House. He enjoyed his time in this house, commenting 'I used to have a good laugh in Hexham. The teachers were all right and Miss Davies is really reasonable. She's fair to you. Now it's different.'[14] Similarly, in the first year at the school he claimed that he had 'a good laugh'[15] but at the same time worked hard: 'Well in the first year, really I was a swot. I used to keep reading and learning. I couldn't learn enough you know. The class that I was in we had a fair laugh and everything.'[16] His remarks on school work were supported by the comments from his teachers in his first-year report. This end-of-year report supports David's views on his first year. He had satisfied his teachers' academic and behavioural expectations and was above average for his year group in all areas of the curriculum. His teachers had used words such as 'good' and phrases such as 'works well' to describe his work. Similarly, in terms of behaviour his house head noted that he had 'behaved well'. This was praise indeed, as Gillian Davies had quickly established a reputation among teachers and pupils for insisting on very high standards of behaviour.[17] David's high grades for effort and attainment together with the comments from his teachers indicated that he was among the more able members of his year. He had filled a 'best pupil' or 'ideal pupil' role[18] which in his terms made him a 'swot'.

In the second year things started to change as David explained:

> In the second year it started to get boring. I got fed up with reading

and all that. There was a trip I was supposed to go on. I paid £2 towards it and they didn't let me go for some reason. When I tried to get the money refunded they said, 'No', so I didn't take much more interest. After that if things didn't start to go my way, I decided not to work. I just threw my cap in.[19]

Although David described a dramatic change in his attitude towards school on the basis of one incident, the teachers' accounts document a gradual change in behaviour and attitude during the second and third years. Their remarks on David's second-year report indicated that he was still among the 'best' pupils in his year. In terms of effort and attainment grades, David had several C grades and he continued to fulfil many of his teachers' expectations, who remarked that he did 'some good work', 'worked well' and 'tries hard'. However, his standards were not as high as in the previous academic year: the report also included remarks like 'could do even better', 'his written work needs to be improved' and 'his attitude to work is too vague'. Despite the fact that teachers had given David a set of grades to indicate he was 'average to good' for his year group, there were also several indications that his work was not of the standard he had previously achieved and that he could do much better. This position was summed up by his tutor, his head of house and the headmaster in his second-year report.

Group tutor: David is a pleasant member of the class and seems to have worked steadily this year. With constant effort he should reach quite a good standard of work.

R. Passmore

Head of house: A satisfactory report which should encourage David to continue his efforts. Pleasant and helpful in the house.

G. Davies
Head of Hexham

Headmaster: He must try to keep up his efforts.

G. Goddard
Headmaster

This summary evaluated the other teachers' comments and indicated that David still fulfilled their academic and behavioural expectations. However, there were indications that David could improve on his performance.

In his house file there were a series of commendation slips that stated he was 'helpful and co-operative'. Furthermore, he was involved in various house activities including working in the tuck shop. But this picture of the intelligent, hard-working, well-behaved pupil was transformed for some of his teachers by a series of incidents that centred around the theft of a wristwatch from another pupil in the middle of the second year shortly after his report had been issued. Although David told me about several of his 'brushes with teachers' he never mentioned this incident, which was fully documented by his house head in a typed note in his personal file.

Sept. 70–71
Uneventful first term in 2HG. Continues to be helpful.
Second term. Stole a £9 wristwatch from Sally Perkins's locker. Wristwatch disappeared. After two days of searching and questioning, Mr Lloyd issued an ultimatum. If it was not returned the police would be called. After school that evening, about 5.15 p.m. Mrs Knight called me down from the staff room. David Jones was waiting and gave me the wristwatch saying the boy who had stolen it had asked him to return it. Spoke to him at some length and asked him if he was the boy but he denied this. Said that the boy concerned would run away from home if his name was given as his father would beat him. David knew the family well and had always taken the other boy's part. David had given a promise that he would not tell on his friend. Gave some vivid descriptions of the beating the thief would get if his parents found out. He told me that his mother had advised him to give back the wristwatch after David had come by it through doing a swop for it with the other boy. He seemed to enjoy every minute of the interview and demanded promises that I would not ask him about it again or go to his house. I found his whole attitude excitable and melodramatic. In the course of the next few days I gave him several opportunities to add to his story but he did not. After a few days I called at his house to thank his mother for making David bring back the wristwatch. The mother kept me standing at the door and her apparent lack of knowledge of the whole thing more or less confirmed what I already thought very possible. Mother was very rambly in her conversation and was frequently interrupted by another son, about fifteen years old, who was only too eager to tell me about the things David gained by the swopping method. House looked very untidy and the mother kept saying that she could not ask me in because it was a mess. On returning to school I saw the boy again and put it to him that it was about time he told the truth and that I had found several discrepancies in talking to his mother. He broke down and admitted that he had taken it. Said that he came back into the hall for his books, opened the wrong locker and saw the wristwatch and was tempted but did not realize its value. I found this hard to believe as previous questioning established that he was one of several who had been examining it when Sally had it in the playground. I came to the conclusion that the

boy lied so easily that to get the real truth was very difficult. Earlier in the business when he realized that I was not satisfied with his explanation he had given me the name of a Southwark boy as the thief. Again he was most elaborate in his description and identification. On checking I found that the boy in question was in the supervision of a member of staff at the time the wristwatch was taken but David would not retract his statement. At one stage in the matter David indicated that he had been wrongfully accused of theft in his junior school.

No further trouble but I found that he had wangled himself on to the tuck shop team without permission from me. As this had to be closed because it was running at a loss I made it clear that he was not one of the team and removed him from the temptation.

Offered to move house. It could be that he wants to turn over a new leaf but he will need careful supervision over money and valuables as he seemed to me in a fantasy world during the wristwatch theft while sounding most convincing. A change might do him good as he is certainly very helpful and willing. Could well have difficulties at home. I got the impression that he was the brightest there and probably doesn't get much encouragement. On free dinners for most of the year.
1.9.1971

G. Davies
Head of Hexham House

This account transformed the official record that was kept on David Jones. It also details an aspect of the work of a house head and the way she modified her perception of David's behaviour. Earlier reports from his teachers indicated that they considered him no problem to the school. Furthermore, in terms of academic work and behaviour he approached the role of model pupil. However, the wristwatch incident transformed his house head's perception of him and the role which he held. The same head of house who had considered him well behaved now considered him a thief and a liar who required 'careful supervision over money and valuables'. Although she claimed that David had 'wangled himself on to the tuck shop team' she had given him a commendation earlier in the term for 'working so hard in the tuck shop'.[20] With the wristwatch incident he was rapidly removed from the tuck shop team and it was implied that he could have been responsible for the financial losses. Despite this major shift in her behavioural perspective of the boy she still believed that he was 'very helpful and willing' and considered he was the most intelligent member of his family.

This incident also changed the perspective from which other teachers viewed David's home and family. His school record card (completed when he entered McGregor), indicated that he was the middle child of a family of three, having an older brother and a younger sister. His father had been a builder but was now permanently off work as he had been seriously injured in an accident. Against the father's name on David's record card was written, 'Welshman, nice, intelligent, f. pleasant'. These notes which were written in pencil (possibly by the headmaster, given the style of writing) indicated that a visit had been made to the boy's home, since there was a note that he lived in a 'fairly good house'. Initially, the family was not regarded as a problem or a potential problem for the teachers. David's file contained a series of notes from home that fully documented the reasons for each of his absences from school and were a further indication of the parents' co-operation with the teachers. Meanwhile, when David had an opportunity to go on holiday during school time in the first year, an educational welfare officer had called at his house. The welfare officer had concluded that the family were 'not particularly well off' and that the holiday was in order. He reported that David's mother was 'most co-operative'.[21] These initial visits were very positive and there were no adverse remarks about the boy's parents or his home.

However, with the wristwatch incident, Gillian Davies called at his home unexpectedly and uninvited. The report which she made on her return to school transformed the image of the family. On the basis of one visit, they were officially recorded as unhelpful to their son and not interested in the school or in education. Judgements were made of the home as she claimed that it 'looked very untidy' and it was 'a mess'. Furthermore, the mother was reported as 'very rambly' which added to the general picture of a family who presented or might present some problems for teachers.

At the beginning of the third year, two new houses opened at Bishop McGregor School and all pupils were given an opportunity to volunteer to move to one of these houses. David Jones was among those who took up this offer and moved to Clifton House. David's records went with him, so that teachers in the new house were alerted to the fact that David and his family could constitute a problem for them. David found the teachers in Clifton very different from those in Hexham. He disliked his tutor and his head of house, before whom he often appeared when he was without uniform, or absent or late for school. As far as he was concerned, his head of house was someone who 'doesn't do much except shout her mouth off from time to time'. However, he explained that this had not prevented him from playing around in other teachers' classes and doing as little work as he could. The results of these activities were reflected in his third-year report.

Third-year report on David Jones

Date 24.ii.72   Age 13 years 11 months

Attendance A (absent for 8 days since September)   Tutor group 3/4/BB

Subject	Grade Effort	Attainment	Comment
Technical drawing	B	C	Quite satisfactory progress.
Metalwork	A	B	Good effort – he enjoys his work.
Religious education	B/C		Good work on the whole.
Maths	C	C	Examination 34%. David works quite well and is making steady progress.
Geography	C	D	David appears to try hard but this is not reflected in his marks. Exam. 27%.
English	43% C	B	I have noticed a deterioration in his work. He is capable of much better work than his examination result indicates.
French	D	D	I do not feel that he has really come to grips with this subject.
Art	A	A	Has great ability here and works very hard.
History	C	C	Examination 45%. 21st out of 32. Tries hard.
Physical education	D	C	David could work a lot harder.
Music	C	C	Examination 48%. This shows what effort can achieve. If applied to classwork the grade would improve.

Group tutor: David has secured good marks in only a few subjects. It appears that he must come to grips with himself and decide to apply more effort if he is to obtain better all-round marks.

P. Horne

Third-year report on David Jones—*(continued)*

Head of house: Some of these results reflect a rather negative attitude. His work must improve and I would like to see him take a more active role in the house.

M. Rolls
Head of Clifton House

Headmaster: David is at the crossroads. The road marked 'EFFORT' means an uphill slog. The other road drifts downhill. Which one will David choose?

G. Goddard
Headmaster

Note: All teachers' initials have been removed.

The teachers' remarks showed a decline in David's academic performance. However, they support David's view that he had given up working and was intent on enjoying himself by playing around with his friends in various classes. No longer did David hold a 'best pupil' role, because his work showed little effort in academic subjects like English, mathematics, geography and history where he had low grades and a series of comments that indicated he was not meeting the teachers' academic expectations. Furthermore, he was not meeting the teachers' behavioural expectations[22] being told that he had to 'come to grips with himself', and that he had a 'negative attitude' towards school and his house.

The only area in which David showed any interest and met with any success was practical subjects. He gained good grades in art, technical drawing and metalwork and teachers praised his efforts. While this did not meet the academic criteria teachers set for potential examination candidates, this record of work and behaviour did meet their criteria for allocating pupils to the Newsom department. A poor performance in academic subjects, a good record in practical subjects and a poor or negative attitude towards school, especially in the third year, was enough to orientate an individual towards the Newsom course. David's performance together with his refusal to work in school or do homework was sufficient for him to be allocated to the Newsom course in the fourth year.

In Newsom, David placed himself on a path of little work and frequent absence from school. Although often absent he was always covered by a note 'from home'. However, there was some doubt about the authenticity of these notes; they were written on pieces of paper torn from a school exercise book. Each note bore David's father's signature but as David explained to me, it was an easy one to forge – a point which he proved when he treated several members of the Newsom group and myself to a free demonstration.

By the middle of the spring term in the fourth year, Maggie Rolls had recognized that there was a pattern of frequent absences against David's name in the register. She therefore wrote to his parents indicating the level of his absence:

> Bishop McGregor School
> Hollybush Lane
> Merston
> 22 February 1973

Dear Mr and Mrs Jones,

Can you let me know why David is not at school? He has been absent for three days now. His attendance has not been good for some time now. Is there a reason for this? Will you contact me as soon as possible?

Yours sincerely,

M. Rolls (Miss)
Head of Clifton House

This letter received no direct response from David's parents. Then followed a series of further notes that claimed David was absent from school because he had the 'flu, was sick, or had stomach pains. Even when David came to school, his attendance was punctuated by periods of lesson truancy. By mid-March events came to a head for David. Maggie Rolls had followed up his activities which were summarized in a note that she sent to Peter Horne (David's group tutor and the deputy head of house):

Re DAVID JONES
On Friday, having sent a letter to his parents, it came to my knowledge that
   (a) he had TRUANTED;
   (b) he had taken a bike at lunch time on Friday without permission.
So I went to see his parents on Saturday – a revelation.
   (a) The place was like a slum house – dirty clothes everywhere, the smell knocked me sick.
   (b) His parents are old – his father broke his neck several years ago and has been an invalid ever since. Came out of hospital (for umpteenth time) this week.
   (c) I felt sorry for them – the poverty, the old woman having to go to work, the father in great pain.
What I discovered re David
   (1) He was genuinely off school on Tues. – ill the day before and his father had not come out of hospital.
   (2) Wed. – VB says he came for his lessons (RIDING)
              – did not appear for registration or for lessons after break.

(3) Truanted Thursday.

(4) VB tells me he took Garibaldi's bike at lunch time without permission.

(5) His dad was very angry with him – actually I could hardly tell what he was saying.

David will receive:

2 strokes on one hand for his TRUANCY

1 stroke on the other hand for taking the bike.

I don't mind when you cane him but I'd like him to admit he thoroughly deserves the cane on both counts.

I did not like the way he answered me back on Saturday – his dad was mad with him too.

The root cause of his absences lie in fact (I *think* anyway)
   (a) Father needs a lot of help at home – mother really too old and too ill-looking to work.

Each time he goes to hospital David seems to be the only one who can help him.
   (b) MAYBE he has truanted before.
   (c) David looks too young to be their son.[23]

This note provides further insights into the relationships between the home and the school, the role of a house head and her relationships with a pupil. Furthermore, it provides evidence on the way in which the problematic character of the family is reinforced within the official house record. Again, a visit by a house head to the Jones household resulted in the values of the school and of an individual teacher being held up against the family who were regarded as 'a problem'.[24] Maggie Rolls attempted to find an answer for David's behaviour, frequent absence and truancy by looking towards his home and family background. This culminated in a further unannounced and uninvited visit to David's home from a house head. On the basis of one brief visit this teacher produced a report for the boy's file that contained numerous assertions about his family. Maggie Rolls appreciated that the family had financial difficulties through the father's continued illness. Although she claimed to be 'sorry for them' she reinforced the image of a 'problem' family. His home was described as being 'like a slum house' because of the dirt, the smell and clothes lying around.[25] The family's life style was also considered deviant because an unfounded assertion about illegitimacy was made when she remarked, 'David looks too young to be their son'. Yet this was entered in an official record.

Maggie Rolls's visit to David's home also had significance for the boy. Maggie had told Peter Horne that when she visited the house David was rude to her and it was this, rather than his truancy and theft, which led her to request that he should admit that he deserved to be caned. David agreed with part of her story but had his own point of view. He hated Maggie Rolls and thought he was justified in being rude to her. He had also kicked her car because 'The only time she talks to me is when she's insulting me or telling me to come to school'.[26] He also told me that he hated the teachers in Clifton House and in particular he singled out his tutor, Peter Horne. David compared this teacher unfavourably with other staff when he remarked:

> Horne he's a different fellow, he says lots of things, but there is a time and place for that and he picks the wrong time and the wrong place. He's an idiot. Even in the third year when I came into school whether I was early or late he'd have me for being late. When I used to truant he used to say if you come in half-way through the day you'll still get your mark. Then one day I came in half-way through the day and he asked me why I was away and he gave me a right doing about lateness. You can't win really.
>
> One day he was caning me and I'd had four. I was only due for three and he said, 'Hold out your hand' and I said, 'No'. I held out me hand and Miss Rolls came in and she said, 'That's enough'. I don't know what he's got against me, silly old goat, I wish he'd do something sensible, like take a walk under a bus.[27]

David had a stock of these 'war stories' in which he 'bullshitted'[28] about his relationship with house staff. In these stories he was always the central figure wronged by teachers who pushed him around, broke promises, lied, cheated, double-crossed and caned him. Some of his stories were exaggerated but others contained elements of truth. Many of his stories highlighted characteristics of teachers, especially house heads who were seen to be attempting to maintain school rules, but regarded as less than honest in their dealings with pupils. Some stories about his punishment were confirmed by the entries in the school punishment book and with accounts that Newsom teachers could provide.[29]

David was launched on a course of regular truancy. Whenever he was absent from school, he was seen by Maggie Rolls and caned by Peter Horne if truancy could be established. But David did not mind being caned for truancy – he saw this as an occupational hazard:

> It's over in a couple of minutes ain't it and it just pains for ten minutes. There have been people who have been truanting from here for about six months. When they come back here they ain't gonna get suspended, they're gonna get caned. Whack, ten minutes that's it. To have six months for ten minutes, it's worth it isn't it?[30]

After Maggie Rolls's report on David in the spring term of the fourth year, his attendance and behaviour did not improve. His absence increased in frequency to a point where it was only interrupted by short periods at school. Even when he was at school he was far from occupied. He claimed that he spent his time 'doing nothing',[31] a phrase which covered a range of non-work activities: talking to friends, looking out of windows, walking around the school with other Newsom pupils, and taunting teachers who were regarded as 'fair game'. Such was the culmination of David's career at Bishop McGregor School.

David's case illustrates the story of a pupil who had the potential to do well in school. However, in answer to the headmaster's question posed in David's third-year report, he chose to go downhill where he followed a path which involved little or no work. The attempts of house staff to get him to conform to school rules and routines met with no success. If anything, they simply reinforced his hatred for teachers and for the school. After spending two years in the Newsom group he formally left school in the summer term 1974 without taking any public examinations. However, he claimed 'I've had two years of no work and I'm still as brainy as some of those in the top sets',[32] a point that it was impossible for his teachers to deny.

Although David could not be regarded as 'typical' of Newsom pupils, he does represent those pupils who had the ability to take public examinations but instead followed the Newsom course. David's case illustrates how a pupil is processed into the Newsom department, highlights the relationship between home and school, and the changing relationship between teachers and a pupil.

The case of Sean Kelly

Sean Kelly was unlike David in almost every way. He was tall and thin and looked perpetually tired. Sean was regarded by other Newsom pupils as 'a right dosser' and was considered by teachers to be one of the laziest members of the Newsom group. Sean made it clear to all that he disliked being in school. He always looked miserable, was renowned for non-cooperation with teachers and spent as much time getting out of work as getting on with it. Sean had always experienced difficulties in schools. Throughout his primary school career he had little success, being confronted with numerous learning difficulties which followed him into Bishop McGregor School, influencing his relationships with teachers.

Sean was frequently around the school site but infrequently in classes. He could regularly be found wandering about the school during lessons or in the café nearby. He had few aims other than to distance himself from school – a point which was revealed by his school 'uniform' of coloured sweater, brown trousers and faded denim jacket with 'I love Tessa' scrawled in ink across the back. The only times he looked pleased was when he came out of school, when he was 'playing up' a teacher or in trouble. On these occasions, he wore a broad mischievous grin. At other times he appeared sullen and bored. By the age of fourteen he had effectively finished school and was just waiting for the leaving date at the end of the spring term in his fifth year.

Sean lived with his father and two brothers; his mother had walked out on the family some years earlier. He was the middle son and like his brothers did not perform well at school. His report card from the local Catholic junior school indicated that he was 'very slow' and 'suitable for the remedial group' when he joined McGregor. It was therefore not surprising that Sean was unconcerned about going to a new secondary school, as he explained in an interview with me:

RB   Did you choose to come here [Bishop McGregor School]?
Sean I didn't mind where I went.
RB   You didn't mind where you went then. Well, when you came here, when you arrived on the first day, what happened?
Sean I didn't come the first day.
RB   How was that?
Sean I was still on holiday.
RB   What happened when you did come?
Sean They didn't know where to put me, didn't know my house or anything.
RB   Where did you eventually go?
Sean I went to Southwark [House].

This was indicative of Sean's attitude to school. His absence on the first morning at his new school was the first of many absences. He was often late for school or for lessons or missing when groups or activities were organized. Sean always managed to be anywhere but the right place at the right time, as far as the teachers were concerned. It was usual for him to be allocated to a task or a group when he arrived in a classroom rather than allowed a choice. This merely confirmed his attitude to school. He did little or no work and spent his time annoying teachers and pupils. In short, Sean's withdrawal from school activities prevented him from exercising choice within the formal timetable.

Sean's lack of involvement with school was attributed by many teachers to his learning difficulties and lack of school success. These problems were well summarized in his first-year report. Sean's teachers regarded his academic work as 'poor' and 'unsatisfactory' compared to that of his peers. Their comments indicated that Sean found most work difficult. However, several teachers considered that these difficulties were enhanced by Sean's negative attitudes to school which were expressed through lack of concentration, effort and hard work. Sean confirmed that he distanced himself from school and school work in an interview with me:

First-year report on Sean Kelly

Date 15.vi.70   Age 12 years 4 months
Attendance B   Tutor group 1ST Southwark

	Grade		
Subject	*Effort*	*Attainment*	*Comment*
Religious education	C		More effort needed on Sean's behalf.
English	D	D	Must try harder in this subject.
French	C−	D	Too easily distracted, must concentrate more.
Art	C	C	Does his best.
Science	D+	D−	Finds difficulty but does not really concentrate or exert himself.
Maths	D−	E+	Lacks the necessary determination to work at a subject in which he is very weak.
Drama			Has made little contribution.
Physical education	C	C	Satisfactory.
Geography	C	C	Tries, must make an effort to improve the presentation of his work.
Music	C	C	Fair.
Technical drawing	C	C	Satisfactory.
History	E	D	Sean will have to apply himself if he is to make any progress.
Technical activities	C	C	Satisfactory.

Group tutor: Sean finds some subjects difficult. To overcome his difficulties he must concentrate on his work and make an effort during lessons.

                                        S. Hawkins

Head of house: Sean is a pleasant, well-mannered boy.

                                        T. Coyne
                     Head of Southwark House

Headmaster: While pleasant, Sean must try very much harder next year if he is to benefit from the opportunities here.

                                      G. Goddard
                                     Headmaster

Note: All teachers' initials have been removed.

RB   What were the subjects that you liked best in the lower part of the school?

Sean   Nothing.

RB   What nothing at all?

Sean   No.

RB   Well what about anything in the first, second, or third year?

Sean   I can't remember, got a bad memory.

School work was defined out of existence. As far as he was concerned, there was nothing of interest and nothing worth doing or talking about in relation to school. To maintain this view, he claimed that he was unable to recall anything that was done. His alleged bad memory was a strategy that was regularly used not merely to 'forget' about school work but also to 'forget' the place where he was supposed to be, the work that he was supposed to be doing and the equipment that he needed.

Sean found school work difficult but his behaviour in the first year met teachers' expectations; he was regarded as 'pleasant' and 'well mannered'. Nevertheless, his difficulties with academic work recurred throughout the second year to such an extent that the headmaster referred him to the child guidance unit because of his reading difficulties. The city's educational psychologist found that according to the test scores, Sean had a reading age of six years one month and reported:

> On the present results Sean is a boy of limited intelligence who is finding considerable difficulty in holding his own in normal school. He enjoys school, especially games, swimming and English but is making little progress. His reading needs special attention because he has only just made a start here. In view of these observations I recommend ascertainment subject to parental consent.[33]

The educational psychologist supported the school's diagnosis of Sean's difficulties with basic subjects and recommended him for a special school place. However, he could not transfer schools without his parents' agreement. The officers of the authority wrote to his father suggesting the transfer but no reply was ever received with the result that Sean completed his secondary education in the remedial and Newsom departments at Bishop McGregor School.

Sean's reports in the second and third years reflected a similar performance in academic subjects. He obtained D and E grades together with comments that indicated a lack of motivation, concentration and application to school work. However, in metalwork where he obtained a grade A he was regarded as 'very good'. His third-year report was summed up by his group tutor, head of house and the headmaster in the following terms:

Group tutor: Sean must make a greater effort not to be distracted since his work suffers. He could also make a greater contribution to house and tutor group activities.

S. Mills

Head of house: Sean's attitude has improved recently – he is more co-operative and less stubborn. I am delighted to see the effort he is putting into his English and his metalwork.

B. Pennington
Head of Southwark House

Headmaster: English and metalwork – fine. Now I hope to hear that other subjects are being given the same energy.

G. Goddard
Headmaster

By the end of the third year Sean was still finding difficulty with school work and his general attitude and personal behaviour were regarded as problematic by his teachers.

When Sean had to choose which courses to follow in the fourth and fifth year, he selected Newsom courses. He explained the process of becoming a Newsom pupil by saying: 'They ask you what you wanna do in Newsom, whether you wanna do exams or no exams, and I said I didn't wanna do any exams so I went into Newsom'.[34] However, when it came to deciding what Newsom was about, Sean demonstrated that he had a different conception of the course from his teachers. In an interview with me we discussed Newsom courses:

RB   What is Newsom?

Sean   You don't have to do exams and you go to classes and go out places. You can get out of lessons.

RB   How's that?

Sean   You can go out somewhere 'cos you're not doing exams.

Newsom was a means of getting outside school and out of doing any work. It was a course which Sean considered did not include lessons. In addition, Sean indicated that he did not work in the core course which was taken alongside the Newsom course:

RB   Do you have to go to any subject lessons?

Sean   Do you mean maths and English?

RB   Yes.

Sean   Yes, you have to go to English and maths and RE.

RB   What do you think about that?

Sean   It's all right. You don't do anything in it anyway.

RB   You must do, surely.

Sean   No, not in English and maths. No, there is nothing to do. I don't do any English.

RB   Do you take religious education?
Sean No, I ain't been there for ages.
RB   Well, where do you go then?
Sean I go and do some work with the teacher. You don't do anything
      in there.
RB   Who is the teacher you go with?
Sean I go with Mr Pennington [his head of house].
RB   What kinds of things do you do then?
Sean Do some painting.

As far as Sean was concerned there was no work for him to do in the core curriculum. However, he was prepared to work on things that interested him like the painting jobs he did around the school for his head of house. Sean's conception of the core curriculum was not shared by his subject teachers. He was so retarded in reading that special provision had to be made for him to have individual classes with Jean O'Rourke. Jean originally thought she could improve his situation by adding three years to his reading age. But she found that Sean rarely attended her classes, choosing instead to spend his time either wandering around the site or playing the pin ball machines in the corner café. When he did attend these classes, she found he had little to contribute. For if Sean did not participate in classes his ignorance would not be revealed. He therefore utilized strategies of non-attendance, non-cooperation and non-participation keeping his position relatively safe and avoiding being the subject of public scrutiny. In this respect, the teachers' strategies for work were swiftly redefined by Sean to mask his inadequacies in the school system.

During the fourth and fifth years not only his work was called into question. Sean's behaviour was also considered problematic by teachers. In the summer term of the fourth year the school buzzed with gossip about Sean and his girlfriend, Tessa, who was also a member of the Newsom group. Sean and Tessa had been seen in the long grass on the edge of the school playing-field by the caretaker's wife, who informed the headmaster that she had seen them kissing, cuddling and petting. Rumour had it that she had claimed 'everything but intercourse took place'. This situation was handled by the pupils' house heads. Tessa's house head said she was no longer to see Sean. But when Sean heard about this instruction he immediately sought revenge, attacking the house head's car and scratching it from end to end. This was followed a few days later when he threw a brick through the house head's study window. The seriousness of this situation was revealed in a letter that the headmaster sent to Sean's father:

30 May 1973

Dear Mr Kelly,
    I am sorry that you could not come last Friday. The matter is one of great seriousness. I have, therefore, to tell you that Sean is not to

return to school until we have met and discussed what shall be done:

(a) with regard to his misbehaviour on Monday 21 May,

(b) the large window that he broke between 10.30 and 10.45 on Wednesday 23 May,

(c) the lies that he told to three of this staff.

The other boy is prepared to pay half the cost of the window so that will reduce the amount falling on Sean.

I feel myself that we have to suspend Sean for a period from school since the throwing of the heavy stone could have seriously injured a member of staff.

Will you please telephone the school on Monday to fix an appointment and arrange for Sean to stay at home until, as I have said above, we have discussed the matter.

Yours sincerely,

G. Goddard

Headmaster

When the headmaster met Mr Kelly it was decided that Sean should be suspended from school for two weeks – a decision that met with Sean's approval because it removed him from the situation he disliked and he could legitimately be absent from school.

On his return, Sean resumed his former attitudes and continued to be inactive in classes. His end-of-year report indicated that he did very little work. His grades consisted of a collection of Es which were followed by such comments as 'unsatisfactory', 'never works', and 'a waster of the first degree'. By the end of the fourth year, Sean was unable to meet any of his teachers' expectations, including those attached to the Newsom department. In all his courses, he refused to do any work beyond annoying the teacher who was taking the class. This was revealed in the concluding remarks on his fourth-year report:

Group tutor: I would have great difficulty in saying something pleasant about Sean's fourth year. He is lazy, resentful of correction and not prepared to make any effort to succeed in life now. He must show some improvement in the fifth year.

D. Gilmore

Head of house: A most deplorable report. We expect a complete change of attitude next year.

B. Pennington
Head of Southwark House

Headmaster: What kind of life is he planning to have if this is
                     how he prepares for it?

                                                        G. Goddard
                                                        Headmaster

These comments summarize the views of Sean's teachers about his
attitudes to school as expressed in his work and behaviour. When he came
to my classes he was late, ill prepared and set on a course of maximum
distraction for me and for the pupils. In my lessons and in other Newsom
teachers' classes he would lie full length on a table or a workbench and
pretend to sleep. None of the Newsom teachers objected to him engaging
in this 'activity' as it allowed other members of the class to continue
uninterrupted with their work. In common with other Newsom pupils,
Sean did what he wanted. However, when he joined sets for core courses
teachers insisted that he participate in the class and at the least sit behind a
desk. For Sean this was difficult. Even in these circumstances he managed
to entertain his classmates. Teachers told me how he often spent time
sitting at his desk combing his hair or counting his money. In one room
with long tables he regularly made paper aeroplanes to float up and down
a bench – an activity which the teacher decided not to stop as she thought
this would cause greater disruption. The most extreme diversion any
teacher observed was in an English lesson. As the teacher read aloud to the
class Sean passed the time producing a number of blond streaks in his hair
with his comb and a bottle of dye. However, he would be outside
classes whenever he could, wandering around the site and making short
excursions to the local café.

This pattern of uncooperative behaviour recurred in the fifth year. In
the first term he refused to follow out a teacher's request which resulted in
a further suspension from school. After a two-week break he returned to a
personal timetable which involved him in building, painting and
decorating jobs around the school – a complete change from his normal
timetable, but a situation that Sean found preferable to classes. However,
when one of his jobs took him up to the cycle sheds he could not resist
starting up the school motorbike and riding around in the top yard. He
was soon caught by a teacher and the autumn term therefore ended with
him being caned again.

In his final term Sean kept out of trouble. He started to attend classes
more regularly and to participate in a very minor way. He was not prepared to be involved in reading or writing but he did help other members
of the group to make cups of coffee, wash up and rearrange desks and
chairs. This was a change for Sean even if it was interspersed with periods
of 'messing about'. His final report summarized the mixed end to his
school career before he left (at the first opportunity) to become a plasterer
(a job which lasted only a few weeks before he was asked to leave).

Fifth-year report on Sean Kelly

Date January 1974   Attendance: Fair

Subject	Set	Grade Effort	Attainment	Comment
Newsom		D	D	Will work only when the mood takes him.
Maths	C		Exam. Abs.	Although Sean has developed a more sensible attitude in class, his past lack of effort rules out any possibility of being able to take a public exam. in this subject.
Religious education		E	E	Rarely present therefore no work handed in.
Building construction		E	E	Rather poor.
Newsom		D	C	Sean can do good work and lately has made good progress.
Games				On the occasions Sean has participated his work has been without any distinction.
English		D	D	Sean muddles through without showing much interest.

Group tutor: I hope I detect some improvement in Sean's attitude recently. Perhaps the new atmosphere of work will encourage the development of Sean's maturity and responsibility.

J. Adams

Head of house: A mixed year. Sean has done some useful work for the house and deserves praise for this, but he has also blotted his copy book on occasions.

B. Pennington
Head of Southwark House

Headmaster: I echo Mr Pennington's remarks and Mrs Adams's hopes.

G. Goddard
Headmaster

Note: All teachers' initials have been removed.

Sean had not found it easy to attend school, to engage in school activities or to work with teachers. The difficulties he experienced resulted in his allocation to the Newsom course. Although the teachers defined the course as an alternative to the conventional school programme, Sean took it further. He established an alternative programme to the Newsom one. He disliked most school activities, did little or no work, created trouble for himself and for others and had poor relationships with teachers. Sean decided to leave school as soon as he could (in the spring term of his fifth year) because he considered this would mean 'I can get a job. Then I can forget school.'[35]

Sean's case has been used to examine the problems that some Newsom pupils had with school and indicates the way in which one pupil reacted to school, schooling and education. It has also brought us towards considering some of the strategies that Newsom pupils used to 'pass the time' in the department and in the school, before leaving at the earliest opportunity. Sean was therefore broadly representative of Newsom pupils who had learning difficulties and as such was the polar opposite of David Jones and his associates.

The case of Mary Rushton

Mary Rushton was often absent from school and was not very well known by her teachers. The records that teachers could keep about her were vague. No school report could be written in the fifth year because of her prolonged absence. Mary had drifted through the lower school, existing in a state of limbo somewhere between the demands of teachers and the demands that were made by her family and her peers.[36] Mary was prepared to work at some subjects to please the teachers. However, if she disliked the teacher she did little work. This state of limbo between conventional and unconventional behaviour coupled with a family history which was regarded by many teachers and by Mary as problematic, was sufficient for her to be placed in the Newsom group.

When Mary Rushton arrived at a lesson she looked as if she was ready to leave. Her outdoor coat was never removed and a battered shopping-bag was always at her side. Any pupil who touched the bag was in trouble as Mary was well built and prepared to use her weight against any boy or girl to protect the bag and its contents. Mary had a reputation as a fighter yet she had earned some 'popularity' with other members of the Newsom group. But her 'popularity' was as shortlived as the cigarettes and matches that she dispensed from her bag. Whenever she was absent from school or out of classes other pupils were ready to tell teachers that they suspected truancy.

Mary's reputation and that of her family had been recorded by her primary school teachers and passed to McGregor on her record card which contained a series of observations. She was the third eldest in a family of eight children and had attended a Catholic junior school in the city centre. The school had no recorded occupation for her father; written against his name was 'not likely to see him, layabout, drinks' and a further note added 'mother finds it difficult to manage moneywise'. Automatically, these remarks conveyed to the teachers at McGregor that Mary came from a 'problem family'. This was confirmed on several occasions by gossip that circulated among teachers about arguments and fights between the parents and violence against the children. Many of the stories originated from Mary who, in conversation with a Newsom teacher, remarked 'My dad's bloody evil, miss'.

Mary's reputation was established at McGregor on the basis of remarks on her record card where it was noted that 'she was involved in several spiteful incidents' and that she was 'rather noisy and cheeky'. If this was her reputation in school, it was subdued in comparison with her life outside. Her parish priest told me about several incidents in which she had been involved at his youth club. In particular, he remembered a fight in which she was a central figure. The fight had reached such proportions that the police had been called. However, Mary's reaction had been to turn to a police officer to instruct him to 'fuck off'. These accounts were used by teachers whenever assessments were given of Mary in staff-room conversation. Most teachers thought she was loud, aggressive and disruptive. In these terms, both the family and the girl were regarded as problematic.

If behaviour was a problem, academic work was not. In the lower school she was considered to be average to below average in comparison with her peers. This was reflected in her first-year report when her teachers considered she was 'average' for her year group. However, several comments indicated that she had not fully met her teachers' academic expectations: remarks were made about 'more effort' and the need to 'stir herself to produce much better work'. Similarly, in terms of behaviour there were no adverse remarks but an indication that greater effort was required.

Mary's personal record indicated that she was 'drifting' through the lower school, doing what was necessary but remaining untouched and uninvolved by school activities. In this respect, her work and behaviour came somewhere between what teachers expected and what was disapproved of. By the end of the third year her report summarized this position.

The third-year report indicated that while Mary had improved in some subjects she had deteriorated in others. Nevertheless, in terms of effort she obtained four B grades, five C grades and two D grades. In particular, there was a distinction between her work in practical subjects – art, home economics and needlework, where she obtained C grades for attainment – and academic subjects, such as geography, science and

First-year report on Mary Rushton

Date 13.vi.70   Age 12 years 0 months
Attendance C

Subject	Grade Effort	Attainment	Comment
English	C	C	Mary's problem is concentration. Her work has improved and if she keeps trying and reading her work will get even better.
Physical education	C	C	Could do better with more effort.
Maths	C	D	Could do better with more effort.
Religious education	C+	C	At times Mary does good work.
Geography	C−	C+	Mary needs to go into more detail.
General science	C−	C−	I am sure Mary could do better.
Art	C−	C−	Could put in more effort.
French	C−	D	Must make more effort.
Home economics	C	C	Rather easily distracted – can produce some good work.
Drama			Keen – took part in school production.
Music	C+	C+	Satisfactory.
History	B	C−	Mary's work has improved. She must try to write more legibly.
Needlework	D	D	Disappointing. I think Mary must stir herself to produce much better work.

Group tutor: Mary is cheerful and has a helpful attitude. I feel that at times she could make more effort to participate fully in class life.
                                                                                       A. Harding

Head of house: Mary must try that bit harder.
                                                                                       T. Coyne
                                                                       Head of Southwark House

Headmaster: Can be good but must try much harder to make full use of her abilities.
                                                                                       G. Goddard
                                                                                       Headmaster

Note: All teachers' initials have been removed.

Third-year report on Mary Rushton

Date February 1972   Age 13 years 7 months
Attendance E

| Subject | Grade | | Comment |
	Effort	Attainment	
Needlework	C	C−	Mary has not decided to make a great effort to improve.
English	C	C	Mary is not working to the best of her ability. She is too easily satisfied with a low standard of work.
Art	B	C	Mary works well.
Music	B	D	Disappointing exam. result.
Geography	D	D	Has not worked. Exam. disappointing.
History	B	C	Mary has tried – result disappointing – 43%, 28th.
Home economics	B	C	57%. Mary works well in class. A very capable and reliable girl.
Maths	C	D	Mary can work well but her written work is often spoilt by its untidy appearance. She can be easily distracted although there has been some improvement here lately and she has shown more interest in what she is doing.
Physical education	C	D	Mary could do better. I'm hoping to see an improvement.
Religious education	C	C	Reasonable work but room for more effort.
Science	D	D	A disappointing standard. Mary can and must show a more willing attitude towards her work.

Group tutor: This is not really a good report. Mary doesn't come to school to work but to waste time. She must improve this attitude. She also does very little when tutor group or house activities are organized.   L. Dowd

Head of house: Mary has a pleasant personality but is obviously too easy-going. Her attendance record must improve.   B. Pennington
                                                Head ot Southwark House

Headmaster: This is not good enough. Much more effort is needed.
                                                  G. Goddard

Note: All teachers' initials have been removed.   Headmaster

mathematics, where she obtained D grades. In academic subjects her work and general attitude were below teachers' expectations in comparison with her peers. This work record was utilized by teachers to decide the courses she could take in her fourth and fifth years. Teachers were convinced that there was little evidence to suggest Mary would be prepared to do sufficient work in school or prepare for public examinations in the fifth year.

The criteria that teachers used to allocate pupils to the Newsom course were a negative attitude towards school work and a facility for practical rather than academic subjects. Mary met all the criteria and was therefore allocated a place on the Newsom course. Her fourth year in the Newsom department was her last 'effective' year in the school. Mary attended classes on a sporadic basis. Often she would be seen around the school but not at lessons. I soon discovered that her lesson truancy was well known by staff and pupils alike. However, the size of the school meant that this behaviour was difficult to prove. In class, she would participate only when she was in the mood or when teachers bullied her into working.

During the fourth year teachers not only became aware of her lesson truancy but also her periods of prolonged absence. When Mary returned from one long absence she told several Newsom teachers that she had 'trouble' at home. She explained that her parents had separated and her mother was left with all the children. In these circumstances, Mary claimed that she needed to take time off school to help her mother look after her younger brothers and sisters. It was therefore her prolonged absence, lack of work and general behaviour that characterized her fourth year and was reflected in her end-of-year report.

This report indicated that Mary was still considered relatively able by her teachers. Indeed, an opportunity had initially existed to enter for a public examination: she had been allocated to the GCE set for religious education and to the third set for mathematics. However, her periods of prolonged absence, her problems at home and the quality of her work resulted in a situation whereby Mary drifted through the fourth year without making any positive contribution to school work.

During the fifth year Mary attended school for a brief period in the first term, followed by a long absence. Rumours were quick to spread. Some pupils claimed that she was just 'wagging it', while others said (enviously) that she had got herself a job.[37] Meanwhile, some of her friends had heard that she had gone to live in Eire with her grandmother. This last story was confirmed by a note from her mother who said that she had gone to live in Eire with her grandmother as 'she was very depressed about me [her mother] and her father breaking up and the welfare lady thought this was a very good idea for a few months'.[38]

By the end of January Mary was back at school. Immediately she returned, she busied herself talking to teachers and pupils about her visit

Fourth-year report on Mary Rushton

Date July 1973
Attendance C

Subject	Grade Effort	Attainment	Comment
Newsom		C	Mary can work quickly and quietly but often chooses not to in order to attract attention.
English	C	C	Works well in spasms – usually arrives inadequately prepared to work properly.
Maths set C		18½% 11%	Can work well but needs to be driven too frequently.
Religious education (GCE C Group)		9%	Mary, while no bother, seems to get very little from this lesson. She is welcome to stay but she has no chance of passing an exam. in this next year. A pity for she has the ability.

Group tutor: Mary must adopt a more consistent approach to her work if she is to benefit satisfactorily. I would like to see the sensible attitude she shows in tutorial time extended to her lessons.

D. Gilmore

Head of house: Mary has had her difficulties this term and she has done well to cope with them.

B. Pennington
Head of Southwark House

Headmaster: Try to keep up your efforts.

G. Goddard
Headmaster

Note: All teachers' initials have been removed.

to Eire. Despite her stories about Eire and her grandmother, teachers and pupils refused to believe them, preferring to think she had held a temporary job somewhere in Merston and had recently been dismissed. Now that Mary was back at school she followed a similar routine to the one she had adopted before her absence; attendance at classes and at school was intermittent. She always maintained that school was of little use to her as she wished to be a hairdresser.

This case study of Mary Rushton is not as detailed as those of David Jones and Sean Kelly, because she was only in school for brief periods during her fourth and fifth year. However, her case is included here because White and Brockington (1978) have suggested that we need to know more about those pupils who rarely attend school and are relatively unknown by teachers. Mary's case illustrates the process by which she became a Newsom pupil, her relationships with teachers and her attitudes to school. Mary was also broadly representative of a group of pupils showing ability in some subjects, but choosing to drift through the school and end their school careers with periods of prolonged absence. As a consequence such pupils were little known by their teachers in the final year. In fact no final report could be issued on Mary Rushton as she had been absent from school for so long.

The significance of the cases

These three case studies might be regarded as extreme examples of Newsom pupils. While each of the cases refers to the characteristics of an individual they are, as has been indicated, broadly representative of different pupils within the department. They had different life histories, experiences of school and sets of relationships with teachers. These cases have also been selected to examine pupil profiles and the way in which pupils were allocated to the Newsom course. David Jones was recognized by his teachers as an intelligent boy who started his secondary school career with good work and behaviour. A series of misdemeanours in his second and third years resulted in several problems for David, among which were his relationships with teachers and the transformation of his identity (as recorded in his personal file). Parallel with these developments, David's academic work reflected a lack of interest or effort. By the end of his third year, David met all the criteria for being placed on the Newsom course. Despite the fact that David liked the Newsom staff and the activities they provided, he still had to attend classes in other parts of the school taken by teachers whom he disliked. The result was that David engaged in prolonged periods of truancy, including lesson truancy from classes that took place outside the Newsom department.

In Sean's case we have a pupil who had experienced educational failure in primary school, reinforced by failure in the secondary school.

During his lower school career at McGregor, he made no progress in basic subjects. As a result of his relative backwardness and his desire to leave school at the first opportunity, he was placed in the Newsom department. Although Sean claimed that he liked the activities provided by the department he would truant from some of these classes as well as lessons taken in subject departments. Sean never found an area of school which captured his interest, with the result that he was in constant trouble with teachers throughout the final stages of his school career.

Finally, Mary's case is illustrative of a girl who lacked commitment to school work. A series of lengthy absences meant that she was known by relatively few teachers. In her last two years at school, she was allocated to the Newsom course. She drifted along in this in much the same way as she had in the earlier part of her secondary schooling. She remained relatively untouched by the school, neither gaining rewards nor having major sanctions imposed against her.

These three portraits raise questions about the way in which pupils were allocated to the Newsom department, their school experiences, their relationships with teachers and the ways in which situations were defined by teachers. This account suggests that teachers allocated pupils to the Newsom course on the basis of an adverse behavioural record, an adverse academic record, lack of motivation, lack of commitment, and prolonged absence. No pupil had to meet all these criteria but a combination of several items was sufficient to be placed on the Newsom course.

In their study of deviant pupils, Hargreaves, Hester and Mellor (1975) suggest that one way teachers classify pupils can be explained through a theory of typing,[39] which is used to make sense of pupils' experiences. The theory suggests that pupils are typed in three stages. Firstly, a stage based on 'speculation' when the teacher initially meets the pupil. Secondly, 'elaboration' when teachers verify their initial impressions and, finally, 'stabilization' when teachers establish a clear identity for the pupil. These stages can be used to understand the processes involved in becoming a Newsom pupil.

Speculation

During this stage the teacher begins by utilizing background information on the pupil. The primary school record may be used together with first-hand impressions of the pupil. At this point, teachers establish hypotheses about pupils that are subsequently checked out. As Hargreaves, Hester and Mellor (1975, 150) remark: 'The initial typing is used to make sense of what the pupil has done so far, but it also points forward in time by suggesting the kind of person the pupil will perhaps turn out to be'. This stage in the pupil's career is apparent in our three case studies. The two pupils whose identities were most easily established

were those of Sean and Mary. In the case of Sean his difficulties with
school work and his limited ability suggested that he would become a
member of the Newsom course. In Mary's case, her record card provided
teachers with details of her difficulties resulting from family circumstances. In both cases, pupils were initially defined as problematic for
teachers.

David was seen in favourable terms by teachers as far as behaviour
and academic work were concerned. However, one incident in his second
year resulted in a situation whereby his house head began to de-typify
him: that is, she began to restructure the identity of this pupil and his
family contained in the official school record.

Elaboration

During this phase, it is argued by Hargreaves, Hester and Mellor (1975)
that teachers verify their initial impressions and are concerned with confirming their initial view. Again, in the cases of Sean and Mary, the
accounts provided by teachers in houses and subject departments suggest
that their initial impressions were confirmed. In Sean's case, the teachers'
impressions of a pupil with severe difficulties were reinforced by confirmation from an external agent (the educational psychologist). Furthermore, his abilities in *practical* rather than *academic* subjects coupled with
his behaviour compared to that of his peers (cf. Hargreaves, Hester and
Mellor 1975, 279–80) was sufficient to confirm the teachers' view that he
was unsuitable for external examinations but suitable for the Newsom
course. In Mary's case, we have a pupil who received few positive or
negative judgements from teachers. However, frequent absence together
with lack of motivation suggested that she was destined for the Newsom
course. Finally, in David's case the impression that had been created by
his first head of house was confirmed for his second house head by actions
and activities considered deviant. He was seen to constitute a problem,
because his behaviour was regarded as unfavourable when compared to
many of his peers. Furthermore, his academic work began to decline, with
the result that by the end of his third year he was seen by teachers as a boy
who could achieve more in *practical* than in *academic* subjects and who
could constitute a behavioural problem for them. In this sense, he was
regarded as a suitable pupil for the Newsom course.

Stabilization

This stage applies when teachers have categorized their pupils; when they
are no longer surprised by their actions or activities. In this respect, it
could be argued that this stage confirms the previous two stages of typing.
The McGregor pupils' position as members of the Newsom department

confirmed their teachers' initial conceptions. All the pupils no longer wished to work, were considered in negative terms as far as behaviour was concerned, lacked commitment to school work and were frequently absent.

Finally, the case studies indicate that the impressions held by teachers in houses and departments during the first three years of secondary schooling were used when decisions were taken about the course that pupils would follow in their final years at school. However, we have tended to dwell more upon the pupils' encounters with house heads and subject department teachers than with members of the Newsom department. We therefore turn now to see who the Newsom teachers were, how they became Newsom teachers and what their views of Newsom pupils were on the basis of their work with them.

Notes

1   See Hargreaves (1977, 279–80), who considers that these processes of typification are based upon (a) familiarity with similar pupils, with the result that pupils who belong to a group are typed on the basis of the teacher's knowledge of a few members of the group, and (b) peer matching where the teachers compare pupils with their peers.

2   Cf. White and Brockington (1978, 19–20).

3   Cf. White and Brockington (1978, 4).

4   See Newsom (1963, 194–233).

5   At this point we might consider the value of such composite pictures and the extent to which they distort reality.

6   For accounts of pupils that correspond closely to Newsom pupils and which begin to address some of these issues see White and Brockington (1978), White (1980) and Willis (1977).

7   For a discussion of the way in which elements of secondary schooling are organized on the basis of gender see Delamont (1980). For a discussion of contradictions in female education see Sharpe (1976, 121–58), and for a discussion of sexism in schools see, for example, Deem (1978, 39–54). For a similar situation in a college of further education see Stanworth (1980). For a discussion of ways in which this can be further investigated see, for example, Delamont (1981, esp. 78–80).

8   For a discussion that considers whether schools should maintain personal records on pupils see Winter (1976).

9   For accounts of life histories and their use see, for example, Becker (1966), Burgess (1982a, 131–5, 146–51), Denzin (1970), Langness (1965) and Mandelbaum (1973).

10 Interview with David Jones.

11 Interview with David Jones.

12 The age group to which David belonged was the last group of Roman Catholic pupils who had to sit the eleven-plus examination in Merston.

13 Interview with David Jones.

14 ibid.

15 Cf. Woods (1976a).

16 Interview with David Jones.

17 This point was confirmed not only by my observations and by remarks made by other teachers but also in a note about pupil behaviour she had written to the headmaster, in which she had remarked that she was 'difficult to please'.

18 Cf. Lacey (1970, 50–1) on 'best pupil' roles, and Sharp and Green (1975, 154) on the 'ideal pupil' role.

19 Interview with David Jones.

20 Comment by the house head on a commendation slip (given to pupils for doing good work) included in David Jones's file.

21 Education welfare officer's report contained in David Jones's personal file.

22 For a discussion of the links between behavioural and academic expectations among pupils see Lacey (1970, 82–5).

23 Copy of internal (hand-written) note from Maggie Rolls to Peter Horne in David Jones's personal file.

24 For an account of pastoral care seen in these terms see, for example, Best, Jarvis and Ribbins (1977).

25 Her views, however, need to be treated with a certain amount of circumspection. For a similar form of teacher opinion see, for example, Moody (1968).

26 Interview with David Jones.

27 ibid.

28 For an account of 'bullshitting' in the form of tall stories see Mukerji (1978).

29 For a detailed discussion of David's punishments see Burgess (1982b).

30 Interview with David Jones.

31 For an account of 'doing nothing' outside school see Corrigan (1979, 119–41).

32 Interview with David Jones.

33 Educational psychologist's report on Sean Kelly.

34 Interview with Sean Kelly.

35 Interview with Sean Kelly.

36 This concept of 'drift' is adapted from Matza (1964, 28–30) who argues that drift is a state of limbo between convention and crime.

37 Some pupils who did not come to school for long periods of time did get themselves temporary jobs which were, of course, illegal. Clive Smith worked on several jobs in his last two years 'at school' as a milk roundsman, a lorry driver's mate and as an industrial cleaner. Alan King was away for several months working as a window cleaner and only returned to school when the man who owned the business got a smaller van and as a consequence could no longer take him along.

38 Letter written by Mary Rushton's mother to the head of Southwark House.

39 See Hargreaves, Hester and Mellor (1975, 140–216). For further developments on the use of the concept of typification in the sociology of education see Hargreaves (1977).

7

NEWSOM TEACHERS AND

NEWSOM TEACHING

In studying the Newsom department I looked at Newsom teachers, Newsom pupils and their relationships with each other. While the previous chapter concentrated on pupils, this chapter focuses on teachers. Both will be brought together again in the final chapter. This separation of teachers and pupils is, as Delamont (1976, 41) suggests, somewhat artificial. However, I have attempted to develop links between the chapters on pupils and teachers by following common themes. In the previous chapter I examined the characteristics of pupils and the way in which they became members of the Newsom department, while in this chapter I am concerned with the characteristics of a Newsom teacher and the processes involved in becoming one. In turn, I examine the understanding that Newsom teachers had of their pupils' problems. A further theme underlying this chapter is the ways in which Newsom teachers defined school activities that were different from those definitions provided by teachers who worked in houses and other departments.

The observations I made in the school and in the department led me to several considerations: what strategies did the headmaster use to staff this department? Who were the Newsom teachers and why did they join the department? What processes were involved in becoming a Newsom teacher? What teaching ideologies were involved in Newsom teaching and how were these formulated by teachers?

Teachers and teaching

Teaching is an occupation, which as Hirst (1971) and Goodman (1971) maintain, takes many different forms. In this respect, there is a diverse literature on teaching, written from an educational as well as from a sociological perspective. Much of the educational material is not concerned with what actually exists or what actually occurs in school but is more interested in what *should* occur. As Morrison and McIntyre (1969, 13) have shown, much educational research on teachers has been devoted to what constitutes the 'good' or 'effective' teacher. Meanwhile, sociological writers have directed their attention towards teachers as an occupational group,[1] the teaching profession,[2] recruitment patterns,[3] teaching as a career,[4] teacher roles[5] and teacher–pupil interaction in the classroom.[6]

The work on teacher roles has stressed the *ideal* situation. Wilson (1962) considers the role of the teacher to be concerned with the transmission of knowledge and values, eliciting respect and establishing rules of personal behaviour which are acceptable to society. Meanwhile, Hoyle (1969, 59–60) lists fourteen subroles that can be attached to the teacher among which are included judge, helper, referee, detective and friend. These abstract analyses indicate the characteristics associated with the teacher, but do not relate to particular teachers in particular schools. Even some of the empirical studies on teacher roles (cf. Musgrove and Taylor 1969; Grace 1972) do not discuss what actually happens to teachers in their everyday work. However, recent studies of classroom interaction have contributed to our understanding of teachers and teaching. Nevertheless, there is a lack of material on teachers working with children who might be described as lower working-class, culturally deprived, low ability, non-academic or problem pupils: the reluctant learners.[7] It is to this task that we now turn.

Teachers for non-academic pupils

Several writers in Britain and the United States have suggested that teacher preparation concentrates on ideal situations. Becker (1952b) remarks that teaching techniques are often aimed at the 'ideal' or 'perfect' client. This results in difficulties for the teacher working with pupils who are not committed to schools and school work. As the pupils in these classes present problems, it is often difficult to recruit teachers specifically to work with non-academic pupils. Indeed, the Newsom committee indicated that average and below-average pupils had a proportion of teachers who could not secure other appointments and a large number of teachers who stayed for only short periods of service. They summed up the problem by saying:

One of the problems, as many heads assure us, in finding teachers for our pupils is just the lack of a sufficiently attractive professional image. Most people enjoy teaching the abler pupils: the response is quicker and surer, interest is more readily established and maintained – and discipline the easier for that reason – and the teacher welcomes the sense of intellectual challenge. (Newsom 1963, 99.)

Fifteen years later the situation showed little change as White and Brockington (1978, 3) reported: 'According to both unions, teacher unwillingness to be involved in the teaching of "low ability" pupils is certainly as endemic as ever'. The Newsom committee (Newsom 1963, 78–108) had argued that average and below-average pupils required highly skilled teachers who could communicate easily and well. However, they maintained that these teachers should have qualifications which cut across the divisions of specialist and non-specialist, practical and academic, and should have experience of the world beyond school.

At McGregor, Goddard wanted teachers with a variety of talents who could work with Newsom pupils. He found from his early experience that 'those who got most success [with Newsom pupils] could roll with the punches. They were people who could understand why a youngster goes to sleep [in a lesson] without taking offence.'[8] But finding such people, getting them to apply for a Newsom post and appointing them to the department was not an easy task. Goddard wished to maintain maximum flexibility and therefore worded his advertisements for Newsom work in broad terms, making reference to the raising of the school-leaving age (ROSLA). One such advertisement was worded:

> ROSLA–Newsom: An interested teacher to join an experienced staff involved in planning the third round of ROSLA activities. ROSLA group teaching is limited to half a timetable and thus other subjects should be stated. Art, games, craft, technical subjects and others advantageous.[9]

This job description attempted to make the post look attractive. Firstly, it involved Newsom (old style) and ROSLA (new style) work.[10] Secondly, the appointee would be involved in curriculum planning as well as teaching. Finally, almost any practical subject was considered advantageous for this post. This strategy prevented anyone who was interested in this work being ruled out by subject requirements. In the further particulars the job was described in more detail. Here, Goddard indicated that teachers appointed to the Newsom department would have to:

help solve such problems as
(a) identification and persuasion of suitable Newsom candidates among present third-year pupils
(b) evaluation of present fourth-year programmes

(c) modifications to fourth-year programmes and individual time-tables for Newsom pupils in the fourth year

(d) design of programmes for Newsom fifth year

(e) organization of resources required/available for Newsom programme

(f) improvements in movement to and from Newsom groups to and from other options

(g) increasing the participation by 'outsiders' in programmes

(h) contributing to 'humanities and recreational' fourth-year programmes and establishing which suit Newsom pupils and which Newsom pupils suit which programmes.

Unlike other positions in the school, Newsom posts were not neatly subdivided into pastoral or academic work, because both elements of the teacher's job were brought together.[11] These posts required skills that were essential for pastoral work, as teachers had to organize and administer courses and establish links with outside agencies. Secondly, in common with subject teachers it demanded skills in curriculum development, design and evaluation, and participation in inter-disciplinary links between the Newsom course and other areas of the curriculum. However, in common with other appointments Mr Goddard wanted teachers whose approach to discipline and attitude to children could be relied upon. To provide some inducement to teachers to take up these duties, scale 2 and scale 3 salaries were available.[12] In short, he was looking for teachers with potential who were interested in developing a career in teaching in general and Newsom work in particular.

The skills that the headmaster sought in the ideal Newsom teacher were detailed in his job descriptions. However, as we shall see, these advertisements did not recruit large numbers of teachers and as a consequence he adopted several strategies for appointing Newsom staff. In turn, when these teachers were appointed they defined and redefined their tasks to achieve some success in their teaching.

Recruitment to Newsom: staffing strategies

Goddard had realized that it would not be easy to recruit teachers to work with Newsom pupils, so he decided to look for potential Newsom teachers when advertising his first posts for the school. All initial advertisements and sets of further particulars therefore asked intending applicants to outline their interest and/or expertise in working on Newsom courses. There was sufficient response from those teachers who were to lead houses and departments to indicate that some form of Newsom programme could be mounted.

Initially, Newsom work was an area of responsibility allocated to a house head who co-ordinated all aspects of curriculum planning. This gave Goddard a breathing-space in which to decide how to organize Newsom staffing; he realized that if he appointed a head of department in this area he or she would have to be incorporated into the departmental decision-making body which he feared was already becoming too large. Towards the end of the second year Goddard decided to appoint a teacher who would be 'in charge' of Newsom courses. This maintained flexibility, although he was still uncertain about the final staffing pattern for the department and the school.

Among a series of applications for a new position of head of house, Goddard received an application from Sylvia Robinson, a teacher who had worked in a neighbouring school at Oldtown where he had been a head. He knew Sylvia from those days and remembered her as 'a bright and breezy and very vigorous PE mistress, who was enormously enthusiastic and a wee bit jolly hockey sticks. Very keen and very enthusiastic.'[13] As Sylvia had more teaching experience than many people already appointed to the staff, she was invited to be interviewed for the post of head of house. However, Goddard told me that when he saw her at the interview he was doubtful if she had the skill and ability to be a house head, a post involving demands from both teachers and pupils. In these circumstances, he decided not to appoint her to this post. However, the Newsom position still had to be filled and Sylvia had expressed interest in this area and careers work. For the position of teacher in charge of Newsom, Goddard explained that he 'wanted someone active, vigorous and outgoing where if something did go wrong it wasn't absolutely critical'.[14] He decided therefore that Sylvia should be offered this position.

Sylvia Robinson had a similar story concerning her appointment but with a slightly different emphasis. She told me that she had originally applied for the post of head of house[15] but had been persuaded by Mr Goddard to take up the joint position in Newsom and careers for a scale 3 – a post which she held until July 1973, after which she merely had formal responsibility for careers. Here, Goddard's initial strategy of appointing someone to lead Newsom was based on persuasion plus financial incentive in the form of a scale post, a strategy that was used again some two years later.

In the spring term of 1973 Sylvia was given the choice of either becoming head of the Newsom department or head of careers, because Goddard now had sufficient points (in what was by now a school of almost 1200 pupils) to create separate posts. As Sylvia decided to take up the careers post,[16] Goddard advertised two new posts of responsibility in the Newsom department to take effect from the autumn term. The advertisement stated that the school had:

Two posts for teachers interested in expanding the present Newsom provision, a scale 2 and a scale 3 are available.

When this advertisement became public Sylvia was quick to criticize. She openly said that the headmaster would be lucky to get anyone to apply for these posts because the financial incentives were not sufficiently high for teachers to be attracted to work with difficult pupils. Other teachers were also interested; they knew that if the posts were unfilled they could be asked to teach Newsom pupils. Gossip continually circulated about the posts. Some staff had heard that no applications had been received, while others maintained that there were no more than a handful of applications. Some of the rumours were confirmed when the shortlist was published on the common room noticeboard. Only three candidates had been short-listed for the two posts: two external candidates and Terry Goodwin who had been appointed to McGregor when it opened. Terry held a scale 1 post[17] in the home economics department and was doing some teaching with Newsom girls for the first time that year.

When I talked to Terry about her application she explained that it had not been her idea to apply for another job in the school but the head-master's. Apparently, Mr Goddard had gone to see her and said that he had had few applications for the Newsom posts. He was pleased with her Newsom work and indicated that she should be able to obtain one of the posts. He suggested that a Newsom post would only involve slightly more Newsom teaching than she was currently doing. However, he did not make any promise of a definite appointment.[18] For Terry, this provided an alternative route for promotion and additional money: she was unlikely to get a similar opportunity in her own department since she had been involved in several disagreements with the head of department. Accord-ingly, Terry had applied for a Newsom post.

On the day of the interview an external candidate withdrew from the field leaving two applicants for two posts. Both candidates were inter-viewed and Terry Goodwin was given the post. Once again, Goddard had overcome part of his staffing problem by further persuasion. On this occasion he had persuaded an existing member of staff to do some more teaching in the Newsom area in return for additional money, by means of the added status of a scale 2 post.[19] In this instance, Goddard's strategy of appointing Newsom teachers from his own staff was by negotiation and exchange; that is, he negotiated the appointment and exchanged additional money in return for Newsom teaching.

These strategies of alternative appointments for external candidates and negotiated appointments for internal candidates to Newsom posts were to be used again. After Terry Goodwin's appointment to the Newsom department, Goddard still had the problem of insufficient teachers to cover Newsom work. Late in the summer term he was still conducting interviews for other positions. This provided a further opportunity to look for Newsom teachers.

Among the posts advertised for September 1973 was a post in technical subjects for which Tony Davis initially applied. Tony told me that he had applied for a series of posts in mathematics, science and technical subjects in other schools to try to obtain promotion and additional money. When Tony was interviewed for the post in the technical department at McGregor, the head had shown an interest in his work with fourth- and fifth-year pupils and with young people in youth groups. During the interview, Goddard had worked his way round to discussing with Tony the possibility of combining some work in technical subjects with some teaching in the Newsom department for a scale 2 post. Tony agreed to take this position but said to me that he only took the Newsom work because of the scale 2 financial incentive. So this appointment was also made by offering the candidate an alternative post with some promotion and additional money in return for a block of Newsom teaching.

While this might have solved most of Goddard's staffing problems in the Newsom department, it did not solve everything. Keith Dryden, who had successfully taught canoeing and boat building to many Newsom boys, had in the late part of the summer term applied for the post of head of art which was advertised with a scale 3 salary. However, Karen Shaw, who had also worked in the art department for the same period as Keith, had also applied for the post. Here, Keith believed that Goddard, not wishing to offend or cause embarrassment, had arrived at a compromise by appointing an external candidate. Karen and Keith were given what Keith termed scale 2 'consolation prizes'. However, Keith was not satisfied as he had only been restored to a point on the salary scale which he held before coming to McGregor.[20] He therefore made an appointment to see the head to discuss opportunities for further promotion.

Keith realized that he was in a strong position to bargain with the head. By the end of the summer term it was well known that Goddard had experienced some difficulty in filling Newsom posts. Keith, who taught canoeing to several Newsom boys, was renowned in the school and in the authority for his success in this area. Some of the boys had recently been chosen for the authority's display team and for this Keith had earned much credit. Keith knew this strengthened his bargaining position and told me that he intended to initiate negotiations for promotion. Indeed, if it was not forthcoming he would threaten to resign. With few teachers able, ready and willing to take Newsom work, Keith had a strong case. When additional appointments were made in the autumn term the head found an additional point to promote Keith, 'from scale 2 to scale 3 with added responsibility for Newsom work in the fourth and fifth years'.[21] With this appointment all the major positions within the Newsom department had been allocated.

Much to Sylvia's disgust and to the disgust of other members of the department, there was no individual who held the post of head of department. All the Newsom teachers, unlike other staff, were expected to work in subject departments together with their Newsom commitments. However, they were placed on a salary career grade in return for taking Newsom classes. In these circumstances the teachers had invested their careers in this department (cf. Woods 1979, 167) because they had been unable to obtain alternative teaching posts. Now they had to develop a strong commitment to Newsom teaching if they were to advance their careers by this route, as Goddard maintained that all Newsom teachers were members of a team holding equal status. The result was a series of internal conflicts between teachers who adopted various career strategies.

Sylvia believed the department needed a scale 4 or 5 appointment if it was to have equal status with other departments. Indeed, she indicated that if it had been a scale 5 position she would have taken it, as it would have provided more money and increased her status. Although Sylvia was not head of the Newsom department she took the lead in all department meetings. This gave her the opportunity to define the business and to attempt to manipulate other teachers in the department. At the first departmental meeting in the autumn term Terry, Tony, Sylvia and myself were present. Sylvia asked: 'How should the department be controlled? Is a leader required?' Before any of us could reply she advanced the view that a head of department at scale 4 or 5 was required. Terry agreed saying that such a post would give status to the department and its work (a comment that suggested she had discussed the matter with Sylvia). Keith Dryden and Tony Davis did not join in these discussions but it was evident from future conversations that Sylvia had encouraged them to think about having a head of department. Indeed, it provided each teacher with an opportunity to think about his or her own chances of promotion.

Terry quickly withdrew from the struggle for promotion. As her husband was going to move south, she started to apply for posts outside the school from the middle of the autumn term. This stepped up the pressure on Tony and Keith. Tony told me that with Terry leaving (quite possibly at Easter) and with Sylvia in charge of careers he could see that the field was wide open for either Keith or himself. Tony thought that if he attempted to reorganize the department it would help him impress the head and so gain the post. He began therefore to busy himself with Newsom administration. A rash of notices suddenly appeared in the common room showing the composition of Newsom groups. All the lists clearly bore Tony's signature and thus his wish to gain credit for his organizing abilities. In addition, Tony also took on the task of liaison with the local technical college which organized 'link courses'[22] for Newsom pupils. Despite his attempts to take charge of the department there was competition from other quarters.

Sylvia still remained the unofficial self-appointed 'head' of the Newsom department. She made a point of discussing Newsom work with many teachers, with the result that those individuals who did a little teaching in the department consulted her about their work. Furthermore, she made it clear to Terry, Tony and myself that the secretarial staff still continued to send her all the letters and invoices which concerned the department. One day she announced that she had been asked by the deputy head to write a paper on Newsom work in the school. This annoyed the other Newsom teachers, because the way she described the invitation implied that she was the officially acknowledged 'head' of department. This was a further indication that Sylvia wanted the status she associated with a head of department and with senior teachers.

When Keith Dryden was given a scale 3 post for his Newsom work, Tony and Terry felt that this was unfair to them. As far as they were concerned, Keith did not take enough Newsom classes to warrant this additional money. However, for Tony the situation was more serious as he considered that Keith would now try to become head of the department. There were few developments in the latter part of the autumn term but by January I was aware that Keith was interested in being head of the department. In conversation with several other teachers who were talking to Keith and myself, it was remarked that Newsom teachers were without a head of department to represent them at the heads of departments' meetings. Several of the others suggested Keith for the job but he indicated that he was only prepared to take this on for added status and additional money.

At a Newsom department meeting, Keith introduced the issues that had been raised in our conversation a few days earlier. He considered it important to have a Newsom representative at the heads of departments' meeting who, he argued, should hold a scale 4 or 5 post. The others agreed, but Tony added that the person appointed should not hold a post in another department. If this was approved, he would be in line to get the post as Keith and Sylvia had some of their points for work in other departments. However, when Keith sent a log of decisions from the meeting to the headmaster, only his initial remarks were included. Goddard never reached any decision that was made public and no head of department was appointed, since he maintained that the Newsom teachers worked best as a team. However, both Keith and Tony still continued to try and gain support for a post at a later date.[23]

These career strategies developed by Newsom teachers contribute to our understanding of the headmaster's staffing strategy within the department. At first sight it might appear that gaining an appointment in the Newsom department was relatively easy, as negotiation between the headmaster and an intending Newsom teacher resulted in promotion and financial incentives for the teacher. In these circumstances, it might appear that the same rewards were there for any teacher prepared to take Newsom groups. However, in making appointments Mr Goddard had only given the teachers one scale point each for their work *within* the department. Each teacher, therefore, had equal formal status in terms of their salary within the department, regardless of their general status within the school, and there was no head of department. These two factors contributed to the conflict and competition among Newsom teachers, because they had to develop a strong commitment to the department if they wished to gain promotion. Goddard's strategy for making appointments to this department was also part of the process of becoming a Newsom teacher to which we now turn.

Becoming a Newsom teacher

The processes involved when an individual takes up a new activity, a new style of life or a new occupation have been widely studied in sociology (cf. Becker 1968; Weinberg 1968). In education there are many studies of teachers and teaching which have focused on induction years (cf. Cornwell 1965; Cope 1971; Taylor and Dale 1971) and the teachers' probationary year (Hannam, Smyth and Stephenson 1976). However, as Lacey (1977, 45) remarks, much of this work has concentrated on teacher attitudes rather than the processes involved in becoming a teacher. Accordingly, his study of student-teacher socialization[24] concentrates upon the novice who searches for different ways to teach and for methods 'to get by'. This approach can also be used to help analyse what happens when teachers obtain new appointments.

Whenever teachers take up new posts they are faced with different classes, new colleagues, new books, new equipment and new ideas. They become novices in the new situation, as they have to orientate themselves to a new set of tasks. When I joined the Newsom staff at Bishop McGregor School, I became aware of several developments in my teaching style. In particular, I found that I shifted towards the 'established' pattern of teaching within the department. It is to this experience and that of other teachers in the department that we now turn to discuss social relations among teachers and between teachers and pupils which contributed to the process of becoming a Newsom teacher.

Initial ideas

For most teachers the words 'Newsom pupils' create an image of pupils who are not prepared to settle into the routine of conventional schooling. Indeed, as we saw in chapter six, Newsom pupils cannot be classified by their ability; they are better classified in terms of their attitudes towards schools, teachers and school work. Newsom pupils were perceived by most teachers at McGregor as unsuitable for examination courses. However, alternative courses had to be provided as there was no 'ready-made' syllabus for them. Newsom teachers were, therefore, required to devise a new programme.

The headmaster gave Newsom teachers no illusions about their pupils. In the summer term before the start of the fifth-year Newsom course, he met all Newsom teachers. As some teachers were new to the department Goddard spent some time talking to us about the pupils. He explained that many of them were in Newsom because 'They have alien-ated their teachers in the lower part of the school'. Terry agreed and remarked, 'It's because of shortcomings like this that they are in Newsom'. She continued by saying that although many of them would often be late for lessons, hate to work and were noisy they were 'a nice bunch of kids'. This was confirmed by Keith and Sylvia who were ready to cite examples of reformed rakes and Newsom pupils whom they would rather teach than pupils in other classes.

It appeared that the Newsom teachers all held a favourable picture of their pupils. This puzzled me, as initially I had found many of the pupils loud-mouthed, perverse, uncooperative and lazy. Tony Davis, who was to join the staff the following term, had come to McGregor for this meeting. He looked bewildered by the teachers' statements. In conversation after the meeting he explained that his experience did not accord with those of his future colleagues as he exclaimed, 'This job involves teaching a bunch of scruffs'. His remark was immediately taken up by Sylvia Robinson who commented, 'They might be scruffs to other people but they are very acceptable to us'. Tony made no reply but looked as if he was waiting to be convinced. In future meetings before the start of the autumn term, Tony made it clear that he had different ideas from his colleagues. He thought the pupils would work at a very low standard and constantly referred to working 'at their level'. Indeed, he did not consider it necessary to have any special skills to teach brickwork, pottery and interior design to Newsom pupils.

At this stage, meetings of the newly formed Newsom department provided an opportunity for staff to discuss freely impressions of their pupils. The teachers appreciated that Newsom pupils constituted a problem to other teachers and to some extent for themselves. However, they were not prepared to see these pupils simply labelled by their deviant activities. Tony was therefore the subject of some criticism for his comments on pupils who at that stage he did not know.

Course planning

Course planning brought the staff closer to the reality of the classroom. Unlike other subjects where teachers had merely to follow an examination syllabus defined by the public examination boards, Newsom teachers had to set about constructing their own syllabus. Here, they looked at their task in ideal terms.

Those teachers who had worked with the Newsom pupils examined their 'successes' and their resources in order to plan the core elements of the course. Terry's classes in cookery and mothercraft were taken as examples of activities that could be developed in the coming year. Terry maintained that it was possible to do continental cookery with the Newsom pupils and that in mothercraft they could be entered for an examination. Sylvia claimed that it was possible for the pupils to take an examination in first aid.

At this stage nobody mentioned the pupils: their qualities, inadequacies, strengths and weaknesses. Instead, the syllabus was constructed around topics that had been previously taught with some success and which we as Newsom teachers might offer. In many cases, the 'subjects' or courses we were prepared to offer were no more than topics based around hobbies, interests and simplified versions of our own subjects.[25] This was the case with the wine-making option which Jim Parkes insisted on taking as he remarked to me, 'I only teach a few periods of Newsom because it gives me an opportunity to follow up my hobbies in school time'. As far as 'subjects' were concerned, Terry was offering a version of home economics and some of Keith's classes were an offshoot of his initial training. Furthermore, Tony Davis who had been trained in technical subjects was prepared to do courses in cabinet making, building and jewellery making. Sylvia had a scientific background and intended to give a basic mathematics course based on the National Savings 'money matters' project. I myself offered a general studies course that had at its core elements of social studies that could be discussed in relation to the locality.

By the end of our planning sessions in the summer term, it appeared that we could cover all the Newsom periods on the timetable. The pupils were to be given a series of courses based on teachers' interests and areas of expertise. However, no account was taken of actual Newsom pupils at this stage. Plans for the curriculum were instead based on what the Newsom teachers thought should be done and what they felt they were capable of teaching.

The first crisis in Newsom

At the beginning of the autumn term we faced reality. The abstract talk of timetables, pupils, syllabi and curricula were brought to bear on real pupils, in real classes. Our ideals took a knock before the first day of term. Much of the equipment which had been ordered during the previous term had not arrived, the rooms which were essential for practical work were not available and because of further modifications to the timetable, additional groups had been allocated to teachers for which there were no plans. Such difficulties demanded an urgent Newsom meeting. Despite the fact that departments could hold pre-term planning meetings, Newsom teachers were unable to come together because their presence was demanded at meetings with other departments for whom they taught. As a result, the first opportunity for Newsom teachers to meet was in their first scheduled session with pupils at the beginning of term. Fortunately, one teacher had been scheduled to use the audio-visual aids room. This allowed us to put all the pupils together with the teacher who screened a film he had found in the stock cupboard that morning. While he 'entertained' the group we retreated to another room to look at staffing, room allocation and curricula once more. This was the reality of being a Newsom teacher where handling minor crises was an everyday activity.

In this meeting we had to deal with a real situation. I describe the situation as I saw it. The group met in Sylvia's room which had been used to store materials for the Newsom department. It contained piles of departmental stock and equipment. One book case was crammed with pink exercise books which had been ordered for Newsom work in the previous year but never used. In the far corner was a pile of games and boxes of unopened Childwall project material[26] which appeared never to have been moved since they were originally dumped in that position.

Although Sylvia was no longer in charge of the department she still assumed control. She placed chairs around in front of her desk, behind which she sat to address Tony, Keith, Terry and myself. Sylvia posed the problems and waited for our answers. 'How are we going to get rooms? How are we going to obtain equipment? What are we going to do with the pupils in extra lessons?' she asked. Terry was the first to respond. She considered that we might subdivide the pupils again and allocate further practical work. Sylvia agreed. She said she could keep one group fully occupied tidying up her study for part of the term, after which she suggested Tony and Keith could come along with a group of boys to decorate it. The very idea sparked off debate. It was evident from the expression on Tony's face that he was not prepared to support this idea. He remarked, 'I think there is already too much practical work in the courses'. Terry disagreed claiming that practical activities were the only way in which pupils could be involved in work. However, Tony managed to persuade the others that more 'theory' work should be done and volunteered to take this on himself. It was reluctantly agreed that this was the only way to solve the problem of inadequate rooms and a lack of equipment.

Keith Dryden had said little up to this point. It was evident that he was quietly fuming. He was still not satisfied with the 'solution' as it was impossible for him to work without adequate rooms and equipment. This started Terry off again because she did not have the equipment which had been ordered for her screen printing. By this time some three-quarters of an hour had passed and Sylvia attempted to sum up our decisions. She said she would be contacting the deputy head to get further rooms for our groups. However, Keith doubted if this would result in any satisfaction. The bell went to signal the end of the 'lesson' and we heard a door burst open followed by shouting and cheering as our Newsom pupils ran out of the block towards the school gate. It was the end of the afternoon. We finished our meeting and left Sylvia in her room. Keith walked away grumbling about the lack of provision. 'How can we teach properly if things are like this?' he asked. We all agreed that something had to be done. Keith remarked, 'Sylvia's all right but we shouldn't leave everything for her to do, otherwise it'll be a mess'. He and Tony therefore agreed to contact the deputy head separately to get further rooms so that we could begin teaching in the second week of term.

This situation revealed some of the main problems in being a Newsom teacher. It was possible to plan a syllabus and to arrange groups for an ideal situation before the start of term but this was subject to alterations in the light of room allocation and staffing changes. Furthermore, a department without a recognized leader received a raw deal when it came to timetables, room allocation, co-ordination and checking up on equipment, stock and facilities. It relied continually on goodwill and volunteers to take on different tasks. Still, this early crisis had been solved but others were to arise before the term was much older.

Handling crises and learning to teach in the Newsom department

In the second week of term we started our Newsom courses. Tony quickly found that he had problems. On Tuesdays he had what he described as his 'worst day' with six periods of Newsom work and a fifth-year tutorial which contained several Newsom pupils. In addition, he thought he had too much Newsom work as all his craft groups were really Newsom classes in disguise. He taught only two classes outside the fourth and fifth year that were not in Newsom. As the weeks went by, Tony began to find further problems. He had come from a school with a 'tough' reputation. Accordingly, his tactics for dealing with fourth- and fifth-year pupils were to 'grind them down', 'keep their noses to the grindstone' and 'prevent them from stepping out of line'. However, these tactics did not work with Newsom pupils at Bishop McGregor School.

By the third week of term, Tony looked tired, drawn and very pale. Each time he came to the staff room to sit down he greeted me with the words, 'Oh dear'. Towards the end of the third week trouble showed up in one of Tony's groups in the shape of Peter Vincent. Tony told me after one lesson that he had sent Peter Vincent to his head of house to be caned. I was puzzled. My time in the school had taught me that this was not the kind of punishment that pupils or subject teachers associated with Newsom teachers, so I enquired what had happened. Tony explained that

Peter had been throwing acorns around the room. Tony had told him to stop and pick them all up. Predictably Peter had refused and remarked, 'You can't make me do that'; a classic ploy.[27] Tony had not been prepared for this reaction from a pupil. He repeated his request but Peter continued to be provocative by threatening to damage Tony's car. This had been as much as Tony could tolerate, with the result that Peter had been sent to Gill Davies (his head of house) and later caned. I listened carefully to the story, which was the first of several accounts I was to hear that day. When Sylvia got to me she recounted the story and added, 'There was no need for this to have happened. You and I know that Peter was only joking. He's not the sort of person to do that kind of damage' (smashing Tony's car). Sylvia thought that Tony had handled the situation badly because in her view Peter had done nothing to warrant being hauled before his house head and caned.

As the term continued, Tony's initial enthusiasm for Newsom teaching began to wane. He repeatedly told me that the courses he had planned were not running smoothly. While he was not getting real trouble from Newsom pupils, he was still finding it difficult to get them to work. I agreed that the pupils could be difficult but provided they were allowed to settle with their own interests they would work in my classes. However, Tony disliked situations where pupils refused to do the work he had planned, lacked proper equipment, and wandered around the classroom or sat and gazed into space. In his view, this was not 'proper teaching': classes were just drifting aimlessly and pupils were not engaged in set work. But he was assured by Keith, Sylvia and myself that this constituted 'real' Newsom teaching. We argued that it was essential to change the pace of classes and allow pupils to engage in a variety of activities alongside the set work. In this respect, Tony was being introduced to the way in which Newsom teaching was the subject of bargains and negotiations between teachers and pupils (see chapter eight).

Tony remained unconvinced. He thought that our approach proved his point. The whole department was drifting, we were not engaged in proper teaching nor in the activities we had planned. He was disillusioned with Newsom teaching. He did not need to say this as the expression on his face clearly told the story. By early October (just six weeks after the term had started) he was contemplating staying away from school but decided against it as he maintained 'Newsom classes are too difficult to leave to other people'. By mid-October the problem was no better. One break time Tony came into the staff room and reviewed his options with me. 'I could always get a job elsewhere or I could get a temporary job as a carpenter until the relevant post comes up', he said. For days he considered resigning but eventually decided against it. He decided that he would try and sort out the department as this might earn him a scale 3 post and additional financial rewards.[28]

Tony Davis's introduction to the Newsom department, to its work and its pupils in the autumn term was similar to my experience in the summer term (see chapter five). During that time I had acquainted myself with some of the norms that were held by Newsom teachers in order to come to terms with the situation and lead a tolerable existence. Firstly, pupils were not forced to follow the curriculum that had been planned but were allowed to engage in a diverse range of activities. Secondly, if pupils did not wish to work for a teacher they were allowed to sit and gaze out of the window or go to sleep, or wander around the room. Thirdly, when they created problems for the teacher in the classroom they were *not* sent to heads of houses – the normal procedure in other classes. They were dealt with in the classroom. Fourthly, punishment of Newsom pupils by Newsom staff was minimal and physical punishment was non-existent. Tony had evidently not observed the actions and activities of his colleagues and was therefore finding it difficult to subscribe to the norms of the department, which contributed to the day-to-day activities of 'teaching'.

In the second half of the autumn term, things were no better for Tony. He existed on a day-to-day basis, hoping that the more difficult pupils would be absent from school when they had lessons with him. He also expected pupils to adhere to the standards of discipline maintained by the house heads; an expectation which continued to present him with problems. As the second part of the term progressed his courses were continually obstructed by the pupils until he reached a stage where he allowed pupils to go to sleep on the benches, laze around in the classroom, go out of the room and wander around the school grounds. However, he explained that he followed this pattern of 'work' because 'It is difficult to know what to do with the fifth-year pupils', and in particular, 'It's too difficult to have to put up with Peter Vincent and Sean Kelly all the lesson if you try and make them work'. By the end of term the titles attached to Tony's courses had little in common with the content. This was discussed by the pupils who had stopped complaining about his classes. His new strategy now earned him a reputation as 'a good teacher' with whom it was possible to 'have a laugh'.[29] When I asked how the classes were different, the pupils told me they were now allowed to sit around, make cups of coffee, listen to records, look through magazines and work when they wanted (a style of teaching that will be explored in more detail in the following chapter). Tony was now a Newsom teacher.

When Tony was appointed to the Newsom department he was a qualified teacher but not a Newsom teacher. In this respect, his first term at McGregor was a period in which he had to learn how to become a 'proper' Newsom teacher who provided pupils with some freedom in the classroom. When plans were made for Newsom work, Tony, in common with other Newsom teachers, conceived the courses in 'ideal terms'.

However, Tony was not in tune with the teaching styles adopted by his colleagues and attempted to put these 'ideal' plans into operation. This resulted in situations where pupils created trouble in his classes and Tony reacted by punishing them. While this was in keeping with the rules adopted by other teachers, it was unusual for teachers in the department. So Tony found Newsom teaching difficult until he adopted the teaching methods used by his Newsom colleagues. His definition of what constituted a class lesson, Newsom work and Newsom activities underwent several changes in the first term until he was teaching in much the same way as other members of the department. In this sense, just as Lacey's student teachers (Lacey 1977) learned new sets of norms, so this teacher had gone through a learning process until he had adopted the teaching style used by other members of the department.

Newsom teachers and teaching styles

The process of becoming a teacher is, as we have seen, developmental. Fuchs (1969) and Lacey (1977, 78–80) consider that the honeymoon period, marked by euphoria and heightened awareness, is the initial experience for teachers. But for the Newsom teacher this period only exists in the pre-pupil contact phase. Indeed, many teachers who are confronted with Newsom pupils suffer culture shock and conflict in the classroom because they do not have their role expectations fulfilled. If Newsom teachers are to obtain some success, they need to redefine the teacher role.

We have already seen how an inexperienced Newsom teacher resolved his problems by taking on the teaching style that was used by other Newsom teachers in the school. This process led me to ask: who are the Newsom teachers? How do the teachers see themselves and how do they define their duties? To address these questions I began to collect brief life histories[30] of Newsom teachers.

A career biography written by Sylvia Robinson focused on her family and educational background:

> Father died when in Seaside in 1939 at the age of 24. Mother as a young widow returned to grandmother in Leyton and my sister aged 5 years and myself aged 2 years. Also in grandmother's house during the war years were two single aunts. Grandmother went blind about 1935. I lived for nine years in the centre of the City of Leyton in a densely populated Catholic area and attended the local school. The only child in the school to pass the 11+ and went to St Cuthbert's High School. First year in which 1944 Act of 'every child sitting the exam' being put into practice. Mother remarried in October 1947 and stepfather agreed to allow me to take up a grammar school place. Left

school December 1953 after completing one term in 6th doing physics, maths, chemistry at 'A' level to take up employment as laboratory assistant with an industrial company. After leaving school did continuous voluntary youth work with 13–18-year-olds as a Grail Member and attended annual leadership courses from 1954–66.

1958–60 – St Joseph's Training College (Advanced Maths, Advanced PE, subsidiary Biology) – awarded gold medal for proficiency in practical teaching.

1960–3 – First post at St Joseph's Convent Grammar School attended by invitation of head. Assistant in middle school maths, science and PE.

1963–6 – Senior mistress co-educational bilateral school – again by invitation.

1966–70 – Returned home because of mother's illness and took up head of PE post in local school.

1970–1 – Amalgamation of boys and girls on one campus.

1971–4 – Interviewed for head of house [at Bishop McGregor School] but agreed to take up care of Newsom as I had been accepted for a one-year course in counselling at a university but could not get secondment. Head of house – a difficult position for release. Newsom and careers responsibility since.

The characteristics in Sylvia's life history in terms of family background, education and educational failure, troubled home life and teaching career had much in common with other Newsom teachers, especially Keith Dryden who wrote in his career biography:

I was born and raised in a mining area, have three brothers and three sisters. My mother is the daughter of a farm labourer and was until marriage a committed Methodist. My father, from a family with ten children, was the son of a lock keeper on the canal system – the family had a thriving business in coal delivery and smallholdings where they kept pigs and other livestock. The family were of no denomination though vaguely (very) deist.

The first home I can remember was on a council estate ('3 bedrooms') quite close to my father's job which was a position of driving-handyman for a firm that made fertiliser (a glue factory is another less-attractive euphemism). The local primary school had obviously expanded to take in 'the bulge' years of 1947–8 when I was born and consisted of one very large three-classroomed unit made of corrugated iron and four joined terrapin huts. The junior section built in 1911 was of the most mundane usual type. Streaming of sorts was employed in the infants, and very rigid streaming in the junior three-form entry, 40ish to a class. I was placed in the upper stream and remained there (usually coming 26–7 in overall class position) until 3rd year (9–10) when I suddenly 'spurted' to occupy one of the top five positions for the final two years. Our year was the first in the local authority not to take the 11+ examination (1958–9) but were transferred to secondary school on recommendations of our teachers. I was sent to the nearest grammar school from my home where alienation set in! I was alienated from home not school however! I took 'O' levels in 1964 and passed the seven we were able to take, after six months' constant battle with home I was allowed under severe sufferance to go into the sixth form where I took chemistry, biology, art, French and general studies, dropped French after a year and then proceeded to pass four 'A' levels with average-ish grades and because I couldn't think of anything else to do I applied to university to do psychology with education and biology 'quelle dommage' – further alienation, too much distraction and a 'poor attitude' and I ended up at training college in Merston the following year.

I had during vacations at school and on every Friday night and all day Saturday worked in a supermarket, a skivvy-cum-warehouse-man. The year I left university I worked on a conveyor belt picking offal from amongst bones before they fell into a crusher to become bone meal. I found the 'academic' standards of Merston Training College very easy to slip into the B–C grade range and so muddled my way through, working as a roof tiler's mate, labourer in a sand-and-gravel quarry and labourer at a concrete block works during the holidays.

I enjoyed teaching practice and after dispensing very quickly with an attempt to assume authoritarian attitudes – it wasn't me and I'm not a good enough actor and don't kids appreciate sincerity? Sometimes?! I then got my first post at St Augustine's Comprehensive, a baptism at the deep end as far as Newsom children go – I had 12 periods in my first year, 16 in my second. I had a head of department who 'didn't like that sort of child'. I got a little fed up of it however and applied to McGregor dropping a scale post. I had two nominal Newsom periods in my first year here and now have ten periods plus a scale 3. I have worked as a stocktaker in a factory and as electrician's mate during my summer vacations since beginning teaching.

While Sylvia and Keith had much in common, I also found that they shared some characteristics with Terry Goodwin and Tony Davis. Furthermore, some of the distinctive traits of the main Newsom teachers were also shared by other staff who took a minor role in the department. Personal experience was used to help understand Newsom work and to contribute to teaching style.[31]

Family background

Both Keith's and Sylvia's family background could be described as working class. Even before I asked for a brief life history Sylvia had talked about her family. Among the string of facts, gossip and innuendo with which she regaled me was the point that her family was working class. She demonstrated her point by talking about her family's poverty, the area in which they had lived, the type of primary school she had attended and her family's attitude towards education. She regularly told teachers that she could get along with Newsom pupils because she could identify with their family backgrounds. 'I've got a similar background to them,' she exclaimed, 'that's what helps me to understand all that they do.' However, these remarks were not reserved for teachers' ears as Newsom pupils often told me, 'Miss Robinson told us all about her family this morning'. Similarly, other teachers told me that they got a résumé of Sylvia's 'life story' from the pupils. Keith considered that this gossip was a strategy which Sylvia used to identify with the pupils. Certainly, it had been of interest when originally told but was no longer 'hot news'. Several pupils pronounced it 'boring' and 'a drag' while one girl summed up most pupils' feelings when she remarked, 'I know exactly what she's going to say as soon as she starts. I've heard so much about her gran that I can say all the words along with her. It's boring.' Nevertheless, in the early days of fourth-year Newsom work, gossip about family life had helped Sylvia to communicate with the pupils.

Keith also came from a working-class family which he claimed helped him to understand what life was like at home for many pupils. He considered that some teachers could not understand what home life was like for pupils who belonged to large families living in small houses. Unlike Sylvia, Keith did not articulate his life story either to the staff or to pupils. However, when he talked to me about his personal account, he did claim that he used his family experience in order to understand his pupils.

Educational experience

Education was naturally a common topic of conversation among the teachers. Often I found the Newsom teachers would illustrate points they wished to make from their own educational experience, while on other occasions they would provide anecdotes about their time at school and college. With this material I could examine the characteristics of their educational careers. In each case the Newsom teachers had confronted some problem in their own educational careers. Sylvia regretted that she was forced to leave school before taking 'A' levels as this made her a late entrant to college and to the teaching profession. Keith's life history also revealed several problems in his educational career. First, the struggle with his family to allow him to take a sixth-form course, followed by a period at university ending in failure in the first-year examinations because he had done so little work.

Terry Goodwin always claimed that she saw no reason to presuppose children would enjoy school because she could remember hating it. As a consequence, she said, she had frequently wasted her time by playing around with other pupils. One day, amid gales of laughter, she told a group of us that her own school career had ended abruptly when she was expelled because she was a disruptive child. Tony Davis had also experienced early educational 'failure' as he had not done sufficiently well in the 11+ examination to gain a grammar school place. Finally, the headmaster, who worked with Newsom pupils each week, had experienced educational failure at a later stage as he had 'cracked up' while studying at university.[32]

For all the teachers who worked in the Newsom area, 'education' had constituted a problem at some stage in their lives. In some cases this included some form of educational failure. However, they considered that these experiences also contributed to their understanding of Newsom pupils who were daily confronted with the problem of school and with their lack of educational success in conventional subjects.

Skills for teaching

Among those teachers who predominantly worked with Newsom pupils and those who assisted in the department there was some common experience in terms of their initial training as teachers. The Newsom teachers recruited to the McGregor staff had been trained either in science or in practical subjects. Among those who had a scientific training were Sylvia Robinson, Jim Parkes and the headmaster, while those with a training in practical subjects included Keith Dryden, Terry Goodwin, Tony Davis and David Smith.

In addition to their initial training, two teachers had also taken a leadership course. Sylvia had attended several leadership courses and had been offered a place on a counselling course at a university before she joined McGregor. Furthermore, she continued to extend her expertise in this area by attending local authority in-service courses on counselling. Meanwhile, Tony Davis told me that he had worked as a youth-club leader before joining Bishop McGregor School.

Initial training together with personal experience helped the teachers to plan Newsom activities. The teachers' expertise was used, as suggested by the Newsom committee, to produce simplified practical courses. Some courses involved the adaptation of scientific principles to practical situations in 'electricity in the home', 'wine making', and 'film making and photography'. Similarly, the teachers' practical experiences were reflected in courses on 'canoeing and boat building', 'food' and 'painting and decorating'. Meanwhile, Sylvia's and Tony's experiences in youth work contributed to the idea that Newsom work could not be fitted into the pastoral/academic dichotomy which was dominant in the school. Certainly, Sylvia made the claim that Newsom work involved as much time talking to pupils (which she termed 'counselling') as it did in transmitting knowledge in a particular subject.

In this respect, Newsom teachers were in some senses an identifiable group. They shared certain characteristics in terms of descriptive social class, family and educational background. Similarly, in terms of their subject qualifications and initial teacher training there was a common body of experience. These common characteristics contributed to their understanding of Newsom pupils and their work in the department. In short, these experiences were 'qualifications' that could be used to develop a teaching style in the Newsom department and which were based on particular teaching ideologies: that is, a set of beliefs and ideas considered to be the essential features of Newsom teaching.[33]

Teachers' ideologies

I found that the way Newsom teachers worked with the pupils was based principally on their ideas about pupils' problems. How they perceived these problems influenced their ideas about the Newsom course and their activities in the classroom. In short, the teachers developed a set of ideologies that guided their activities: what they thought *should* be planned and done and what *was* done in the classroom.[34]

A recent account on ROSLA/Newsom work by White and Brockington (1978, 4) states that the central problem for Newsom pupils is being in school. Certainly, this reaffirms the evidence provided in part one of the Newsom Report where a conversation is quoted between a boy who had just left school and his former headmaster. When the headmaster asked the boy what he thought of the new school buildings he replied, 'It could all be marble, sir, but it would still be a bloody school'.[35] This remark summarizes the feelings many Newsom pupils had about school. Indeed, the Newsom teachers at McGregor agreed that the main problem for their pupils was the fact that they had to come to school. However, some Newsom teachers considered the school constituted the problem for the pupils, while others thought the pupils and their home backgrounds were the cause of problems in school.

The school as a problem

Newsom teachers frequently discussed the reasons for pupils' problems. Keith Dryden considered that he was a 'liberal' as far as educational philosophy was concerned. He was taking several of the social science based education courses with the Open University where he had become acquainted with some of the 'radical writing' on schools and education.[36] He was convinced that the central problem in education had been correctly diagnosed by the radical writers in their accounts of schools. Keith therefore considered that at McGregor it was the organization, rules, routines and values which constituted a problem for Newsom pupils. He saw that whatever Newsom teachers provided was only a temporary solution to the school 'problem', because pupils were confronted with another form of education and schooling when they went to other departments and to their houses. Keith Dryden summed this up by stating, 'When they [the Newsom pupils] are here [at McGregor] they have to be a part of the school'. Keith explained that although the Newsom pupils worked separately in Ushaw block they were still part of the formal structure of the school when they joined other fourth- and fifth-year pupils in houses and departments. He considered that problems arose when Newsom pupils had to participate in house assemblies and subject classes. Here, they were bound by the same rules which governed the actions and activities of other pupils.

Terry Goodwin agreed with Keith's diagnosis. She thought many Newsom pupils hated school because the experience was alien to them.[37] She supported her view with examples of things which pupils were expected to do in other departments and in houses. This led her to conclude that no sane person would make the demands on pupils made by some teachers. She indicated the rival expectations that were held by departments. Some insisted that no ball-point pens were to be used while others permitted their use. In some departments, she said dates were to be placed on the right-hand side of pages, while in others the opposite instruction was given. Similarly, in some departments titles were to be underlined while in others no underlining was requested. She considered these different routines would puzzle most people and constituted a particular problem for Newsom pupils.

The problem of the home and family

Sylvia Robinson and Tony Davis held a different view. They were prepared to agree that many of the pupils disliked school for the reasons which Terry and Keith had advanced. However, they also thought that problems with schooling had much to do with the individuals themselves. Sylvia could give examples of Newsom pupils whose parents were separated or divorced and where the children had been central to arguments. Sylvia quoted the case of Sean Kelly. She said that Sean's mother had walked out on the family leaving the children with the father. As a result, Sean was expected to look after the younger children during his father's absence. This 'evidence' allowed Sylvia to conclude that Sean found difficulty in adjusting to school and to relationships with teachers. Secondly, she recalled the case of Alan King who, she explained, had good relationships with women teachers but very poor relationships with men. She accounted for this by making reference to the poor relationship which Alan had with his father. For Sylvia, the family was the root cause of her pupils' problems.

In addition, Sylvia also looked at individual children's deficiencies to account for their problems with school. One pupil Sylvia frequently discussed was Janet Merritt, who was often absent because she had to attend hospital for special treatment. Sylvia said that Janet considered her weakness in school subjects could be attributed to her prolonged absence and therefore her parents were prepared to allow her to stay at school for a longer period so that she could follow CSE courses. Sylvia disagreed with this plan and told Janet that she did not consider her capable of CSE work as she had a spelling problem. Sylvia perceived the situation in similar terms for other Newsom pupils who she considered had problems with reading, writing and basic number work.

Tony Davis shared Sylvia's views on the pupils and their parents and looked towards them for an answer to the pupils' problems. He considered that the pupils' behaviour was as much a cause for concern as their work. He thought many pupils were too familiar with their teachers; a situation which he attributed to their relationships with parents. Similarly, he complained that Newsom pupils were often late for lessons, lacked equipment of their own and rarely wanted to work. So he concluded that it was the pupils' own shortcomings which accounted for their problems with school. Tony reached a similar conclusion to Sylvia: the Newsom pupils' problems with school could be linked to their family background and their personal deficiencies, and these deficiencies were highlighted in the school.

The Newsom staff were therefore agreed that their pupils were confronted with a problem through the very fact of having to be in school. The reasons they gave for their pupils' problems were diverse: some located these problems at the level of the school while others put them with the individual pupils and their family backgrounds. However, they all agreed that it was their task to provide some 'solutions'. This created problems for the teachers which Keith summarized by saying, 'What can you do with the pupils? What can you get them to do?' He explained that even when these questions had been resolved a series of further problems were presented: 'What standards do you aim at? What do you do if they [the pupils] say they don't want to do anything? What are the limits to which you are prepared to go?'[38] The teachers attempted to answer these questions in their day-to-day activities with the pupils. At McGregor, the Newsom staff claimed that their attempts to overcome the problems of school were for the benefit of the pupils, other teachers and ultimately other members of the school. Sylvia claimed, 'We keep our pupils occupied which allows the subject departments to get on uninterrupted. That way everybody is happy.' Such a remark led me to examine the different ways in which the Newsom teachers 'occupied' the pupils and engineered a 'solution' to the problem of school (see chapter eight).

Summary and conclusion

This chapter has focused on Newsom teachers and the ways in which they defined their activities. In particular, space has been devoted to the ways in which these teachers' appointments were different from those in other departments and in houses. An analysis of the way in which teachers were appointed to the Newsom department has provided an opportunity to examine the headmaster's staffing strategies. While it was relatively easy to obtain an appointment in the department, it was difficult to gain further promotion. The head's staffing strategy, therefore, promoted commitment to Newsom work among the Newsom teachers.

While teachers were appointed to the Newsom department, it still did not make them Newsom teachers. To become a Newsom teacher demanded a period of learning and a period of re-socialization by pupils and teachers; training and qualifications were not enough. Teachers of Newsom courses needed to draw on their own personal resources to teach the pupils. The final part of this chapter has therefore involved brief life histories of individual teachers. An analysis has been made of the way in which these teachers' personal and educational experiences contributed to their understanding of their pupils and their pupils' problems. In turn, their ideas about their pupils contributed to the way in which they defined the situation in the department, devised the Newsom programme and adopted a teaching style, all of which are examined in chapter eight.

Notes

1 See, for example, Tropp (1957).
2 See, for example, Kelsall and Kelsall (1969).
3 See, for example, Floud and Scott (1961).
4 See, for example, Kelsall and Kelsall (1969, 82–136).
5 There are countless discussions of teacher roles. See, for example, Kob (1961), Wilson (1962) and Hoyle (1969).
6 See, for example, the papers in Chanan and Delamont (1975), Stubbs and Delamont (1976), Hammersley and Woods (1976), Woods and Hammersley (1977) and Woods (1980a, 1980b).
7 For two studies produced by teachers see White and Brockington (1978) and White (1980). Both discuss work at the Bayswater Centre in Bristol where an attempt is made to provide an alternative education with 'problem pupils'.

8 Interview with the headmaster.

9 Advertisement sent to the local education authority's staffing office, 3 April 1973.

10 'Newsom' was taken from the Newsom Report (Newsom 1963) while ROSLA was taken from the decision to raise the school-leaving age to sixteen (Department of Education and Science 1971: Circular 8/71).

11 This supported the Newsom committee's recommendations. See Newsom (1963, 78–108).

12 In 1973–4 when the research was done, scale 2 salary was £1446 to £2533 and scale 3 salary was £1718 to £2658.

13 Interview with the headmaster.

14 ibid.

15 Sylvia Robinson always wanted to be a house head or a senior teacher in the school. During 1973–4 she applied for further senior posts: head of Arundel House and director of studies (a post at senior teacher level). She claimed that all these posts involved work that she already did, so much so that she regarded the job description for director of studies as a thinly veiled description of her post. However, she was never promoted above her careers post and therefore resigned from the staff to take up a job with a neighbouring authority, which carried with it a possibility that she might be upgraded to senior mistress. However, she always associated with senior members of the school (see chapter three).

16 Although head of careers, it was agreed with the headmaster that she would still take a large number of Newsom classes.

17 In 1973–4 the salary for a teacher on scale 1 was £1306–£2406.

18 This was a statement that the head had made in the first set of further particulars for teaching posts. However, many promotions were internal to the school.

19 In 1973–4 promotion from a scale 1 to a scale 2 post merited an additional salary increment of approximately £235 depending on the incremental point an individual teacher was placed upon.

20 On coming to McGregor, Keith had gone down from a scale 2 to a scale 1 post.

21 List of additional positions filled within the school and posted in the staff common room, 2 November 1973.

22 Link courses were developed in technical colleges with a view to bridging the gap between school and work for pupils who had to remain at school and who were not taking public examinations.

23 At the end of the academic year Sylvia and Terry left the school, so the race for promotion was more open. In the following year Keith obtained a degree and a post of responsibility in the sixth form, while Tony was given a scale 3 post to be in charge of the Newsom department.

24 See Lacey (1977) and Lacey, Horton and Hoad (1973).

25 For a discussion of the way in which teachers modify the subject matter for different groups of pupils see Keddie (1971), and on Newsom courses see Burgess (1984b).

26 Project material which was specially purchased for use with the Newsom pupils.

27 For an account of strategies deployed by pupils with a new teacher see Ball (1980).

28 In 1973–4 promotion from a scale 2 to a scale 3 post merited an additional salary increment of approximately £415 depending on the incremental point an individual teacher was placed upon.

29 Cf. Woods (1976a).

30 For a discussion of this approach see Bertaux (1981), Burgess (1982a, 131–5, 146–51) and Mandelbaum (1973).

31 For a similar approach used by free school teachers see Swidler (1979, 55–82).

32 Account provided by the headmaster in his career biography.

33 For a further account of teaching ideologies see Sharp and Green (1975, 68–9).

34 Cf. the account of infant teachers' ideologies (King 1978, 10–15).

35 See Newsom (1963, 2).

36 See, for example, Holt (1969, 1970), Illich (1973) and Reimer (1971).

37 Cf. Wilmott (1969, 77) who states: 'Run bureaucratically with a formal structure of authority, with "morning assembly" and dinner queues and bells marking off the day, it is a strange and very different world from that of Mum and Gran and the corner shop'.

38 Fieldnotes.

8

TEACHERS, PUPILS

AND THE NEWSOM COURSE

This chapter is concerned with bringing Newsom pupils and their teachers together to analyse what happens when they meet each other in the classroom. Many studies of classrooms (cf. Hargreaves, Hester and Mellor 1975) have divorced classroom activities from the schools, the educational system and the society in which they are located. Furthermore, accounts of classroom interaction do not link the patterns of social interaction to the curriculum which is presented within the classrooms (cf. King 1978). These trends are related, in part, to the way classrooms have been studied. Some researchers have used observation schedules and structured research instruments to study classroom interaction,[1] while others have become so captivated by interactionism[2] that they have failed to locate their classrooms in a broader context.[3] This study has already located Bishop McGregor School within the Merston comprehensive system and the Newsom department in relation to the school. As a consequence, the activities that occurred in Newsom classrooms can be located within a social context.

My early impressions of the school, the Newsom department, its teachers and its pupils, raised several questions which I used to orientate my study. I began by asking: what is the Newsom course? How is this course seen by different members of the school (the headmaster, Newsom and non-Newsom teachers and Newsom pupils)? What counts as working on the Newsom course? What are the patterns of social relations that occur between the teachers and pupils in the Newsom department? Do the work and the relationships within the department influence patterns of teaching in other departments of the school? Although these questions were useful, I found that they needed to be supplemented by questions relating to definitions, negotiations and strategies between teachers, pupils, and teachers and pupils. Further questions that emerged included: how do teachers define the Newsom course? How do pupils define and redefine the course? What strategies, negotiations and bargains are used by the teachers and pupils? To what extent do activities in the Newsom department influence work within the core courses which Newsom pupils attend? This brings us full circle to a consideration of the influence of the Newsom department, its pupils and teachers upon the actions and activities of teachers in other parts of the school.

Defining the Newsom course

The headmaster's conception

We have already seen how the headmaster used positive definitions to communicate his ideas about the Newsom course to parents and pupils. Newsom courses were 'for young adults', 'to help pupils to mature' and 'for pupils to understand themselves and their world'. When talking to teachers and when advertising positions within the department, Mr Goddard still promoted a positive image. Newsom was an area for innovation and curriculum development, for experiment and ideas. Indeed, Goddard not only discussed these elements with his teachers but also showed how his hopes could be realized as Newsom teaching always featured on his own timetable. It was another area where he demonstrated how his ideas could be put into operation.

When writing about the department he defined its work in the following terms:

> For better or for worse we at McGregor use the word Newsom and define it as work on non-examination material designed for pupils for whom the maximum expectation of success in public examinations seems likely to be three CSE grade 5s or less.[4]

Here, despite all the positive attributes, the department and its pupils were defined in negative terms. In the Newsom course, pupils were to work on non-examination material because he thought they would meet with relatively little success in examinations compared with other pupils. This definition separated the Newsom course from the examination work of other fourth- and fifth-year pupils. This 'official' school definition was readily accepted by subject teachers as it legitimized their activities when they labelled a pupil 'suitable Newsom material'. Furthermore, pupils lacking conventional academic skills required for success in public examinations but possessing practical skills could be easily allocated to the Newsom course.

Goddard's definition provided a framework for Newsom teachers within which they could work. The definition helped them to identify pupils and their weaknesses in conventional secondary school work. In addition, it pointed to a demand for a course that would allow pupils to receive some positive evaluation from teachers. While there had been several recommendations (Newsom 1963, xvi–xviii) and suggestions for courses with 'average' and 'below average' pupils,[5] there was no set syllabus to which McGregor teachers could turn. The first task was to design a Newsom course; an activity that allows us to examine the model Newsom teachers used when discussing their pupils, the curriculum they designed and the strategies they planned to use to help their pupils achieve some success.

The Newsom teachers' conception of the course

As several new appointments were made to the Newsom department for the academic year 1973–4, some planning had to take place. The latter part of the summer term was therefore a time when Newsom department meetings were held to discuss the curriculum, the organization of teaching groups, staffing and resources. As a member of the department I was automatically involved in these discussions which revealed the teachers' philosophy together with the assumptions that they made about their pupils. There were two interrelated themes in these planning meetings: an analysis of the pupils' experiences of school and a discussion of the Newsom curriculum.

The pupils' experiences of school

In the first departmental meeting in the summer term, teachers who already taught Newsom pupils gave an account of the pupils to those who were new to this work. The focus was upon pupil characteristics and reasons for their being allocated to the department for the last two years of their schooling. This allowed some comparisons to be made between Newsom teachers' views of their pupils and those of their colleagues. In short, contrasting teacher typifications of Newsom pupils were examined. Sylvia Robinson indicated that many teachers were pleased when pupils were allocated to the Newsom department because this allowed examination classes to continue without those who were regarded as 'slow', 'rowdy', 'nuisances', 'troublemakers' and 'thicks'. While it was evident that Newsom pupils were disliked and considered in negative terms by house and departmental staff, it was equally apparent that they were regarded in positive terms by the Newsom teachers. Keith commented that they were 'nice ordinary kids'. At this remark, the headmaster laughed and said, 'What you've got to remember is that they might be a nice bunch of kids to you, but in the lower part of the school they have alienated many of their teachers'. He explained that conflict between pupils and teachers, together with poor home backgrounds, poor attendance and poor work records, accounted for pupils being allocated to the Newsom course.

Sylvia was happy to support his ideas. For her, it was the deficiencies of individuals and their families that made them potential Newsom pupils. Sylvia explained that Newsom pupils were frequently late for lessons, unprepared to work and difficult to motivate. Terry Goodwin remarked, 'It's because they are late and because they have failings that they are in Newsom'. Several of the others agreed as they knew that their pupils were perceived in this way by most teachers, who compared them unfavourably with their peers.

Having discussed the Newsom pupils, we were aware of our task. The children we had to teach were viewed in negative terms outside the department, experienced difficulties in meeting the main academic and behavioural expectations of their teachers, and as a consequence had little academic or personal success in the school. Faced with this situation Keith Dryden argued that members of the department had a duty to create situations for the pupils where they could gain some success. He was interrupted here by Sylvia who considered that it was important to decide on the characteristics of teaching groups before moving on to discuss course content. Sylvia advanced the view that Newsom pupils, although in a co-educational school, did not react well to being taught in mixed groups. Furthermore, she considered that the situations which the department provided for single-sex groups, such as mothercraft for girls and boat building for boys, had met with most success.[6] Jim Parkes agreed with Sylvia but for different reasons. He thought his courses in photography and wine making were more suited to boys than to girls or mixed groups. Keith Dryden and Terry Goodwin were opposed to such a move. They argued that within a mixed school it was unnatural to teach pupils in single-sex groups.

These early discussions helped me to identify the different positions and perspectives adopted by Newsom teachers. In turn, these differences influenced their relationships with each other, with pupils, with the groups they taught, and the content of the courses subsequently offered. As we shall see, the strategies teachers were able to adopt with pupils in their classrooms rested, in part, on the relative success of the strategies they adopted in meetings with their colleagues. If they were to teach particular courses to specific groups using certain rooms it was important to 'capture' facilities in departmental meetings. Planning meetings were important as the curriculum content and teaching programme were influenced by the decisions taken at departmental meetings.

Curriculum content

Further planning meetings in the summer term involved discussions about curriculum content. Here, the teachers began to establish their own initial definitions of the Newsom course. As Newsom was a course and not a subject, taken by all Newsom pupils alongside the core curriculum, it influenced teachers' plans. The Newsom teachers considered that their curriculum had to complement the core course and had to satisfy several criteria. Firstly, it had to allow pupils to utilize their practical skills in

Table 8.1   Areas in the Newsom curriculum at Bishop McGregor School, 1973–4

Areas	Subjects to be covered
1 Government, law and general studies	History, geography and social studies
2 Money matters	Basic mathematics and basic English
3 Mothercare/wood carving/ jewellery making/food	Woodwork, home economics, art
4 Going to work	Careers
5 Leisure	Physical education: swimming, horse riding, art and craft: light craft

which, it was generally agreed, they had more success. Secondly, the curriculum had to offer courses which would prepare pupils for work and adult life. Finally, it had to provide centres of interest through which history, geography and science could be taught, and in which pupils could gain some success. Sylvia advanced the view that the staff should sub-divide the curriculum into five areas (see table 8.1).

This five-fold division of the Newsom course was considered by teachers to be a 'balanced' curriculum, because it was their version of the principal academic, practical and recreational activities taken by other fourth- and fifth-year pupils outside the core course. This plan appeared to support the idea that school knowledge is stratified and subdivided into high-status and low-status knowledge, as the Newsom courses contained simplified material compared with that provided in examination classes. In short, curriculum content reinforced the distinction between the Newsom department and other departments.[7]

The curriculum which each Newsom pupil was to follow was to be based on one course from each of the five areas. However, each of these courses could only operate within the constraints of the school timetable, the staff that were available at given periods of the day (having been released from work within subject departments) and the resources which were available. School policy dictated that the timetable followed by fourth-year pupils would automatically be followed in the fifth year.[8] However, this was not a simple operation. New teachers had been appointed to the school and to the department and this was the first year in which a fifth-year Newsom course had to be offered. Staffing was therefore a major consideration and serious constraint on the type of Newsom courses that could be provided.

When the timetable became available at the end of the summer term, it was found that most Newsom classes were to be taken by teachers who held posts of responsibility within the department. However, some 'outside' help would come from the headmaster and members of the science, physical education and music departments. This knowledge helped the staff construct specific courses to cover the Newsom periods which appeared on the fifth-year timetable. The plan is summarized in table 8.2.

Within each double period some choice was involved as two or three courses were simultaneously on offer. Each pupil was to follow a range of courses where the emphasis was upon practical rather than academic work (at which they had failed in the lower part of the school).[9] Although these ideas were discussed in the summer term, nothing could be finalized until the following September when pupil numbers and room allocations would be available. However, teachers had to order equipment that was not held in the school since it would otherwise be impossible for the courses to take place. Accordingly, they decided to spend the departmental capitation allowance by ordering the following equipment:

Photographic and wine-making equipment
First-aid books
Textiles
Jewellery-making equipment
Woodwork vice
Books and film (on work)
Record player

However, some equipment never arrived as nobody took responsibility for processing the order.

By the start of the autumn term there was little equipment available for use on the courses. Further complications arose as the rooms that had been allocated to the department were unsuitable for practical classes. Keith complained that it was impossible to run boat-building classes in rooms that were normally used by subject departments. However, the

Table 8.2 Courses offered in Newsom time for fifth-year pupils at Bishop McGregor School, 1973–4

Day	Periods	Courses	Staff
Monday	1 + 2	Individual projects (job cards)	Headmaster
		Careers/television	Sylvia Robinson
Monday	3 + 4	Television/consumer project	Tony Davis
		Money matters	Sylvia Robinson
		Screen printing	Terry Goodwin
Tuesday	3 + 4	Jewellery making	Tony Davis
		Cookery	Terry Goodwin
		Film making/wine making	Jim Parkes
Tuesday	6 + 7	Social services	Headmaster
		Merston project	Bob Burgess
Wednesday	1 + 2	Leisure (swimming, hobbies, craft)	{ Sylvia Robinson
			{ Peter Horne
		Horse riding	Veronica Bateman
Wednesday	5 + 6	Practical electricity	David Evans
		First-aid theory groups	Tony Davis
Thursday	1 + 2	Boat building (boys)	Keith Dryden
		Careers/television/ Childwall project (girls)	Sylvia Robinson
Thursday	3 + 4	Money matters	Tony Davis
		Music	Mollie Richards
		General and local studies	Bob Burgess
Friday	1 + 2	Link courses (boys)	Technical college staff
		Mothercraft (girls)	Terry Goodwin
			Sylvia Robinson
Friday	3 + 4	Practical work	Tony Davis
			Sylvia Robinson

Note: Bishop McGregor School operated on a timetable that had seven periods each day and where each period was forty minutes long.

Newsom teachers decided that they should still try and offer the courses since much time and effort had been given to their initial plans.

The day before the autumn term started a series of staff meetings were held so that essential decisions could be taken concerning the organization and operation of the school. On this particular day, houses and departments were scheduled to hold meetings and finalize arrangements for the new term and academic year. This caused difficulties for the Newsom teachers. It was impossible to meet in departmental time because they were involved in subject department meetings. Some Newsom teachers also claimed that no further planning could be done until they met the pupils. We turn, therefore, to the first day of term when Newsom teachers and pupils met each other.

Meeting the pupils

Sylvia Robinson considered it important to explain to Newsom pupils something about their courses. She knew that the headmaster had talked to them about Newsom as a course that was essential for young adults. But she also appreciated that Goddard's definition of Newsom contained several ambiguities. She explained to me that it was quite logical for a pupil to ask why they should do the Newsom course when it was so different from the examination courses provided for most other pupils. Furthermore, Newsom pupils often asked why they should do any work.

She persuaded her colleagues that it was important to meet the pupils to explain what Newsom teachers thought their courses were about. On the first day of term we therefore met in the audio-visual aids room where Sylvia addressed the pupils. She told them that:

> Newsom may mean that you are doing two CSEs or perhaps three or perhaps four, not because you haven't the ability to do any more but because that is what you can cope with best. It's all done for you to cope with CSE and to follow other courses at the same time. Some of the courses will be for examinations and some will be non-examination courses. There will be some written work to do and some practical work to do.[10]

At this point, Sylvia attempted to 'sell' the department. She knew the Newsom course was viewed unfavourably by other teachers and pupils and she therefore tried to make it very positive. Like the headmaster, she made a comparison with examination courses but her emphasis was different. She stressed the way in which Newsom courses could help pupils to cope with their examination work. In this context, an attempt was made to build a bridge between the Newsom courses and other courses in the school. She claimed the Newsom course involved examination work which provided a further link with the main school curriculum. Finally, she maintained that it involved written and practical work as did other courses. In this respect, Sylvia was attempting to divest the Newsom course of some of the characteristics that separated it from the main school courses by defining it in terms different from those used by the headmaster.

Once the major orientation of the department had been explained other teachers gave five-minute talks about the courses they were to offer. Jim Parkes discussed his wine-making and film-making courses. He emphasized how it would be possible to make wine which would be suitable for Christmas presents. Keith Dryden also made his boat-building course sound attractive as he said that it might be possible to take an examination in this course which would help when it came to getting a job. Keith also emphasized that he would be happy to run other short courses according to pupil demand during the year. Next, Terry Goodwin explained how her food course would involve planning, cooking and eating meals each week. The mention of making mountains of chips seemed to cheer up most pupils who appeared bored by these course descriptions. Indeed, some pupils had already started to rest their heads on the desks.

Tony Davis talked next about jewellery making. He stressed how cheap it was to make jewellery which would involve design as well as production. Then I got an opportunity to talk about my course. In common with other teachers I focused on the practical element of the local studies option and how it would include many visits out of school. The words 'day out of school' were sufficient to generate some nods of approval from the pupils. Finally, Sylvia talked about her 'money matters' course. This would allow pupils to do some work in English and mathematics on topics like wages, insurance contributions and savings. Finally, she said that all these courses were designed to get them a better job. However, here was a further contradiction which the pupils were quick to raise: if you could get a better job by following the Newsom course, why was it only followed by pupils who took few examinations?

Several aspects of the Newsom course had been discussed in these meetings among teachers and between teachers and pupils. Firstly, the teachers planned an ideal course to be taught. Secondly, while the Newsom teachers defined their work they were forced to adopt the criteria used by teachers in subject departments: namely to make comparisons between their courses and examination courses. However, I still needed to follow up a series of questions like: how were the courses taught? What was the *actual* content of the courses? What was the relationship between the Newsom teachers and their pupils? What did the Newsom pupils think of the Newsom course? It is with these questions in mind that we turn to an analysis of the Newsom course.

Teaching strategies on the Newsom course

Teachers establish their own style of teaching by interpreting the rules, routines and curricula in a school. Clearly, this is possible in the 'private' world of the school classroom as Moody (1968, 953) shows in her discussion of life in a comprehensive school. She claims that:

> Apart from the informal pressures it is relatively easy for a teacher to behave and teach differently from other teachers – simply because in

the classroom she is king of the castle. There is no need to talk about it; you can just do it – quietly.

However, as Becker (1952a) and Woods (1977) have indicated, if teachers are going to remain teaching lower class, difficult or problem pupils, they have to accommodate to the situation. Becker (1952a, 474–5) maintains that this involves developing new techniques of teaching and discipline, being prepared to accept less work and rationalizing the pupils' behaviour. This complements the notion of teacher strategies[11] which include confrontation avoidance,[12] negotiation, truce and indulgence,[13] fraternization,[14] domination[15] and humour.[16] Woods considers that strategies are developed by teachers so that they can 'survive' in the classroom. Among the survival strategies he identifies are negotiation, fraternization, ritual, routine and morale boosting. However, survival strategies are linked to teacher control in the classroom.

I found that Newsom teachers at McGregor used several strategies in the course of their work. But to equate these strategies with teacher survival and the control of pupils would be far too limiting. Newsom teachers modified the curriculum they planned, had it modified for them and accordingly modified their teaching styles. The strategies that accompanied these processes of definition and redefinition were used to help create an 'alternative' pattern of schooling within the 'conventional' school. In short, the strategies adopted by teachers were used to provide some 'solution' to the problem of being in school.

Adapting the rules

We have already seen that the headmaster had a series of points of practice for all pupils which expressed the norms and values of the school. These were regularly reinforced by the head in his weekly assembly and by house heads in their assemblies (see chapters two and three). Newsom pupils were confronted with a series of expectations and the penalties involved for not fulfilling them. While I was at McGregor, smoking was common among pupils. Teachers regularly saw pupils heading for the boiler house – the meeting place for pupils who wished to smoke. To begin with only the location was acknowledged but no evidence of its use was available. However, by the spring term much evidence, in the form of cigarette ends and empty cigarette packets, was scattered around for all to see. When teachers walked up to the boiler house, pupils could be seen smoking, but by the time they arrived all the evidence had disappeared. Most young teachers were tired of existing in a situation where their authority was visibly challenged. They wanted some action taken against the smokers. A petition was therefore circulated by these teachers calling for support from the head and his senior staff. Many signatures were collected and the petition presented to the headmaster. In response, the house heads planned an 'attack' on the smoking area with the result that many smokers were caught and caned.

In the Newsom department there was a different routine. The pupils told me that David Smith (an art teacher who took Newsom classes) did not object to them smoking in his room during lunch breaks. Similarly, Keith Dryden told me that he adapted the no-smoking rule. He explained that he allowed Newsom pupils to go to the toilets for a smoke in the middle of lessons. Furthermore, the pupils told me that Tony Davis smoked in lessons that were held in the workshops and that he did not object if they used his stock cupboard as a place to smoke.

As I had doubts about the authenticity of these stories, I decided to check reports about Newsom teachers who allowed pupils to smoke. When I called on Tony Davis during a Newsom lesson in his workshop, I found him working at a bench with a cigarette balanced carefully on the edge. He would talk to the pupils, take a few 'drags' from his cigarette and return it to the bench. This was not the only smoke in the room. It appeared that some pupils had been smoking.

I found that I could check the smoking stories in my own course. When I took a group of Newsom pupils into the town we had to travel on the local service bus. The pupils boarded an empty bus at the terminus which was some distance from the school. They dashed up to the top deck of the bus and sat in the back seats. I followed and sat just in front of them. As the bus moved off, a boy leaned over my seat with a cigarette in one hand and cigarette lighter in the other. 'Do you mind if I smoke, sir?', he asked. I was uncertain about what to do. I knew the school rules and realized that if I allowed him to smoke I would be breaking the rules. Furthermore, if this was reported to the head by other passengers I would be in trouble and perhaps lose my right to do research.[17] On the other hand, I knew how smoking was treated in the department. To break with this tradition would create problems for my identity as a Newsom teacher. But I was unsure about what staff allowed pupils to do outside the school so I replied, 'You do whatever you would with other Newsom teachers'. 'Thanks very much', he said, lighting his cigarette. Soon the back of the bus was full of smoke as other pupils followed his example. 'You're just like Miss Robinson and Mr Dryden', remarked the pupils. They told me that Sylvia allowed them to smoke when they went on walks and that Keith took them round to his house where they could smoke. However, I still had to check these stories. A few days later when I was talking to Sylvia, I told her what had happened on the bus. The story amused her and she confirmed that smoking regularly occurred when she took pupils out of school. Similarly, Keith also confirmed the story about allowing pupils to smoke. The pupils and staff in the Newsom department had therefore adapted the no-smoking rule.[18]

The no-swearing rule was also adapted. Here, the staff inverted the rule which Goddard had enunciated in an assembly. The head explained that in future he would regard swearing at teachers as seriously as any assault upon their persons. He ended his talk by saying, 'I don't want to be head of a school where people swear at each other'.

I had been the only Newsom teacher in this assembly and so I was asked by my colleagues what Goddard had talked about. When I recounted the story Sylvia laughed and said, 'I'd hate to tell him that he is head of a place where people swear at each other'. I nodded in agreement. I had seen situations in the Newsom department and in my own lessons where arguments occurred between pupils resulting in a considerable amount of swearing. Similar situations were also discussed in many of the diaries that teachers kept for me.[19] They reported that pupils not only swore at each other but also at teachers. Tony Davis's diary indicated that swearing at him and to him was part of the daily routine. In particular he remarked of one class: 'The majority of boys worked on wood carving. Peter Vincent continued on coffee table amidst swearing and bad-tempered outbursts which is normal for the class.'[20] Tony indicated that this behaviour was 'normal' for the class, a point that could be supported on the basis of other conversations I witnessed between Newsom teachers and their pupils. Listening to Keith Dryden talk to two boys one evening, I noticed that he only swore on two occasions but covered it with the phrase, 'oops, that just slipped out' as a means of excusing himself when he swore in front of or at the pupils. This was a linguistic device that I also heard pupils use and which allowed them to swear in the presence of Newsom teachers without fear of sanctions being brought against them.

In these circumstances, Newsom pupils were prepared to redefine the situation. In a conversation with John Slattery, he explained that he had sworn at a teacher:

John   I told Mr Gear to well . . .
RB   What was this?
John   Well we were all supposed to do games last two periods on a Monday, about a couple of months ago. It was really wet so we couldn't go outside and I brought a note in saying I didn't want to do games.
RB   A genuine note?
John   Oh yes, written by me Mam. There was nothing wrong with me though, I just didn't wanna do games and so we all decided we wanted to play table tennis but Mr Gear wouldn't let me play so I said, 'Oh for fuck's sake'. He said, 'Would you mind repeating that?' I said, 'As long as I don't get into trouble'. He said, 'You're chicken' and I said, 'Well as long as I don't get into trouble' and he said 'Go on'. So I said it again and he told me to get out.[21]

This story was an accurate account of what had occurred in the lesson as it was repeated to me in similar terms by the teacher concerned. Despite the change in relationship between the teacher and the pupil further negotiation took place. The pupil was only prepared to repeat the obscenity in return for immunity from punishment. Here, the teacher was ready to comply with the pupil's wishes. The Newsom teachers had redefined the school rule but in turn the pupils had redefined the situation.

Flexibility

The Newsom teachers were convinced that one of the reasons for their pupils' failure in school was because they were forced to follow activities in subject departments. As a consequence, it was considered that the 'problem' which Newsom pupils encountered was the monotony of fixed routines. It soon became part of the Newsom teachers' philosophy that flexibility was the 'solution'. Sylvia Robinson set the keynote for this style of work by explaining to other Newsom teachers that Newsom teaching could not be subdivided into pastoral and academic work. She argued that Newsom teachers might find it necessary to work with groups as well as individuals and would be involved with subjects, pastoral care, counselling and administration. For her, flexibility was not only required in course planning but also in teaching methods. She thought that all lessons should involve different activities.

The idea of flexible arrangements for Newsom work was subscribed to by other Newsom teachers although they each interpreted this in different ways. Terry Goodwin considered that in lessons with Newsom pupils you had to be prepared to cover a range of activities besides working on the material which was the subject of the lesson. As a result, her lessons included having a chat, listening to the radio and looking at magazines – a range of activities to help most pupils pass the time in a double lesson. Keith agreed with this approach because his boat-building classes usually involved a few boys working on boats, some chatting, some making coffee, a group playing cards and others just sleeping or 'doing nothing'.[22] Flexibility involved being prepared to allow a range of activities to take place in any one class.

Jim Parkes had a different approach. He organized short courses for the Newsom pupils so that they could follow a range of different activities in the same class throughout the year. Similarly, Tony Davis ran different courses at different times of the year. A further approach was adopted by Sylvia Robinson and Michael McGovern which involved a bargain being established with pupils. They explained that they agreed to allow pupils to play table tennis in their basic mathematics course during alternative weeks. Pupils were allowed to play table tennis, provided a suitable amount of work had been completed during the previous week. Similarly, other teachers interspersed class lessons with a 'games lesson', because they found it helped them to get to know the pupils and ensured that some 'work' would be done. I found that Newsom teachers and pupils attempted to persuade me this was a useful strategy to obtain work. However, once teachers redefined the curriculum it provided a base for further redefinition by pupils who entered into manipulative strategies with their teachers.

In some classes, the flexible approach gave pupils the opportunity to extend, expand and elaborate some of the activities which teachers had decided could take place alongside 'work'. However, the planned activity often took second place. The pupils found it particularly easy to manipulate the situation where teachers were prepared to sit and talk, with the result that they encouraged teachers to continue talking in order to avoid 'real work'. The Newsom girls boasted that they were particularly good at developing this strategy. They were even prepared to listen to teachers talking about things that they had heard before. This was particularly true of Sylvia Robinson's classes as one girl commented, 'I've heard some of the things that many times I could say it all with her'. Other members of the group agreed but considered that engaging in repetitive conversations was much better than working. Similarly, the girls found they could get Terry Goodwin talking in classes. However, they could only persuade her to talk for part of the lesson, but at least this allowed them to avoid work for one lesson in every two. Terry's diary reflected this pattern of class 'work', remarking about one lesson:

> Impromptu chat session at the beginning of the lesson on the discipline of infants leading on to a discussion of wife beating and the position of the law as regards these matters (goods and chattels). 'Chat' – which got quite heated at times – lasted one lesson. The work intended was finally started. Planning of a meal, food orders, worked. The subject of the lesson 'a meal to represent dishes of a particular region'.[23]

In a subsequent discussion of this and other diary entries Terry claimed that this was a 'typical Newsom lesson' in which the pupils manipulated the situation to delay the work she had planned.

In some teachers' classes, situations were redefined to such an extent that the classes were completely transformed. Not only lesson content but course content was redefined. Tony Davis's classes were examples of such situations. One of the courses which Tony had planned for his Newsom classes was jewellery making. However, the course got off to a bad start. The room allocated to him was a standard classroom inappropriate for practical work. There were also very few materials for the pupils to work with. Despite these problems, Tony started the course with several pupils who soon lost interest when they discovered that the work involved care and concentration. Gradually, Tony found that he could only continue the course with pupils who were interested. So other pupils were allowed to engage in a number of activities in his classes. The result was that he gave up teaching the course to the whole group and his lessons became a series of separate activities. Tony recorded in his diary that in one lesson where all the pupils should have been doing jewellery making, 'The girls played records and chatted' and 'Sean Kelly fooled around with the girls which caused screams and races around the room'.[24] This account was also substantiated by the pupils as one of the girls in this class told me: 'Well, with Mr Davis we are supposed to be doing jewellery making but he can't be bothered with us so we bring up the record player and play records'.[25] Tony told me that the girls had nagged him for weeks to allow them to give up jewellery making. At first he insisted they should do the work he had planned. But he eventually agreed the girls could do something else in his classroom, provided they brought their materials with them. In this instance, he explained that the girls usually arrived each week with the record player, a pile of records and some magazines. This allowed them to listen to records and look through magazines. Often there were inter-ruptions and arguments among pupils. He did not object to the shouting and screaming as pupils chased each other round the room, provided it did not interrupt other classes or spill over into the school grounds.[26] The pupils had therefore successfully changed the content of their course by redefining the situation.

Another way in which manipulation arose was through a staff-initiated programme. The pupils realized that relative to other classes in the school the teachers had made a number of changes to their lessons. While the teachers redefined the 'traditional' curriculum the pupils redefined the Newsom curriculum that had been introduced by their teachers. There were several examples of teacher–pupil redefinition using manipulative strategies. In my local studies course I went beyond practical work in the classroom by making a series of outside visits in connection with our work. During alternate weeks we visited the city centre, the newspaper office, the local football ground and department stores. These activities pleased the pupils as 'it gets you out of school' and in their eyes was 'better than school work'. The term they used to describe these visits was indicative of their attitude to 'work'. While I saw our journeys as educational visits which were part of the course, the pupils referred to them as 'trips' that provided a break from school. The purpose of these visits was also redefined by the pupils. It was my intention that the time should be used to complete various exercises. However, they quickly took the opportunity to use these 'trips' to conduct their own activities. On a visit to conduct a survey of shopping facilities in the city centre some pupils went shopping. One girl brought a pair of shoes to be repaired as her mother thought this would save a further bus fare. Other pupils used the opportunity to visit record shops and some went for a coffee (and a cigarette) when they had 'completed' their work.

This situation illustrated the process of schooling within the Newsom department. It appeared that the conventional school curriculum was initially redefined by Newsom teachers. But the pupils manipulated the teachers' definitions of the Newsom curriculum with the result that these were redefined. This process also occurred when Keith Dryden modified the curriculum by allowing Newsom pupils to make cups of coffee in his classes. Initially, he decided that whenever pupils worked hard he would give them a cup of coffee. This approach was warmly received by the Newsom pupils who saw it as a kind, reasonable and decent act by a teacher. In turn, Keith considered that by allowing pupils to make cups of coffee, it would help to produce an informal atmosphere in the classroom and would help to develop relationships between teachers and pupils and between pupils who would need to co-operate while making coffee.

When Keith Dryden introduced this idea into his classes in the autumn term, it was a rare event. By the end of term it had escalated into a situation whereby pupils were making cups of coffee in almost every class in the Newsom department. Keith found that pupils would volunteer to go and make coffee. Often they would come to classes fully equipped with milk, sugar, coffee, mugs and a kettle. So that rather than being a reward for hard work the pupils had redefined the situation to such an extent that they did little else but make coffee. Originally, coffee making was limited to ten or fifteen minutes at the end of a lesson, but by the end of term it had become the main activity in a double lesson. Several pupils would be involved in making coffee, clearing things away and cleaning up. Meanwhile, other pupils had to go outside the school for supplies of milk. Often there were fights and arguments over who should make coffee, which cups could be used and who should clean up at the end of a lesson. Keith admitted that his anticipation of being able to create relationships among teachers and pupils had failed.

However, coffee making did not stop at Keith's class. After making coffee with Keith, pupils came along to other Newsom teachers with a similar request. They told me that because they were allowed to make coffee in Keith's lessons it helped them to work better and to work harder. Here, the cause 'hard work' and the effect 'making coffee' had been transposed with the result that I, together with other Newsom teachers, agreed to coffee making being done in classes. This brought a radical change to Newsom lessons: no longer were cups of coffee the central interest, but coffee making itself. Pupils were no longer concerned with a privilege, since they had manipulated themselves into a situation where coffee making was a substitute for doing class work. In addition, making coffee also brought more freedom. Pupils could now legitimately leave the site to purchase milk, coffee and sugar when further supplies were required. This brought further rewards in the shape of opportunities for pupils to smoke during school time. Also, if you could not get outside school with your coffee-making 'job', it did, nevertheless, provide some freedom on the site as it was possible to go around the school collecting essential equipment from other Newsom teachers. In this sense, what the staff regarded as a failure the pupils saw as a success, having redefined the activities within Newsom classes.

Developing relationships

The headmaster was convinced that the Newsom department needed teachers 'who can be flexible and who don't easily take offence especially if a youngster goes to sleep [in a lesson]'.[27] He considered that Newsom teaching was based on pupils developing relationships with teachers who understood their attitudes to school, schooling and school work. Accordingly, he believed that Newsom teaching was 'a situation where you have to do what they will allow you to do'[28] and that success was more probable if teachers had developed relationships with their pupils rather than having well-worked-out syllabuses and projects.

All the Newsom teachers agreed with the head's ideas about Newsom teaching. Developing relationships with pupils was essential if other work was to follow. They thought many of their pupils found it difficult to develop and sustain relationships with teachers, especially those who were house heads. They agreed with Moody (1968) that house heads were the people who were paid to do pastoral work but were too close to the control mechanism to develop positive relationships with Newsom pupils.[29] As we saw in chapter six, the Newsom pupils had not developed positive relationships with either house or departmental staff, rarely being able to fulfil these teachers' expectations in terms of behaviour or academic work. As a result, the Newsom teachers considered it essential to establish relationships with their pupils.

Sylvia Robinson told me that Newsom staff found their pupils distrusted all teachers by the time they reached the fourth year. The result was that a considerable amount of time had to be spent getting to know the Newsom pupils. Different teachers adopted different strategies. Sylvia was renowned for her down-to-earth approach with the pupils. In many of her classes she simply exchanged gossip. She would tell them something about herself and her family and in return they would tell her stories about themselves. If the pupils told Sylvia a story she would usually tell a story in return. While this was the way she got to know the pupils and give them advice, it was not always appreciated. On several occasions, girls remarked, 'Miss Robinson's been prying into our business again' to which another girl added, 'Our mum said I weren't to tell her anything. She should mind her own business.' Others thought that not all Sylvia's tales were true, claiming that whatever happened to them or their friends had always happened to her and her friends. Sarah Molinski summed this up by saying: 'I bet if I told her I had a friend who had two noses and three eyes, she would say she knew somebody like that'. These points about Sylvia's classes were often made to other teachers as Keith told me that the girls often moaned about her prying into their sexual affairs with offers of moral advice.

Keith adopted a different strategy. He deliberately set out to make friends with Newsom pupils to such an extent that he found his activities frowned upon by other staff. Keith's approach involved joking with pupils about their girl friends and boy friends and about things they told him about life beyond school. Often he could be seen walking across the school surrounded by Newsom pupils which inevitably meant that someone was leaning on his shoulder or catching hold his arms. Stories also circulated about the way in which Keith engaged in 'friendly' fights with some of the boys. This earned him the reputation of being 'a good bloke'. Similarly, David Smith was also regarded by the pupils as a good teacher and a good friend. David not only fraternized with the pupils but also entertained them. One boy told me how he would organize water fights in art lessons, while another explained how he would never take sweets away from pupils provided he was offered some. David told me one day how he had entertained some Newsom pupils (and pupils in neighbouring classrooms) when he had climbed on to a window ledge on the first floor of the art block and pretended to fly.

While some teachers remained friendly with pupils, others were familiar and flirted with them. Keith Dryden was in his element with a class of Newsom girls, winking at some and making eyes at others. Meanwhile, Terry Goodwin flirted with the boys.[30] She laughed as she told several teachers how she allowed Newsom boys to come into her room and greet her by throwing their arms around her. She was also amused by one boy who had come into her room and lifted up her long skirt just to see what her legs were like. However, she had reprimanded him as she thought this might lead to gossip amongst other teachers. Yet on reflection she was sorry she had reprimanded him as she thought he would get this reaction from other teachers.

Teaching in the Newsom department was different from the teaching in the rest of the school. The Newsom teachers had established a curriculum that involved a 'liberal' approach to academic subjects where the emphasis was upon practical work. They thought this would help to 'solve' their pupils' problems with school. While the teachers redefined the school curriculum and devised different strategies to communicate it to their pupils, so the pupils took things one stage further, utilizing manipulative strategies to redefine the situation. The result was a Newsom course viewed differently by teachers and pupils.

Perceptions of the Newsom course

As it appeared that teachers and pupils in the Newsom department wished to establish a different curriculum, I decided to explore in more detail the ways in which they perceived the course. On an individual basis the Newsom teachers were prepared to discuss their own shortcomings and misgivings about each other and about Newsom work. However, it was very different when they came together in a departmental meeting to discuss their work with the headmaster. In a meeting that I attended after I had been in the school for half a term each Newsom teacher talked about their work with the pupils.

Sylvia talked about swimming lessons and outside visits she had organized for her classes. She reported that pupils were becoming much more 'mature' and 'responsible' – a direct result of the courses provided by the department. In particular, she singled out Peter Vincent and Terry Nicholls who were regarded by other teachers as notorious trouble-makers. She claimed they were settling down to their work and becoming much more mature. This was agreed by other teachers, although in private they were prepared to report their misgivings about it.

Terry Goodwin talked about the girls' group she had taken for home economics. Part of this course was said to include continental cookery and first aid. Terry thought first aid was very popular as the pupils could combine practical work with some written work to gain an examination certificate. She reported that most pupils had enjoyed the written and the practical work and had successfully gained certificates.

Keith Dryden was next. He supported the views already advanced. He said that he found all the Newsom pupils were 'nice kids' who were prepared to get as much as they could out of their courses. It was then my turn to say what I was doing. I realized that the strategy was to provide an edited report that was positive about the pupils. I talked about the success I had with outside visits and how the pupils had produced a reasonable amount of written work. I claimed that the success of the course could be attributed to the fact that I had the opportunity to get to know my group as people rather than pupils.[31] This report was warmly received by the others, especially since I had talked about 'people' rather than 'pupils' – the terms that they utilized. Finally, the headmaster talked about a course he had organized with the fire service. Here again, we were to hear that all had gone well and that the pupils had gained certificates from the fire service (to show that they had successfully completed the course). The head also reported that much written work had been done. However, the only examples of the 'work' publicly available were a series of photographs of the pupils at the fire station.

These remarks were all part of the teachers' evaluation of the Newsom course. All the comments about courses and pupils were in positive terms.

Initially, I was surprised by these remarks as I had received very different reports from teachers when they returned from their classes. The same people who had previously experienced problems now found an alternative version of their activities. The accounts suggested that the teachers were in control of the situation and pupils were obtaining some success. Many pupils, it was said, had improved their behaviour and earned certificates. The staff were thus engaged in a particular strategy. Woods (1979) has talked about teachers' survival strategies with pupils, but here the strategy of survival was being played with the headmaster.

In contrast, the pupils had a very different perspective of the Newsom course and the teachers' work. When I talked to Sheila Brown, Jenny Nelson and Sarah Molinski I found they held similar views of the Newsom course. Sheila summed it up for the group by saying:

> It was great in the fourth year because we had plenty of stuff to do especially in Newsom, but now we have gone into the fifth year we are just coming on like a drag. The fourth year this year are getting treated just like we did last year. They really had time for us, them teachers, the teachers who take Newsom. They do a lot for the fourth year and they are just leaving the fifth year. They don't care for us as much as they did before. They don't care for the ones that are leaving school this Easter either. They have just pushed us on the side now 'cos they know we are leaving. They think, 'They're leaving and we can't do much for them' and so just push us off. They just pay attention to those that are staying on, it's ridiculous really.[32]

Similarly, Jenny indicated that the teachers and the Newsom course did very little for them:

> We just go in and they don't seem to care about anything. We can do what we like and when I can do just what I like, I don't like it. When we leave school people are going to be asking what we learnt in the last year. Gonna have to tell them we never did nothing really. You know things like first aid, mothercare, home economics. We can't really say that we did a lot 'cos we never.[33]

These remarks are interesting on several counts. First, they accord generally with the remarks that were made by the boys in Hargreaves's study,[34] by the girls in Furlong's work[35] and the pupils in Corrigan's study.[36] Secondly, the remarks highlight inactivity and passivity on the part of teachers. Indeed, teachers are criticized for allowing situations to be redefined despite the fact that Jenny had negotiated, manipulated and redefined many situations in the classroom. Thirdly, these remarks are different from those of their teachers. In departmental meetings, Sylvia Robinson and Terry Goodwin had talked about the work which was done in first aid, mothercraft and home economics. The criticism was made here

that very little was done, to a point where the pupil claimed that they did
nothing. For these pupils, courses were seen as a means of passing time at
school.[37]

The position for many pupils on the Newsom course was summed up
by Sarah when she said: 'People say to us "Why are you so dull?" and we
say, "Yes, we're so dull because we don't learn anything, we don't even
take exams and things. All Newsom is for, is the dumb people who are
thick." '[38] The theme of 'doing nothing' arises here in a slightly different
form being seen as not learning and not taking examinations. Direct
comparison is made between Newsom work and examination work.
Furthermore, this girl believed that the teachers' negative image of their
pupils had resulted in the Newsom course. In further discussions,
Newsom work was criticized for not being similar to history and geography which were regarded as 'proper' subjects. Similar statements were
made by the boys. Sean Kelly considered that Newsom was where 'You
don't have to do exams and you go to classes and go out places. You can get
out of lessons.'[39] He equated Newsom with a situation where pupils did
no work. This position was also taken by several other pupils who saw the
Newsom course as a place for 'doing nothing', compared with 'work' in
subjects for public examinations.

The Newsom course was defined and redefined by teachers and
pupils who adapted and adopted different perspectives towards it. The
Newsom teachers had two views of the course; publicly, they thought it
was highly successful, whereas in private they expressed their reservations. For themselves, the Newsom pupils did their best to avoid the
work planned for them but were critical of their teachers and the course,
which they claimed involved little work. Nevertheless, they attempted to
extend the ethos of the Newsom course to their core courses.

Newsom pupils and the core course

The activities that took place within the Newsom department were
acknowledged by teachers and pupils to be different from the activities
that took place in houses and other departments. Alongside the Newsom
course Newsom pupils had to follow the core course with other pupils
from their year group. This situation raised a question about the relationship between work in the Newsom department and work in the core
subjects: to what extent did the Newsom course influence the core
curriculum?

I came to know best the teachers in the English department, who took
the Newsom pupils for their common-core English periods. In particular,
Paul Klee, who took the bottom set in the fifth year, would come and talk to
me about his experiences with the class. After a double lesson with the
Newsom group in the first two periods on a Tuesday morning, Paul would

usually greet me with the expression, 'They're on form today'. He would then proceed to relate the incidents that had occurred in his class. The everyday incidents included pupils running around the room, 'sleeping' on desks and floating paper aeroplanes through the air. Paul was convinced that these pupils did not want to work because in every lesson attempts were made to sabotage the activities he had planned. In one class, Sean Kelly was playing around with his hair; when he went to the back of the room to see what Sean was doing he found he had a bottle of dye on the desk and was in the process of dyeing his hair. In most lessons, Paul found that the pupils constantly complained about having to sit at their desks and work. The result was constant interruption and mis-behaviour. Terry Nicholls made his intentions clear when he told Paul that his aim was to do 'As little as possible for as long as possible' in English lessons.

The situations Paul described cannot be seen as isolated incidents. Staff in the English department who were taking or had taken Newsom classes had similar experiences. Several teachers in other departments who had to teach Newsom pupils with their year group had met a similar fate. Jean Chapman (senior mistress responsible for school discipline) took the bottom set for fifth-year mathematics. She explained that it was impossible to attempt a regular pattern of work as pupils were frequently absent, misbehaved or would not work. As a consequence she tried to 'battle' with the pupils to get them to work. However, there were few rewards for her efforts. She decided, therefore, to help those pupils who wished to work, while those who did not wish to do any work were allowed to do so. The pupils who worked were seated at the front of the room, while the non-workers lay around on desks, looked through maga-zines and in one class flicked a piece of paper up and down a table for a single period. Staff in the physical education department were confronted with similar experiences. Newsom pupils came to games lessons without equipment, and with notes 'from home' to excuse themselves from the lessons. However, those pupils who took part in the classes were prepared to argue and swear at teachers and other pupils.

When Newsom pupils joined the common core they were usually in the bottom sets. Here, classes were much larger than in the Newsom department, because in subject departments there was no special arrange-ment to teach pupils in small groups. Subject teachers found Newsom pupils frequently absent from classes and when they did attend produced behaviour and standards of work which did not meet their expectations.

Jane Adams summed up the ethos of her English classes with members of the Newsom group when she wrote in her diary:

There are nominally twenty-five in the class but fortunately they are never all here together. Five of the boys have been entered for CSE and one or two of them may have a slight chance. These five always sit at the back and are supposed to work on a piece of work I set each week but they can't always resist the comedy show put on by the rest of the class.

Only eight of the class are girls and they are generally quiet, either gossiping or sitting quiet or even working. They very rarely take the initiative in discussion or even trouble-making, though one or two sometimes reply vigorously to the boys' remarks.

Here, the strategy adopted by the teacher bore a marked resemblance to that described by Jean Chapman in the mathematics class where workers and non-workers were separated from each other. In these circumstances, the teachers approached each lesson anticipating trouble, disruption, absence and little work from the group in question.

When some activity was attempted by the teachers there was constant interruption as shown in the following extract from Paul Klee's diary:

Continued with reading of *Day of the Triffids*. Fairly obvious that most find it difficult to maintain concentration. Horns of a dilemma. If I read it gives them a chance to talk, sleep etc. If they read it serves to almost kill the story. Long description or philosophical conjecture in the novel is greeted with yawning or such generalizations as, 'Do we always have to read?' or 'Sir, what is this book about?' (Sarah Molinski). Sarah turned up today for the first time in a month.

This account of 'work' in an English lesson was substantiated by several of the pupils that I interviewed. The story is recounted by two girls:

Sheila   It is the same year after year here, you do the same work over and over again.
RB   The same work?
Sheila   It is the same work, like English, we should be doing writing and learning, but all we are doing is reading out of books.
RB   What, just reading books?
Sheila   Yes, isn't that true Jenny?
Jenny   Um. We read books and he writes questions on the board and we write down in our books what we think. It is the kind of work that we did in the first year. You learnt to put in your capital letters and full stops, your commas and that, but we are doing that all over again.[40]

These extracts bear a marked resemblance to discussions that Woods[41] had with non-examination pupils. Here, as in Woods's study, the pupils found the work repetitive, dull and boring as it had been covered in the lower school. But to the teacher, repetition was essential, because in his terms the pupils had not acquired the basic skills. As a tactic to generate some interest among his pupils, the teacher had started to read a novel to the class with the idea that they should sit and listen. However, the pupils found a passive role boring and not 'work' so they frequently interrupted the class and made requests to go back to writing.

As a consequence of their boredom, the pupils often engaged in alternative activities which the teachers recorded in their diaries. Jane Adams records one boy's activity in a reading lesson in the following terms:

> Clive Smith wielded his screwdriver to great effect and removed all the screws from several ink wells. When discovered he said cheerfully, 'Anything for you, miss' and put most of them back – but five screws were left on the table at the end of the lesson.[42]

In another class Paul Klee described a reading lesson as: 'Silent reading?! Sean counted his money and combed his hair. The scissors have disappeared of late.'[43] Pupils expressed their disinterest by establishing their own alternative activities. Often teachers avoided intervening, thinking this would result in no work being done by anyone in the class. However, many teachers quietly disapproved of the activities as shown by Jane Adams's remarks in her diary when she reported, 'unspeakable lesson – no work done' and on another occasion, 'noise, annoyance, virtually no work done – UGH!' It was therefore rare for the pupils to meet the academic and behavioural expectations of the teachers in subject departments.

Newsom pupils not only attempted to do little work in the subject departments but tried to develop similar relationships with the teachers as those they enjoyed with Newsom teachers. Jane Adams indicated how pupils talked to her when she recorded in her diary: 'The other boys were mildly awkward, e.g. Peter insisted on asking me if I read *Playgirl* magazine and describing a sexy secretary at the place where he had been working'. When Jane talked to me about this particular entry in her diary she said that Peter had actually remarked: 'You should see the knockers on the secretary where I work'.[44] Jane indicated that she would not have expected this remark to be made to her in other classes nor would she have tolerated it from other pupils. But with Newsom pupils she was left with little choice as she thought that any attempt to stop such remarks would have been greeted with uproar. Similarly, John McGuire indicated that in games lessons Newsom pupils were not concerned about the presence of teachers. He illustrated this remark with the following comments in his diary:

> If something goes wrong or against them [the Newsom group] some, notably Malcolm Jackson, lose their temper and usually start swearing

at other people and threatening them but also they tend to sulk and to take little part after the incident has occurred, e.g. if a goal has been given when he thought it shouldn't then Malcolm will stop playing and wander about doing very little but shouting at other people.

John McGuire was new to teaching and realized that this kind of behaviour was not usually tolerated in the physical education department or in the school except among Newsom pupils. He recorded how during one week he attempted to stop this behaviour by not holding a games lesson. However, a week after the abandoned class he recorded that their behaviour had returned to 'normal' with further arguments and obscenities being hurled across the football pitch at himself and other pupils.

These accounts of classes in the common core reveal several patterns. Firstly, the teachers attempted to teach their subject rather than to modify or simplify it, as was done in Newsom courses. Secondly, the pupils attempted to employ similar strategies with subject teachers to those they used with Newsom teachers in an attempt to redefine the situation. Both their academic work and their behaviour were regarded as unacceptable, but very seldom was anything done to punish these pupils because it was thought this would provide an excuse for the 'uneasy peace' to escalate into a state of 'war'. Several subject teachers attempted to rationalize the situation, claiming they liked the pupils despite finding them difficult to work with. This situation was summarized by Jane Adams when she wrote at the end of her diary:

> Now I hand it in, I feel that this is a depressing account. It's a good job that other classes I teach are more interested and less hard work. But I do find a distinct liking for some of the kids in 5I. Whether I have in any sense at all contributed to any aspect of 'education' is one problematic.

Summary and conclusion

This chapter has examined Newsom classes and the experiences of Newsom pupils and their teachers in the Newsom department and in subject departments. The time which Newsom pupils spent in the school was subdivided between activities that took place in the Newsom department and those taking place in subject departments when the pupils joined their year group.

The Newsom staff appreciated that many of their colleagues were not prepared to tolerate their pupils and their behaviour. As a result, they could see that their pupils were presented with many problems in the traditional school curriculum. Newsom teachers therefore attempted to create a new-style curriculum which was based on a 'liberal' education and orientated towards practical skills. In turn they held different expectations of their pupils compared with other teachers.

This situation was used by the pupils to negotiate with, bargain and manipulate the teachers and to redefine the Newsom curriculum. The result was that effective control of the curriculum passed from the teachers to the pupils. With a change in the content of the curriculum went a change in the style of relationships between teachers and pupils. Despite the fact that pupils had manipulated the situation they still complained about their school experience and how they had not learned anything that would be of use. The teachers found it almost impossible to teach the pupils. But for survival in individual classes and in their careers it was important to perceive this work in terms of some success.

Subject teachers held different sets of academic and behavioural expectations. However, Newsom pupils brought to these classes the same kind of behaviour and work ethic that they used in the Newsom department. In this context, they merely reinforced the stereotype which most teachers held of them. The phrase 'That's just Newsom' was used to characterize a situation where there was noise, disruption and little work among Newsom pupils. While this would not be tolerated in other classes, it was allowed in classes where Newsom pupils 'worked', because it was a means of containing pupils who were unwilling to comply with teachers. This highlighted the difference between members of the Newsom department and other members of the school. In these circumstances, the separate curriculum, work rates and behavioural standards might be said to have created an alternative form of schooling within Bishop McGregor School.

Notes

1 For a discussion of research instruments used to conduct classroom research see, for example, Flanders (1970), Wragg (1975) and Cohen (1976). For a critique see Delamont and Hamilton (1976).
2 For a discussion of a similar point see Woods (1979, 12–15).
3 For a discussion of the failure to set teachers, classrooms and schools in a broader context or to link together macroscopic and microscopic analyses in the sociology of education see Banks (1978).
4 Further particulars for a Newsom post.
5 See, for example, Rowe (1959, 55–228), Taylor (1963, 82–102) and White and Brockington (1978, 182–96).
6 For a discussion of the way in which sex and gender are used by teachers to legitimate divisions see Delamont (1980, 24–44). Later, several teachers including the headmaster discussed Sylvia's intervention with me. They considered that she only wanted this grouping adopted because she experienced few difficulties with single-sex groups but had problems with mixed groups.

7 For further discussions of the curriculum in similar terms see Ford (1969), Young (1971, esp. 32–41), Bernstein (1971), Keddie (1971) and Bellaby (1977).

8 This strategy was used to ease timetable planning.

9 This emphasis on practical work was in line with the education that had been considered appropriate for secondary modern school pupils. See, for example, Newsom (1963) and Taylor (1963). However, for reservations about designing a curriculum for academic pupils and another type of curriculum for non-academic pupils see, for example, Shipman (1971, esp. 103–5), Shipman (1980) and Mortimore and Blackstone (1982, 54–102).

10 Fieldnotes.

11 For a discussion of teacher strategies see Woods (1980a) and for a review see Hammersley (1980).

12 See Hargreaves (1979) and Stebbins (1975).

13 See Hammersley (1976) and Woods (1979).

14 See Woods (1979).

15 See Waller (1967), Webb (1962) and Woods (1979).

16 See Walker and Goodson (1977), Woods (1979) and Stebbins (1980).

17 For a discussion of this and other ethical problems in the conduct of field research see, for example, Burgess (1981b). For further material see Barnes (1979) and Dingwall (1980).

18 For another account in which a no-smoking rule is adapted by the participants see Gouldner (1954, 182–7).

19 For a discussion of diaries kept by informants see Burgess (1981a, 1984a).

20 Extract from Tony Davis's diary.

21 Interview with John Slattery.

22 For an account of 'doing nothing' outside school see Corrigan (1979, 119–41).

23 Extract from Terry Goodwin's diary.

24 Extract from Tony Davis's diary.

25 Interview with Jenny Nelson.

26 This contrasts with the situation discussed by Webb (1962), who looked at the way in which teachers wanted chaos kept in the playground and not brought into the school; a point which was reinforced by house heads at McGregor.

27 Interview with the headmaster.

28 ibid.

29 Cf. Best, Jarvis and Ribbins (1977).

30 For a discussion of similar strategies see Delamont (1980, 54–60).

31 This raises questions about the relationship between truth-telling and lying in fieldwork. See, for example, Bok (1978) and Burgess (1984c).

32 Interview with Sheila Brown, Jenny Nelson and Sarah Molinski.

33 ibid.

34 See Hargreaves (1967, esp. 101–2).

35 See Furlong (1976, esp. 165–9).

36 See Corrigan (1976, 103–5) and Corrigan (1979, 119–41).

37 Cf. Corrigan (1976; 1979, 119–41).

38 Interview with Sheila Brown, Jenny Nelson and Sarah Molinski. Sarah acknowledges by implication the importance of examinations and school as a means to an end. Cf. Quine (1974).

39 Interview with Sean Kelly.

40 Interview with Sheila Brown, Jenny Nelson and Sarah Molinski.
41 Cf. Woods (1979, 32–3, 66–7).
42 Extract from Jane Adams's diary.
43 Extract from Paul Klee's diary.
44 Diary interview with Jane Adams. For a detailed discussion of the diary-interview see Zimmerman and Wieder (1977) and Burgess (1981a, 1984a).

CONCLUSION

This study has focused on experiences of comprehensive education. In this conclusion I discuss some of the main themes and some areas that could be investigated in further ethnographic studies of comprehensive schools. Finally (and somewhat briefly), I raise a series of issues concerning the practical implications of this study for those who live and work within our schools.

The influence of social context on comprehensive schooling

Although this has been an ethnographic study of a comprehensive school where the bulk of data has been gathered by participant observation, I also collected some historical and documentary evidence in order that the school and the events I witnessed could be placed in a social context.[1] This style of data collection may appear to depart from the 'classic' model of ethnographic research[2] where relatively little, if any, historical material has been used. However, as Thernstrom[3] has demonstrated, the neglect of historical data has resulted in some situations and events being misinterpreted by ethnographers.[4] A further problem that especially concerns small-scale studies of schools and classrooms is a failure to situate microscopic analyses within broader sets of social relationships.[5] In this context, Banks (1978) has warned of the dangers of over-simplifying situations with the result that the constraints operating upon schools, classrooms, teachers and pupils are taken for granted or ignored completely. Indeed, one of the dangers of conducting ethnographic research from an interactionist perspective is that too much autonomy can be attributed to the members of a school (cf. Banks 1978, 39–41). To avoid this problem and to illustrate the ways in which the members of Bishop McGregor School were constrained by decisions that were not of their own choosing, situations and events have been located within a social context.

The development of comprehensive schools in Merston was part of the broader framework of the reorganization of English secondary education that dominated educational debate after the second world war.[6] The Merston authority needed to establish new schools and proposed that these should be along comprehensive lines. However, they were only allowed to establish comprehensive schools on the understanding that the scheme would be experimental and that the schools would be constructed in such a way that they could be subdivided into separate grammar and secondary modern schools if this proved desirable. This point, together with questions of size, influenced the physical structure of Merston's comprehensive schools. All new secondary schools, including those in the Catholic sector, had a physical house system which officers of the authority thought would influence the recruitment of teaching staff and the way in which teachers and pupils lived and worked within the schools. In short, it was considered that the physical structure of schools would influence their social organization.

So Bishop McGregor School needed to be considered against this background. The school had been built on the Merston model which utilized the house system. The headmaster's staffing patterns therefore operated within the constraints of local authority policy. Furthermore, the way in which the headmaster defined school organization was constrained by the physical structure of the school. It can be argued in turn that the definitions and redefinitions of the situation advanced by teachers were influenced by the setting which had been established by the Merston authority.

The activities of members of the Newsom department could not be understood without reference to the school. Newsom teachers and pupils established an alternative version of schooling to that provided in other parts of the school. In this sense, their actions and activities can be seen as a reaction to the pattern of schooling established by other teachers. In short, I would maintain that the situations I witnessed at Bishop McGregor School and the definitions of situations put forward by teachers and pupils were not merely the products of internal interaction but part of a broader set of relationships within the educational system.

Divisions in the comprehensive school

In concluding his study of a secondary modern school, Woods (1979, 256) suggested that divisions between teachers and pupils, public and private spheres of life, between choice and direction, laughter and conflict, gave rise to his concept of the 'divided school'. Indeed, he thought these divisions were such that they might increase with comprehensivization.

At Bishop McGregor the physical subdivision of the school into houses and departments was used to come to terms with the problem of school size and influenced patterns of school organization, staff appointments and patterns of work. Physical territory was marked out between house heads and heads of departments and for that matter between the heads of houses. The headmaster used these basic physical divisions to subdivide formal responsibility for the implementation of behavioural and academic norms. Indeed, the heads of houses and heads of departments acknowledged these subdivisions in their formal activities within the school. These subdivisions were also reflected in the informal social groups among the staff.

In turn, these divisions were important, as different groups of teachers presented different versions of the same school to the pupils. For those who were responsible for the house system, discipline and order were vital, while for the departmental staff academic achievement 'measured' in terms of success in formal examinations was their central concern. By focusing on the teachers in houses and departments it was possible to see the way in which different versions of the school were being presented to the pupils. By also looking at three critical situations in the school, the activities of the teachers could be seen to reinforce the basic division between houses and departments. In particular, the different ways in which teachers were prepared to put school norms into operation were vital.

This theme was also followed up within the Newsom department. The headmaster had created a department here which was different from other departments. Newsom teachers recognized the artificial division between houses and departments and argued that their own work embraced both pastoral and subject work. In this respect, it appeared that the Newsom department was another division within the school, because the teachers and pupils within the department attempted to establish an alternative education different from other parts of the school. As a consequence, the activities of the Newsom department could not be neatly allocated to either the houses or the departments. Indeed, the pupils were often in conflict with teachers who worked within both areas.

Definitions and redefinitions of the situation

This study has used the concept of the definition of the situation to look at the meanings attached to situations and their significance for social action. I have therefore examined the ways in which situations were defined and redefined by different members of the school operating at different levels within the school structure. The first part of this study focused upon the ways in which the headmaster, the heads of houses and teachers in departments defined and redefined aims, objectives and routines within the school. I followed the ways in which these definitions were used, modified, appeared and reappeared. Similar themes were explored in relation to the Newsom department, although at this point the focus changed from examining relationships between teachers to looking at the ways in which teachers and pupils defined and redefined situations. Looking at definitions and redefinitions of situations within the school and the Newsom department allowed me to focus on processes common to both and to examine the strategies, negotiations and bargains that took place between teachers, and teachers and pupils.

The headmaster provided the framework within which teachers and pupils should operate. Indeed, the material that is discussed in chapter two indicates the way in which he thought the school *should* operate. In subsequent chapters I have explored the extent to which his ideas and ideals were used, modified and redefined. The three crisis situations that are discussed in chapter four indicate the ways in which the headmaster defined how the school *should* work, witnessed the manner in which redefinition took place and then attempted to modify the situations by negotiation, manipulation and bargaining strategies to bring members of the school back closer to his initial ideals.

These processes operated among teachers but they also occurred between teachers and pupils. By looking at the activities of the Newsom department, it was possible to consider the ways in which Newsom teachers redefined the versions of school to which they and their pupils were exposed. In turn, the pupils within the Newsom department were also engaged in further modification and redefinition through the strategies, negotiations and bargains that they deployed in classes.

These members of Bishop McGregor School all had different under-standings of the school and its purpose. While different models of comprehensive education have been advanced – the meritocratic, the integrative and the egalitarian (Ball 1981, 6–10) – it is difficult to attach any one of these labels to the activities within McGregor. For although it may be argued that these models represent basic principles upon which com-prehensive education and schooling have developed, the situation in McGregor, as in most comprehensive schools, is, as Ball (1981, 10) suggests, a mixture of these basic philosophies. Indeed, as the headmaster indicated, his version of comprehensive schooling could not be neatly placed into a single category. Furthermore, different definitions of the school and school activities were advanced by different groups of teachers and pupils. For those who were house heads it was the tone of the school that mattered. They were intent on implementing school-wide norms that were established by the headmaster. Discipline and the control of pupils was at the heart of their work. For as one house head had expressed it, academic work was not important. However, this brought them into conflict with their colleagues in departments who considered they were doing the real teaching. So at least two competing models of the school were advanced. However, the Newsom department did not fit neatly into either of these models. Teachers and pupils within the department had to work within the school structure but advanced a different version of schooling: an alternative to the pattern of discipline and control in houses and academic work within departments. There was little evidence that teachers or pupils could put together these different elements of schooling, with the result that different versions of Bishop McGregor School co-existed upon the same site. At this point, we might recall the main strands in the debate for comprehensive education: namely the abolition of the tripartite system and the bringing together of different pupils and teachers within one school rather than within separate schools. While it was evident that the pupils and teachers had been brought together on one site it was doubtful whether one school was in operation. It would in fact appear that the label 'comprehensive' merely covered a number of diverse activities that took place on one site. Further research on comprehensive schools might therefore consider the relationship between the schools which were planned by politicians and administrators and the extent to which teachers and pupils have been able to put their ideas and ideals into operation.

Further ethnographic research in comprehensive schools

This study has attempted to gather basic ethnographic material on school organization and the work of the Newsom department in a comprehensive school. Subsequent studies might follow up some issues that have been excluded:

(a) The meaning of headship in a comprehensive school; questions of leadership and management and the internal and external relations in which headteachers engage.
(b) The house system and the meaning of pastoral care for teachers at different levels in the school and for pupils in different groups.
(c) The departments and the similarities and differences that exist between different subject and non-subject areas could be explored for both teachers and pupils.
(d) Different categories and groups of pupils and their experience of comprehensive schooling could be investigated. Here, comparisons might be made over time which would, of course, require some long-term field research. Furthermore, questions of sex, gender and pupils' school experience could be examined.
(e) Research among teachers, examining teacher careers in the comprehensive school[7] and in particular the development of teaching styles could be analysed.

(f) The curriculum and the extent to which comprehensive education has resulted in a 'common' curriculum for pupils who attend these schools demands attention (cf. Hargreaves 1982).

If we are to develop our understanding of comprehensive schools, much research still needs to be done on the social processes involved in comprehensive schooling. But teachers might argue that an understanding of the schooling process is not enough. The final section therefore deals briefly with some issues raised by my study.

Issues for discussion

On the basis of my study, numerous issues will, no doubt, be the subject of debate among sociologists, among teachers and among policy makers. Yet such debates are not enough. We need some interchange *between* the different groups so that some dialogue may occur beyond the artificial boundaries that keep many members of these groups away from one another. In the hope that a vigorous dialogue may begin between these groups I have four items to place on the agenda for *active* consideration.

(1) The comprehensive schools that were developed by the Merston authority were subdivided into houses and departments. The evidence suggests that this results in different versions of the same school being presented to pupils. We therefore need to consider the principles along which these schools could operate and the practical implications of the implementation of these principles.

(2) The structure of Merston's comprehensive schools placed great emphasis upon the pastoral system. However, in Bishop McGregor School no teacher had been specifically trained for a pastoral role (cf. Marland 1980, 182–5). Indeed, many house heads equated pastoral care with school administration and the exercise of social control. In this respect, we need to consider the extent to which teachers should be specifically trained for these posts. Also, those involved with the provision of initial teacher education courses and in-service training need to consider the extent to which courses in pastoral care should be provided alongside courses on aspects of the school curriculum.[8]

(3) In Bishop McGregor School a specific department was created for pupils who did not follow examination courses. Some teachers might think that all pupils should be placed in examination courses, while others might argue that such pupils could be best educated in 'alternative' units outside the formal framework of the school. We need to give further consideration to the courses provided for children who were in McGregor's Newsom department.

(4) The approach which has been used to study this school could be used by teachers to engage in school-based research. Indeed, there are now

a number of courses available where teachers can acquire skills in ethnographic research which will assist them in monitoring their own work. If teachers are to be involved in this type of work some consideration needs to be given to the support they require within and beyond the classroom and to ways in which they can be assisted to collect, analyse and present data.[9]

If these issues are considered in more detail it will, I hope, help to continue the debate about comprehensive schools, patterns of schooling and the education of teachers and pupils in the English educational system.

Notes

1 For a discussion of historical and documentary materials in ethnographic research see Burgess (1982a, 131–60).
2 For a 'classic' model of ethnographic research in sociology see Whyte (1955).
3 For criticism of Whyte (1955) regarding the absence of historical data see Thernstrom (1968).
4 For a discussion of the neglect of historical materials in ethnographic studies see the analysis of Lloyd Warner's *Yankee City Studies* in Thernstrom (1965).
5 For a discussion of the problems concerning relationships between macroscopic and microscopic analyses in the sociology of education together with a possible solution see Karabel and Halsey (1977, esp. 61–72).
6 See, for example, Archer (1979, 583–95, 756–64).
7 For a start on this theme see Lyons (1981) and Riseborough (1981).
8 For a preliminary discussion see the papers in Best, Jarvis and Ribbins (1980).
9 For a discussion of ways in which teachers can monitor their own classroom activities see Stenhouse (1975, esp. 142–65), Harlen (1978), Burgess (1980a) and Nixon (1981). For a discussion of some of the methodological difficulties that need to be confronted in this approach see Burgess (1980b).

BIBLIOGRAPHY

Anderson, N. (1923) *The Hobo: The Sociology of the Homeless Man*, Chicago, University of Chicago Press.

Archer, M. S. (1979) *The Social Origins of Educational Systems*, London, Sage.

Auld, R. (1976) *Report on the Inquiry into William Tyndale School*, London, Inner London Education Authority.

Ball, S. J. (1980) 'Initial encounters in the classroom and the process of establishment', in Woods, P. (ed.) *Pupil Strategies: Explorations in the Sociology of the School*, London, Croom Helm, 143–61.

Ball, S. J. (1981) *Beachside Comprehensive: A Case-Study of Secondary Schooling*, Cambridge, Cambridge University Press.

Ball, S. J. and Lacey, C. (1980) 'Subject disciplines as the opportunity for group action: a measured critique of subject sub-cultures', in Woods, P. (ed.) *Teacher Strategies: Explorations in the Sociology of the School*, London, Croom Helm, 149–77.

Banks, O. (1976) *The Sociology of Education*, 3rd edn, London, Batsford.

Banks, O. (1978) 'School and society', in Barton, L. and Meighan, R. (eds) *Sociological Interpretations of Schooling and Classrooms: A Reappraisal*, Driffield, Nafferton Books, 37–46.

Barnes, J. A. (1979) *Who Should Know What?*, Harmondsworth, Penguin.

Baron, G. (1955) 'The English notion of the school', unpublished paper, University of London Institute of Education.

Baron, G. (1970) 'Some aspects of the "headmaster tradition"', in Musgrave, P. W. (ed.) *Sociology, History and Education*, London, Methuen, 183–92.

Barry, C. H. and Tye, F. (1973) *Running a School*, 2nd edn, London, Temple Smith.

Bazalgette, J. (1978) *School Life and Work Life: A Study of Transition in the Inner City*, London, Heinemann.

Bechhofer, F. (1974) 'Current approaches to empirical research: some central ideas',

in Rex, J. (ed.) *Approaches to Sociology: An Introduction to Major Trends in British Sociology*, London, Routledge & Kegan Paul, 70–91.

Becker, H. S. (1952a) 'The career of the Chicago public school teacher', *American Journal of Sociology*, 57, 470–7.

Becker, H. S. (1952b) 'Social class variations in the teacher–pupil relationship', *Journal of Educational Sociology*, 35 (4), 451–65.

Becker, H. S. (1966) 'Introduction', in Shaw, C. R. *Jack-Roller: A Delinquent Boy's Own Story* (orig. pub. 1930), Chicago, University of Chicago Press, v–xviii.

Becker, H. S. (1968) 'Becoming a marijuana user', in Rubington, E. and Weinberg, M. (eds) *Deviance: The Interactionist Perspective*, New York, Macmillan, 262–9.

Bell, C. (1968) *Middle Class Families*, London, Routledge & Kegan Paul.

Bellaby, P. (1977) *The Sociology of Comprehensive Schooling*, London, Methuen.

Benn, C. and Simon, B. (1972) *Half Way There: Report on the British Comprehensive School Reform*, 2nd edn, Harmondsworth, Penguin.

Berg, L. (1968) *Risinghill: The Death of a Comprehensive School*, Harmondsworth, Penguin.

Bernbaum, G. (1974) 'Headmasters and schools: some preliminary findings', in Eggleston, J. (ed.) *Contemporary Research in the Sociology of Education*, London, Methuen, 228–44.

Bernbaum, G. (1976) 'The role of the head', in Peters, R. S. (ed.) *The Role of the Head*, London, Routledge & Kegan Paul, 19–36.

Bernstein, B. (1971) 'On the classification and framing of educational knowledge', in Young, M. F. D. (ed.) *Knowledge and Control: New Directions for the Sociology of Education*, London, Collier-Macmillan, 47–69.

Bertaux, D. (1981) (ed.) *Biography and Society: The Life History Approach in the Social Sciences*, Beverly Hills, Calif., Sage.

Best, R., Jarvis, C. and Ribbins, P. (1977) 'Pastoral care: concept and process', *British Journal of Educational Studies*, xxv (2), 124–35.

Best, R., Jarvis, C. and Ribbins, P. (1980) (eds) *Perspectives on Pastoral Care*, London, Heinemann.

Blackie, P. (1977) 'Not quite proper', *The Times Educational Supplement*, 25 November.

Blishen, E. (1971) *This Right Soft Lot*, London, Panther.

Blumer, H. (1969) *Symbolic Interactionism: Perspective and Method*, Englewood Cliffs, New Jersey, Prentice-Hall.

Bok, S. (1978) *Lying: Moral Choice in Public and Private Life*, Hassocks, Harvester.

Boyson, R. (1974) *Oversubscribed: The Story of Highbury Grove*, London, Ward Lock Educational.

Braithwaite, E. R. (1962) *To Sir, With Love*, London, Four Square Books.

Bulmer, M. (1980) 'Comment on "The ethics of covert methods"', *British Journal of Sociology*, 31 (1), 59–65.

Burgess, R. G. (1979) 'Gaining access: some problems and implications for the participant observer.' Paper prepared for SSRC Workshop on Participant Observation, University of Birmingham, September.

Burgess, R. G. (1980a) (ed.) 'Symposium on teacher-based research.' Special issue of *Insight* 3 (3), 1–34.

Burgess, R. G. (1980b) 'Some fieldwork problems in teacher-based research', *British Educational Research Journal*, 6 (2), 165–73.

Burgess, R. G. (1981a) 'Keeping a research diary', *Cambridge Journal of Education*, 11 (1), 75–83.

Burgess, R. G. (1981b) 'Ethical "codes" and field relations.' Paper prepared for 41st Annual Meeting of the Society for Applied Anthropology, University of Edinburgh, April.

Burgess, R. G. (1981c) 'An ethnographic study of a comprehensive school', PhD thesis, University of Warwick.

Burgess, R. G. (1982a) (ed.) *Field Research: A Sourcebook and Field Manual*, London, Allen & Unwin.

Burgess, R. G. (1982b) 'The practice of sociological research: some issues in school ethnography', in Burgess, R. G. (ed.) *Exploring Society*, London, British Sociological Association, 115–35.

Burgess, R. G. (1984a, forthcoming) *In the Field: An Introduction to Field Research*, London, Allen & Unwin.

Burgess, R. G. (1984b) 'It's not a proper subject: It's just Newsom', in Goodson, I. and Ball, S. J. (eds) *Defining the Curriculum*, Lewes, Falmer Press.

Burgess, R. G. (1984c) 'The whole truth? Some ethical problems of research in a comprehensive school', in Burgess, R. G. (ed.) *Field Methods in the Study of Education*, Lewes, Falmer Press.

Cassidy, P. (1967) 'The school assembly', in Konstant, D. (ed.) *A Syllabus of Religious Instruction for Catholic Secondary Schools*, London, Burns & Oates and Macmillan, 59–68.

Chanan, G. and Delamont, S. (1975) (eds) *Frontiers of Classroom Research*, Slough, National Foundation for Educational Research.

Chetwynd, H. R. (1960) *Comprehensive School: The Story of Woodberry Down*, London, Routledge & Kegan Paul.

Cohen, A. (1982) 'Drama and politics in the development of a London carnival', in Frankenberg, R. (ed.) *Custom and Conflict in British Society*, Manchester, Manchester University Press, 313–43.

Cohen, L. (1976) *Educational Research in Classrooms and Schools*, New York, Harper & Row.

Colgate, H. A. (1976) 'The role of the secondary head', in Peters, R. S. (ed.) *The Role of the Head*, London, Routledge & Kegan Paul, 109–26.

Cope, E. (1971) *School Experience in Teacher Education*, Bristol, University of Bristol publication.

Cornwell, J. (1965) *The Probationary Year*, Birmingham, University Institute of Education.

Corrigan, P. (1976) 'Doing nothing', in Hall, S. and Jefferson, T. (eds) *Resistance through Ritual: Youth Subcultures in Post-War Britain*, London, Hutchinson, 103–5.

Corrigan, P. (1979) *Schooling the Smash Street Kids*, London, Macmillan.

Coulson, A. A. (1976) 'The role of the primary head', in Peters, R. S. (ed.) *The Role of the Head*, London, Routledge & Kegan Paul, 92–108.

Cressey, P. G. (1932) *The Taxi-Dance Hall: A Sociological Study in Commercial Recreation and City Life*, Chicago, University of Chicago Press.

Davies, H. (1976) *The Creighton Report*, London, Hamish Hamilton.

Davies, L. (1979) 'Deadlier than the male? Girls' conformity and deviance in school', in Barton, L. and Meighan, R. (eds) *Schools, Pupils and Deviance*, Driffield, Nafferton Books, 59–73.

Dawson, P. (1981) *Making a Comprehensive Work: The Road from Bomb Alley*, Oxford, Basil Blackwell.

Deem, R. (1978) *Women and Schooling*, London, Routledge & Kegan Paul.

Delamont, S. (1976) *Interaction in the Classroom*, London, Methuen.

Delamont, S. (1980) *Sex Roles and the School*, London, Methuen.

Delamont, S. (1981) 'All too familiar? A decade of classroom research', *Educational Analysis*, 3 (1), 69–83.

Delamont, S. and Hamilton, D. (1976) 'Classroom research: a critique and a new approach', in Stubbs, M. and Delamont, S. (eds) *Explorations in Classroom Observation*, London, Wiley, 3–20.

Denzin, N. (1970) *The Research Act*, Chicago, Aldine.

Department of Education and Science (1965) *The Organisation of Secondary Education*, Circular 10/65, London, HMSO.

Department of Education and Science (1971) *Raising the School Leaving Age to 16*, Circular 8/71, London, HMSO.

Department of Education and Science (1974) *Statistics of Education 1973 Schools: Volume 1*, London, HMSO.

Department of Education and Science (1979) *Aspects of Secondary Education in England: A Survey by HM Inspectors of Schools*, London, HMSO.

Dingwall, R. (1980) 'Ethics and ethnography', *Sociological Review*, 28 (4), 871–91.

Easthope, G. (1975) *Community, Hierarchy and Open Education*, London, Routledge & Kegan Paul.

Education Act (1944), London, HMSO.

Eggleston, J. (1977) *The Sociology of the School Curriculum*, London, Routledge & Kegan Paul.

Eggleston, J. (1979) (ed.) *Teacher Decision-Making in the Classroom*, London, Routledge & Kegan Paul.

Ellis, T., McWhirter, J., McColgan, D. and Haddow, B. (1976) *William Tyndale: The Teachers' Story*, London, Writers and Readers Publishing Co-operative.

Fenwick, I. G. K. (1976) *The Comprehensive School 1944–1970*, London, Methuen.

Flanders, N. A. (1970) *Analysing Teaching Behavior*, Reading, Mass., Addison-Wesley.

Fletcher, C. (1974) 'Fool or funny man: the role of the comedian', in Fletcher, C. *Beneath the Surface*, London, Routledge & Kegan Paul, 147–61.

Floud, J. and Scott, W. (1961) 'Recruitment to teaching in England and Wales', in Halsey, A. H., Floud, J. and Anderson, C. A. (eds) *Education, Economy and Society*, New York, Free Press, 527–44.

Ford, J. (1969) *Social Class and the Comprehensive School*, London, Routledge & Kegan Paul.

Frankenberg, R. (1957) *Village on the Border*, London, Cohen & West.

Frankenberg, R. (1982) (ed.) *Custom and Conflict in British Society*, Manchester, Manchester University Press.

Fuchs, E. (1969) *Teachers Talk: Views from Inside City Schools*, New York, Doubleday Anchor.

Furlong, V. (1976) 'Interaction sets in the classroom: towards a study of pupil knowledge', in Hammersley, M. and Woods, P. (eds) *The Process of Schooling*, London, Routledge & Kegan Paul in association with the Open University Press, 160–70.

Gannaway, H. (1976) 'Making sense of school', in Stubbs, M. and Delamont, S. (eds) *Explorations in Classroom Observation*, London, Wiley, 46–82.

Geer, B. (1964) 'First days in the field', in Hammond, P. (ed.) *Sociologists at Work*, New York, Basic Books, 322–44.

Gluckman, M. (1942) *An analysis of a social situation in modern Zululand*, Rhodes-Livingstone Paper 28.

Gluckman, M. (1945) 'The seven-year research plan of the Rhodes-Livingstone Institute', *Rhodes-Livingstone Journal*, 4, 1–32.

Gluckman, M. (1961) 'Ethnographic data in British social anthropology', *Sociological Review*, 9 (1), 5–17.

Gluckman, M. (1964) (ed.) *Closed Systems and Open Minds: The Limits of Naiveté in Social Anthropology*, London and Edinburgh, Oliver & Boyd.

Gluckman, M. (1967) 'Introduction', in Epstein, A. L. (ed.) *The Craft of Social Anthropology*, London, Tavistock, xi–xx.

Goffman, E. (1952) 'Cooling the mark out: some aspects of adaptation to failure', *Psychiatry*, XV, 451–63.

Goodman, P. (1971) 'Comments on the science of teaching', in Wax, M., Diamond, S. and Gearing, F. O. (eds) *Anthropological Perspectives on Education*, New York, Basic Books, 118–20.

Gouldner, A. W. (1954) *Patterns of Industrial Bureaucracy*, New York, Free Press.

Gouldner, A. W. (1965) *Wildcat Strike: A study in worker–management relations*, New York, Harper & Row.

Grace, G. (1972) *Role Conflict and the Teacher*, London, Routledge & Kegan Paul.

Gretton, J. and Jackson, M. (1976) *William Tyndale – Collapse of a School or a System?* London, Allen & Unwin.

Halsall, E. (1973) *The Comprehensive School*, Oxford, Pergamon Press.

Hammersley, M. (1976) 'The mobilisation of pupil attention', in Hammersley, M. and Woods, P. (eds) *The Process of Schooling*, London, Routledge & Kegan Paul in association with the Open University Press, 104–15.

Hammersley, M. (1980) 'Classroom ethnography', *Educational Analysis*, 2 (2), 47–74.

Hammersley, M. (1981) 'Ideology in the staffroom? A critique of false consciousness', in Barton, L. and Walker, S. (eds) *Schools, Teachers and Teaching*, Lewes, Falmer Press, 331–42.

Hammersley, M. and Woods, P. (1976) (eds) *The Process of Schooling*, London, Routledge & Kegan Paul in association with the Open University Press.

Hannam, C., Smyth, P. and Stephenson, N. (1976) *The First Year of Teaching*, Harmondsworth, Penguin.

Hannerz, U. (1980) *Exploring the City: Inquiries Toward an Urban Anthropology*, New York, Columbia University Press.

Hargreaves, A. (1979) 'Strategies, decisions and control: interaction in a middle-school classroom', in Eggleston, J. (ed.), *Teacher Decision-Making in the Classroom*, London, Routledge & Kegan Paul, 134–69.

Hargreaves, D. H. (1967) *Social Relations in a Secondary School*, London, Routledge & Kegan Paul.

Hargreaves, D. H. (1972) *Interpersonal Relations in Education*, London, Routledge & Kegan Paul.

Hargreaves, D. H. (1977) 'The process of typification in classroom interaction: models and methods', *British Journal of Educational Psychology*, 47, 274–84.

Hargreaves, D. H. (1980) (ed.) 'Classroom studies', *Education Analysis*, 2 (2), 1–95.

Hargreaves, D. H. (1982) *The Challenge for the Comprehensive School: Culture, Curriculum and Community*, London, Routledge & Kegan Paul.

Hargreaves, D. H., Hester, S. K. and Mellor, F. J. (1975) *Deviance in Classrooms*, London, Routledge & Kegan Paul.

Harlen, W. (1978) (ed.) *Evaluation and the Teacher's Role*, London, Macmillan.

Hines, B. (1969) *A Kestrel for a Knave*, Harmondsworth, Penguin.

Hirst, P. H. (1971) 'What is teaching?', *Journal of Curriculum Studies*, 3, 5–18.

Holt, J. (1969) *How Children Fail*, Harmondsworth, Penguin.

Holt, J. (1970) *How Children Learn*, Harmondsworth, Penguin.

Holt, M. (1978) *The Common Curriculum: Its Structure and Style in the Comprehensive School*, London, Routledge & Kegan Paul.

Homan, R. (1980) 'The ethics of covert methods', *British Journal of Sociology*, 31 (1), 46–59.

Hoyle, E. (1969) *The Role of the Teacher*, London, Routledge & Kegan Paul.

Hughes, M. G. (1976) 'The professional-as-administrator: the case of the secondary school head', in Peters, R. S. (ed.) *The Role of the Head*, London, Routledge & Kegan Paul, 50–62.

Illich, I. D. (1973) *Deschooling Society*, Harmondsworth, Penguin.

Jenkins, D. and Shipman, M. D. (1976) *Curriculum: An Introduction*, London, Open Books.

Karabel, J. and Halsey, A. H. (1977) 'Educational research: a review and an interpretation', in Karabel, J. and Halsey, A. H. (eds) *Power and Ideology in Education*, Oxford, Oxford University Press, 1–85.

Keddie, N. (1971) 'Classroom Knowledge', in Young, M. F. D. (ed.) *Knowledge and Control: New Directions for the Sociology of Education*, London, Collier-Macmillan, 113–60.

Kelsall, R. K. and Kelsall, H. M. (1969) *The School Teacher in England and the United States: The Findings of Empirical Research*, Oxford, Pergamon Press.

King, R. (1969) *Values and Involvement in a Grammar School*, London, Routledge & Kegan Paul.

King, R. (1973a) *School Organization and Pupil Involvement: A Study of Secondary Schools*, London, Routledge & Kegan Paul.

King, R. (1973b) 'The headteacher and his authority', in Fowler, G., Morris, V. and Ozga, J. (eds) *Decision-Making in British Education*, London, Heinemann, 422–46.

King, R. (1978) *All Things Bright and Beautiful? A Sociological Study of Infants' Classrooms*, Chichester, Wiley.

Kob, J. (1961) 'Definitions of the teacher's role', in Halsey, A. H., Floud, J. and Anderson, C. A. (eds) *Education, Economy and Society*, New York, Free Press, 558–76.

Konstant, D. (1967) (ed.) *A Syllabus of Religious Instruction for Catholic Secondary Schools*, London, Burns & Oates and Macmillan.

Lacey, C. (1970) *Hightown Grammar: The School as a Social System*, Manchester, Manchester University Press.

Lacey, C. (1977) *The Socialization of Teachers*, London, Methuen.

Lacey, C. (1981) 'Foreword', in Ball, S. J. *Beachside Comprehensive: A Case-Study of Secondary Schooling*, Cambridge, Cambridge University Press, xi–xiv.

Lacey, C., Horton, M. and Hoad, P. (1973) *Tutorial Schools Research Project*, vol. 1: *Teacher Socialization: The Postgraduate Training Year*, London, SSRC.

Lambart, A. M. (1970) 'The sociology of an unstreamed urban grammar school for girls', unpublished MA thesis, University of Manchester.

Lambart, A. M. (1976) 'The sisterhood', in Hammersley, M. and Woods, P. (eds) *The Process of Schooling*, London, Routledge & Kegan Paul in association with the Open University Press, 152–9.

Lambert, R. (1966) 'The public schools: a sociological introduction', in Kalton, G. *The Public Schools: A Factual Survey*, London, Longman, xi–xxxii.

Langness, L. L. (1965) *The Life History in Anthropological Science*, New York, Holt, Rinehart & Winston.

Lawton, D. (1973) *Social Change, Educational Theory and Curriculum Planning*, London, University of London Press.

Lawton, D. (1975) *Class, Culture and the Curriculum*, London, Routledge & Kegan Paul.

Loudon, J. B. (1961) 'Kinship and crisis in South Wales', *British Journal of Sociology*, 12, 333–50.

Loukes, H. (1956) *Secondary Modern*, London, Harrap.

Lyons, G. (1981) *Teacher Careers and Career Perceptions*, Slough, National Foundation for Educational Research.

Mandelbaum, D. G. (1973) 'The study of life history: Gandhi', *Current Anthropology*, 14, 177–96.

Mannheim, K. and Stewart, W. A. C. (1962) *Introduction to the Sociology of Education*, London, Routledge & Kegan Paul.

Marland, M. (1980) 'A programme for a community of schools', in Marland, M. (ed.) *Education for the Inner City*, London, Heinemann, 163–211.

Matza, D. (1964) *Delinquency and Drift*, New York, Wiley.

Mays, J., Quine, W. and Pickett, K. (1968) *School of Tomorrow: The Study of a Comprehensive School in a North West Newtown*, London, Longman.

Ministry of Education (1945) *The Nation's Schools: Their Plan and Purpose*, Pamphlet no. 1, London, HMSO.

Ministry of Education (1947) *The New Secondary Education*, Circular 142, Pamphlet no. 9, London, HMSO.

Mitchell, J. C. (1956) *The Kalela dance*, Rhodes-Livingstone Paper 27.

Monks, T. G. (1968) *Comprehensive Education in England and Wales: A Survey of Schools and their Organization*, Slough, National Foundation for Educational Research.

Monks, T. G. (1970) (ed.) *Comprehensive Education in Action*, Slough, National Foundation for Educational Research.

Moody, E. (1968) 'Right in front of everyone', *New Society*, 12 (326), 952–3.

Morgan, D. H. J. (1972) 'The British Association scandal: the effect of publicity on a sociological investigation', *Sociological Review*, 20, 185–206.

Morrison, A. and McIntyre, D. (1969) *Teachers and Teaching*, Harmondsworth, Penguin.

Mortimore, J. and Blackstone, T. (1982) *Disadvantage and Education*, London, Heinemann.

Mukerji, C. (1978) 'Bullshitting: road lore among hitchhikers', *Social Problems*, 25 (3), 241–52.

Murphy, J. (1971) *Church, State and Schools in Britain 1800–1970*, London, Routledge & Kegan Paul.

Musgrave, P. W. (1973) *Knowledge, Curriculum and Change*, London, Angus & Robertson.

Musgrove, F. and Taylor, P. (1969) *Society and the Teacher's Role*, London, Routledge & Kegan Paul.

Nash, R. (1974) 'Camouflage in the classroom', in Eggleston, J. (ed.) *Contemporary Research in the Sociology of Education*, London, Methuen, 245–50.

National Union of Teachers (1958) *Inside the Comprehensive School: A Symposium Contributed by Heads of Comprehensive Schools in England and Wales*, London, Schoolmaster Publishing Co. Ltd.

Newsom, J. (1963) *Half Our Future*, Report of the Central Advisory Council for Education, London, HMSO.

Nixon, J. (1981) (ed.) *A Teachers' Guide to Action Research*, London, Grant McIntyre.

Ottaway, A. K. C. (1960) 'The aims and scope of educational sociology', *Educational Review*, 12 (3), 190–9.

Park, R. E. (1952) 'The city: suggestions for the investigation of human behavior in the urban environment', in Park, R. E. *Human Communities*, New York, Free Press, 13–51.

Partridge, J. (1968) *Life in a Secondary Modern School*, Harmondsworth, Penguin.

Patrick, J. (1973) *A Glasgow Gang Observed*, London, Eyre Methuen.

Pedley, R. (1978) *The Comprehensive School*, 3rd edn, Harmondsworth, Penguin.

Plath, K. (1965) *Schools Within Schools: A Study of High School Organization*, New York, Bureau of Publications, Teachers College, Columbia University.

Pons, V. (1961) 'Two small groups in Avenue 21: some aspects of the system of social relations in a remote corner of Stanleyville Belgian Congo', in Southall, A. (ed.) *Social Change in Modern Africa*, London, Oxford University Press, 205–16.

Pons, V. (1969) *Stanleyville: An African Urban Community Under Belgian Administration*, London, Oxford University Press.

Popkewitz, T. S. and Tabachnick, B. R. (1981) (eds) *The Study of Schooling: Field Based Methodologies in Educational Research and Evaluation*, New York, Praeger.

Quine, W. G. (1974) 'Polarised cultures in comprehensive schools', *Research in Education*, 12, 9–25.

Rée, H. (1956) *The Essential Grammar School*, London, Harrap.

Reimer, E. (1971) *School is Dead*, Harmondsworth, Penguin.

Richardson, E. (1973) *The Teacher, the School and the Task of Management*, London, Heinemann.

Richardson, E. (1975) *Authority and Organization in the Secondary School*, London, Macmillan.

Riseborough, G. F. (1981) 'Teacher careers and comprehensive schooling: an empirical study', *Sociology*, 15 (3), 352–80.

Rock, P. (1979) *The Making of Symbolic Interactionism*, London, Macmillan.

Rowe, A. W. (1959) *The Education of the Average Child*, London, Harrap.

Scharff, D. E. (1976) 'Aspects of the transition from school to work', in Hill, J. M. M. and Scharff, D. E. *Between Two Worlds: Aspects of the Transition from School to*

Work, Richmond, Careers Consultants Ltd, 66–332.

Schutz, A. (1972) *The Phenomenology of the Social World*, London, Heinemann, originally published 1932.

Schutz, A. and Luckmann, T. (1973) *The Structures of the Life-World*, London, Heinemann.

Scott, J. F. and Homans, G. C. (1947) 'Reflections on wildcat strikes', *American Sociological Review*, 12, 278–86.

Sharp, R. and Green, A. (1975) *Education and Social Control: A Study in Progressive Primary Education*, London, Routledge & Kegan Paul.

Sharpe, S. (1976) *'Just Like a Girl': How Girls Learn to be Women*, Harmondsworth, Penguin.

Shaw, C. R. (1930) *Jack-Roller: A Delinquent Boy's Own Story*, Chicago, University of Chicago Press.

Shaw, K. E. (1969) 'Why no sociology of schools?', *Education For Teaching*, 69, 61–7.

Shipman, M. (1968) *The Sociology of the School*, London, Longman.

Shipman, M. (1971) 'Curriculum for inequality', in Hooper, R. (ed.) *The Curriculum: Context, Design and Development*, Edinburgh, Oliver & Boyd in association with the Open University Press, 101–6.

Shipman, M. (1980) 'The limits of positive discrimination', in Marland, M. (ed.) *Education for the Inner City*, London, Heinemann, 69–92.

Smith, L. M. and Keith, P. M. (1971) *Anatomy of Educational Innovation: An Organizational Analysis of an Elementary School*, New York, Wiley.

Spindler, G. (1982) (ed.) *Doing the Ethnography of Schooling: Educational Anthropology in Action*, New York, Holt, Rinehart & Winston.

Spradley, J. P. (1979) *The Ethnographic Interview*, New York, Holt, Rinehart & Winston.

Spradley, J. P. (1980) *Participant Observation*, New York, Holt, Rinehart & Winston.

Stacey, M. (1960) *Tradition and Change: A Study of Banbury*, Oxford, Oxford University Press.

Stanley, A. P. (1903) *Life of Dr Arnold* (ed. A. Reynolds), London, Hutchinson.

Stanworth, M. (1980) *Gender and Schooling: A Study of Sexual Divisions in the Classroom*, London, Women's Research and Resources Centre.

Stebbins, R. A. (1967) 'A theory of the definition of the situation', *Canadian Review of Anthropology and Sociology*, 4, 148–64.

Stebbins, R. A. (1974) *The Disorderly Classroom: Its Physical and Temporal Conditions*, Newfoundland: Faculty of Education, Memorial University of Newfoundland.

Stebbins, R. A. (1975) *Teachers and Meaning: Definitions of Classroom Situations*, Leiden, E. J. Brill.

Stebbins, R. A. (1976) 'Physical context influences on behaviour: the case of classroom disorderliness', in Hammersley, M. and Woods, P. (eds) *The Process of Schooling*, London, Routledge & Kegan Paul in association with the Open University Press, 208–16.

Stebbins, R. A. (1980) 'The role of humour in teaching: strategy and self-expression', in Woods, P. (ed.) *Teacher Strategies: Explorations in the Sociology of the School*, London, Croom Helm, 84–97.

Stenhouse, L. (1975) *An Introduction to Curriculum Research and Development*, London, Heinemann.

Stevens, F. (1960) *The Living Tradition: The Social and Educational Assumptions of the Grammar School*, London, Hutchinson.

Stubbs, M. and Delamont, S. (1976) (eds) *Explorations in Classroom Observation*, London, Wiley.

Swidler, A. (1979) *Organization Without Authority: Dilemmas of Social Control in Free Schools*, Cambridge, Mass., Harvard University Press.

Taylor, J. K. and Dale, I. R. (1971) *A Survey of Teachers in their First Year of Service*, Bristol, University of Bristol publication.

Taylor, W. (1963) *The Secondary Modern School*, London, Faber.

Taylor, W. (1973) *Heading For Change: The Management of Innovation in the Large Secondary School*, London, Routledge & Kegan Paul.

Taylor, W. (1976) 'The head as manager: some criticisms', in Peters, R. S. (ed.) *The Role of the Head*, London, Routledge & Kegan Paul, 37–49.

Temperton, P. (1981) 'A sordid and futile business', *The Times Educational Supplement*, 17 July, 16–17.

Thernstrom, S. (1965) 'Yankee City revisited: the perils of historical naiveté', *American Sociological Review*, 30, 234–42.

Thernstrom, S. (1968) 'Quantitative methods in history: some notes', in Lipset, S. M. and Hofstadter, R. (eds) *Sociology and History: Methods*, New York, Basic Books, 59–78.

Thomas, W. I. (1928) *The Child in America*, New York, Knopf.

Thrasher, F. (1927) *The Gang*, Chicago, University of Chicago Press.

Tibble, J. W. (1970) (ed.) *The Extra Year*, London, Routledge & Kegan Paul.

Tropp, A. (1957) *The Schoolteachers*, London, Heinemann.

Turner, V. W. (1957) *Schism and Continuity in an African Society: A Study of Ndembu Village Life*, Manchester, Manchester University Press.

Turner, V. W. (1971) 'An anthropological approach to the Icelandic saga', in Beidelman, T. O. (ed.) *The Translation of Culture: Essays to E. E. Evans-Pritchard*, London, Tavistock, 349–74.

Turner, V. W. (1974) *Dramas, Fields and Metaphors: Symbolic Action in Human Society*, Ithaca and London, Cornell University Press.

Tyler, W. (1982) *The Sociology of the School: A Review*, London, Social Science Research Council.

Van Gennep, A. (1960) *The Rites of Passage*, Chicago, University of Chicago Press.

Van Velsen, J. (1967) 'The extended case method and situational analysis', in Epstein, A. L. (ed.) *The Craft of Social Anthropology*, London, Tavistock, 129–49.

Wakeford, J. (1969) *The Cloistered Elite*, London, Macmillan.

Walker, R. and Goodson, I. (1977) 'Humour in the classroom', in Woods, P. and Hammersley, M. (eds) *School Experience: Explorations in the Sociology of Education*, London, Croom Helm, 196–227.

Waller, W. (1967) *The Sociology of Teaching*, New York, Wiley, originally published 1932.

Watson, L. E. (1973) 'Office and expertise in the secondary school', in Fowler, G., Morris, V. and Ozga, J. (eds) *Decision-Making in British Education*, London, Heinemann, 405–21.

Watson, S. W. B. (1958) 'Courses for pupils who do not intend to attempt any external examinations', in National Union of Teachers, *Inside the Compre-*

hensive School: A Symposium Contributed by Heads of Comprehensive Schools in England and Wales, London, Schoolmaster Publishing Co. Ltd, 55–60.

Webb, J. (1962) 'The sociology of a school', *British Journal of Sociology*, 13 (3), 264–72.

Weinberg, M. (1968) 'Becoming a nudist', in Rubington, D. and Weinberg, M. (eds) *Deviance: The Interactionist Perspective*, New York, Macmillan, 240–51.

White, R. (1980) *Absent With Cause: Lessons of Truancy*, London, Routledge & Kegan Paul.

White, R. and Brockington, D. (1978) *In and Out of School: The ROSLA Community Education Project*, London, Routledge & Kegan Paul.

Whyte, W. F. (1955) *Street Corner Society*, 2nd edn, Chicago, University of Chicago Press.

Willis, P. (1977) *Learning to Labour*, Farnborough, Saxon House.

Willmott, P. (1969) *Adolescent Boys of East London*, Harmondsworth, Penguin.

Wilson, B. (1962) 'The role of the teacher', *British Journal of Sociology*, 13, 15–32.

Winter, R. (1976) 'Keeping files: aspects of bureaucracy in education', in Whitty, G. and Young, M. (eds) *Explorations in the Politics of School Knowledge*, Driffield, Nafferton Books, 75–86.

Wirth, L. (1928) *The Ghetto*, Chicago, University of Chicago Press.

Wolcott, H. (1973) *The Man in the Principal's Office: An Ethnography*, New York, Holt, Rinehart & Winston.

Wolcott, H. (1975) 'Criteria for an ethnographic approach to research in schools', *Human Organization*, 34(2), 111–27.

Woods, P. (1976a) 'Having a laugh: an antidote to schooling', in Hammersley, M. and Woods, P. (eds) *The Process of Schooling: A Sociological Reader*, London, Routledge & Kegan Paul in association with the Open University Press, 178–87.

Woods, P. (1976b) 'Pupils' views of school', *Educational Review*, 28 (2), 126–37.

Woods, P. (1977) 'Teaching for survival', in Woods, P. and Hammersley, M. (eds) *School Experience: Explorations in the Sociology of Education*, London, Croom Helm, 271–93.

Woods, P. (1979) *The Divided School*, London, Routledge & Kegan Paul.

Woods, P. (1980a) (ed.) *Teacher Strategies: Explorations in the Sociology of the School*, London, Croom Helm.

Woods, P. (1980b) (ed.) *Pupil Strategies: Explorations in the Sociology of the School*, London, Croom Helm.

Woods, P. and Hammersley, M. (1977) (eds) *School Experience: Explorations in the Sociology of Education*, London, Croom Helm.

Wragg, E. C. (1975) 'The first generation of British "interaction" studies', in Chanan, G. and Delamont, S. (eds) *Frontiers of Classroom Research*, Slough, National Foundation for Educational Research, 13–24.

Young, M. F. D. (1971) 'An approach to the study of the curriculum as socially organised knowledge', in Young, M. F. D. (ed.) *Knowledge and Control: New Directions for the Sociology of Education*, London, Collier-Macmillan, 19–46.

Zimmerman, D. H. and Wieder, D. L. (1977) 'The diary: diary-interview method', *Urban Life*, 5 (4), 479–98.

Zorbaugh, H. W. (1929) *The Gold Coast and the Slum*, Chicago, University of Chicago Press.

NAME INDEX

SUBJECT INDEX